DESIGNWHYS

DESIGNING WEB SITE INTERFACE ELEMENTS

FOR GRAPHIC DESIGNERS | **ERIC EATON**

First published in the United States of America by
Rockport Publishers, Inc.
33 Commercial Street
Gloucester, Massachusetts 01930-5089
Telephone: (978) 282-9590
Fax: (978) 283-2742
www.rockpub.com

Library of Congress cataloging-in-publication data
are available

ISBN 0-201-79303-2

10 9 8 7 6 5 4 3 2 1

Cover Design: Elisabeth Gerber
Book Design: Elisabeth Gerber
Layout and Production: *tabula rasa* graphic design
Series Editor: Cynthia Baron

Printed in China

CONTENTS

introduction

WHAT'S IN AN ELEMENT?

If you eavesdrop on other people's conversations on commuter trains or grocery store waiting lines, you may hear grandmothers grousing about a confusing transaction interface, or pre-adolescents bragging about their mastery of an online game. Awareness of the value of interface design is migrating from MIT lecture halls to brew pubs.

Interface design matters to people. Where successful interaction was once measured by a nebulous sense of accomplishment on the part of anyone who successfully completed a computerized task, the average person has a growing awareness of the ways interfaces should respond to input, and can pinpoint the moment at which an interaction fails. This awareness is breeding more powerful users. They are increasingly focused on the pieces that make an interface work—the interface elements.

As awareness of interface design grows, designers are finding themselves in new territory: The virtual tools they design must live up to objective standards. Before interactive media, it was hard to chart the consequences of design. With print, the only reaction the designer had to contend with at the project's end was the client's. Virtual online tools are a different story. Their success and failure are immediately felt, in such things as the duration of visits, the number of pages viewed, and the amounts of transactions and money exchanges, all of which are instantly recorded by Web servers and analyzed by experts.

Granted, good design is not the sole guarantor of success. But design is the one factor that falls to us. In virtual tools, design—the form of the product—is the sum of its interface elements.

Interface elements are the levers and knobs of virtual tools. They allow a person to access databases, scripts and applications. A button may close a window, a slider may increase volume, and a checkbox may turn a feature on and off. Interface design's purpose is to present these levers and knobs in a way that accurately conveys their function and makes them easy to use.

While most interface elements are familiar enough that people expect them to behave in certain ways, interfaces combine those elements to achieve unique purposes that users can't anticipate. To convey an interface's purpose, designers must familiarize themselves with the intricate behaviors and effects of interface elements, as well as with basic theories of interface design and the laws that govern interface use.

Legacy Interfaces

Most people use and perceive virtual tools largely through habit. The way we use our preferred operating system dictates how we approach similar-looking elements on the Web. For this reason, designers of new operating systems and applications generally strive to adhere to established methods of interface design—which further reinforces habits of use.

Web interfaces are easier to construct than application interfaces, and Web designers don't necessarily follow established paradigms of interface and interaction design. But whether the goal is to follow established systems or invent new ones, a Web designer would do well to look at the origin of the standard elements.

Most virtual tools—like the mouse—can be traced back to Xerox's Palo Alto Research Camp (PARC) and Larry Ellison's early inventions. Apple and Microsoft have been swimming in this gene pool for years. Because of them, nearly everyone with a computer has learned to use the same PARC-derived interface, on which usage standards for all Graphic User Interfaces (GUI) are based.

Because of this common experience, most people have clear expectations for individual elements, even in a new interface. Although the average user would be at a loss to define a successful interface or describe the correct behavior of a given element, he or she has no problem identifying failures. A designer can therefore learn as much as about interface design from observation and empathy as from reading a stack of books on CHI (Computer Human Interface).

In this book, I invoke the user at every turn. (The word "user" appears in this book well over 500 times—surpassed only by "the.") The user's understanding of, comfort level with, and interest in an interface trumps everything else, including superficial style—except for aesthetics.

Should aesthetics be limited to establishing visual hierarchy and organizing the page for readability, or should the designer inject his personal sense of aesthetics, regardless of opposition from the usability side? This is a topic for another book, but the answer is "yes, sometimes; probably; maybe"—if you want to create a brand on the Web, you have to create a distinctive visual language.

Writing about interface design has been approached from a psychological perspective, through the study of reaction times, and as a cognitive science. Here, I study interfaces backwards, looking at the pieces to understand their effect on the whole. However, this is not a study of widgets.

I also address the effects of visual design on utility. It is impossible to talk about interface elements without looking at how they are effected by color, language, context, and the user's temperament.

The Sum of the Parts

This book takes a pragmatic view of interface elements, their design, functionality, and use. Sounds a little like analyzing the nails before building the house, doesn't it? The focus of architecture is the house as a whole and how it is used. Why look at the nails?

When you get right down to it, Web interfaces aren't houses. They are unlike anything else on earth. We can certainly trace their computer lineage, but we must also acknowledge the legacies of calculators and microwave ovens, not to mention elevators and transit maps. At their best, Web interfaces are so varied and multi-functional that they embody everything that's useful and comfortable in the tools of everyday life. At their worst, they can elicit the same frustration and disappointment as clocks on VCRs. Usage techniques cross over from the material to the virtual world, too. The method most people use to clear a calculator—punching the "C" button half-a-dozen times in rapid succession—is the unconscious model many of us bring to the computer: if an interface does not respond the way we expect it to, we pound the button a half dozen times until it does (it won't).

Now, let's go back to that house. Interface elements aren't just the nails. They're the light switches, the outlets, the sink—the devices that make the space livable. Interface elements are also the windows, doors, stairs, stair rails: things that allow us to move from place to place, to see where we are going, and to enjoy the view once we get there.

We don't play with light switches just to hear them click. We use them to turn on a light so we can see to read. As with light switches, Web site interface elements are most successful when the user is only subliminally aware of their presence—when they invisibly facilitate the usability of a site.

Experts judge a Web site as a whole, taking into consideration how well it addresses users' needs and how well it fits their personality. Users judge a site on details. Just like a light switch at the wrong end of a room, a badly-designed element will make its presence known. When the user becomes aware of and distracted by the parts, it's a sign that something is seriously wrong.

Technology

This book takes an agnostic stance towards proprietary technologies like Java, Macromedia Flash, and JavaScript. Circumstances and ability should determine how and when you use these technologies. But remember that HTML was envisioned as a scalable platform to allow documents to be read by a universal browser. This scenario is far preferable to that of a Web where we juggle several versions of a site to ensure that it will run on every possible platform, and where users have to find and download new plug-ins every six months.

When I started designing Web interfaces, many of my counterparts, who also came from print backgrounds, were reluctant to learn HTML. They saw the Web as nothing more than a delivery method. They designed 'zines in QuarkXPress and Adobe Illustrator, packaged them as PDF files, and expected users to download them, print them, and read them just like old media.

That didn't work.

Designers who weren't afraid of HTML but hated its aesthetic limitations, crafted large, static images in Photoshop—pictures of interfaces—pasted them into the background of the browser, and placed on invisible buttons to facilitate interaction. That didn't work either.

Today, interfaces that work perfectly on every browser and every platform usually fall into one of two categories. In the first, the interface uses extensive browser targeting and conditional code to customize a slightly different version for each possible environment. The second category is the all-text HTML site, which uses almost no visual formatting for fear that it will break in one browsing environment or another. Every designer must weigh the benefits of these two approaches and the gray areas in between.

I can't predict the future of the Web, but the past has shown us that the Web is not just a delivery system. Technologies that treat it as such are difficult to manage, particularly on large-scale sites. Web sites built primarily in HTML and CSS connect more easily to other sites, and can easily be repackaged to work in new browsing environments, such as handheld devices and cell phones. While Flash can be enhance usability or create a unique user experience, many interfaces can be built just as effectively with HTML and CSS. Whatever the future holds in authoring technologies, designers should look for the most ubiquitous, democratic, and bandwidth-friendly way to render an interface.

SECTION I:
Interface Design Principles

Rules-of-thumb abound in design. Principles of language, semiotics, color, psychology, and formalism influence our design decisions both unconsciously and consciously. We memorize names of fonts, systems of measure, theories about color and communication, and techniques of reproduction. Now designers have to master the principles of the use and perception of virtual tools. Though it's not the goal of this book to turn graphic designers into computer scientists, the better you understand usability, the more successful your interface design will be.

There are already a lot of books on the subject. I've drawn on some of the best, such as Debra Mayhew's roadmap for interface design, *The Usability Engineering Lifecycle* (Morgan Kaufmann Publishers, Inc., 1999).

The process she advocates is solid:
1) Define usability requirements
2) Set usability goals
3) Identify platform constraints
4) Re-engineer the user's existing task
5) Design and mock up conceptual models
6) Define screen design standards and make prototypes
7) Develop a style guide
8) Develop a detailed interface design
9) Evaluate the design

Read her book. But don't despair when you discover the following hard reality: By the time the average Web endeavor enlists a designer, opportunities to follow a proper usability design process have generally disintegrated, either for lack of time or lack of understanding. In these cases, it will comfort you to know that usability design uses many of the analytical skills that have become second nature to designers.

You don't have to get wrapped up in the science of Computer-Human Interaction. While scientists want to quantify interactive behavior, most designers are comfortable with the notion that there are no hard-and-fast laws in communication. We already base our work on an understanding of the behaviors people demonstrate as they read and interact with designed information. With these behaviors in mind, we scrutinize our works-in-progress with the eyes of the end reader, and ask questions about hierarchy, clarity, and flow. We make adjustments, re-scrutinize, ask other people for their perspectives, and readjust the design.

As it happens, users approach interfaces in much the same way as they approach books or posters, and show many of the same behavioral tendencies. The point here isn't that you should design virtual tools to look like books or posters, but that, with a little modification, processes familiar to us from print design can be applied to interface design.

In this book, we'll focus on the things that make interface design different from print. For one thing, the consequences of interacting with a Web site are somewhat different than with a book. Further, the ambiguity and discord that make 2-D design interesting are just plain inconvenient to a Web site user, who might be trying to buy a book or transfer money from one account to another. More importantly, the success or failure of an interface is measurable because we can track its usage in real time.

A book is a static arrangement of type and imagery that presents information from a single source in a predefined sequence. An interface is an active arrangement of a set of virtual tools that lets people get things and do things from a variety of sources. Interface elements are the levers and switches that enable direct interaction—buttons, links, and menus. These active elements, their behaviors, and their relationships to one another, connect the user to whatever is offered on the site,

and subsequently to the organization that provides it. To design useful online tools, you have to understand how people have used similar tools in the past, what problems they've had with them, and how you can improve upon them with new interactive technologies.

The first two chapters of this book with deal with the relationship of the design process to overall interface development. They cover the influence of strategic goals, technological constraints, and established usability paradigms on interface design. As you read about these ideal models, though, be aware that interface design in the trenches is anything but orderly and methodical. Put a bunch of designers in a room to talk about their experiences, and the stories will range from tales of Kafka-esque bureaucratic debacles to the saga of a single guy who designed, coded, and wrote a two-hundred-page site in ten days.

chapter 1

DEFINING THE PROJECT

It is tempting in the early stages of development to build prototypes so the team can see immediate forward motion. The immediacy of the Web is alluring; within a few minutes, a working model of an interface concept can be produced and distributed with an ease unheard of in print design. But without a strategic and functional framework for the interface—a definition of what it should accomplish, who it will serve, and what technology will best ensure its success—rapid development is a red herring. Before an interface can begin to take shape, the framework must be defined.

As in product development, the first step is to identify the market niche the site will fill, then come up with a clear definition of the user's needs. The end user—the person for whom the site is being built—provides the yardstick for measuring success. Who do you want to attract? How, when, and why will they use your facilities and services?

Once the usage and demographic decisions have been made, developers turn to technology. In interface development, if the site will allow users to launch applications from a button bar, for instance, you have to establish prerequisites for the platform and Web development applications. Other projects are more nebulous. The designer will have to make some investigations to determine the most appropriate technologies.

Most interfaces take shape in leaps during different phases of development. Some aspects can be determined very early— well before any designers are involved. While it isn't common for specific interface elements to be defined before design begins, it does happen. To understand when and how such prerequisites arise, it is helpful to identify some of the circumstances that play a defining role in the process, and to discuss each phase of Web site development.

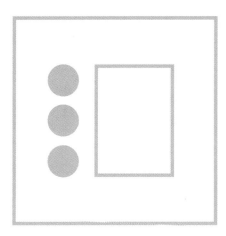

Development Phases

Once deployed, the interface form may seem inevitable, but in fact it is the result of a long and thoughtful process in which many technical, operational, economic, and procedural factors are worked through. Sometimes it comes together quickly, other times it moves like molasses, and often designers aren't involved as early as they should be. But however it goes, Web development happens in four phases:

Defining the Scope of the Project
Defining Strategic Goals
Defining Technical Specifications
Design and Production

The design and production phases themselves have several phases, which tend to overlap and repeat. For instance, the final phase of production, quality assurance, often leads to minor redesign and subsequent re-production. It is not the goal of this book to reproduce the development cycle. Instead, the issues surrounding design and production of interfaces and interface elements at every phase are incorporated into every chapter.

Field Journals

> B.T.E. will distinguish itself by offering real-time field communications between excursionist and the online community. Competitors' of B.T.E. have a RCYR (repeat client per year rate) of 15%. Competetors' new clients referred by past clients rate is estimated at 10%.

> By building an online community though real-time field communications, B.T.E. expects to build a repeat client rate of 30%, and a referral rate of 40%. By involving friends and family of excursionist, through real-time connectivity, B.T.E. can capture new clients by placing the tools for booking excursions next to log entries.

Big Trout Excursions.com

M. C. Nutter
33, from Beverly, MA

Sept. 31, 2002 | 6:50am
After 4 hours charging up stream over 10 miles of tidal estuary, we made camp about 50 feet from what we *thought* was the high water mark. Without getting into too much detail, we retrieved the canoe this morning, and the tent is once again on solid ground.

N

Book an Excursion

FIGURE 1.1

A project scope is not a creative brief or a technical specification. However, literal interpretations of the desired effects may suggest interface solutions that can function as guides for later phases. At the very least, the mental images created at this point will provide a conceptual legacy throughout the project.

Project Scope

Every online endeavor has a scope, or purpose: a desired effect from the point of view of both the company and the end user. The effect can be multifaceted or simple. A company's first Web product may simply provide clear, up-to-date information to its public. For instance, a small bed-and-breakfast on Big Trout Lake might need a six-page site with directions, photos, calendar, rates, and contact information. Though none of this information suggests what form each page will take, you can make certain assumptions: the interface elements will be a mix of unobtrusive navigational links, the focus of the site being on the text and photos.

A company that plans to take advantage of online technologies such as order processing will need a more extensive Web site. Big Trout Excursions Inc., a guided fishing service, plans to use the Web to provide hourly weather updates, last-minute availability, and an online field journal and log book for each excursion, in addition to basic descriptions. A scope for this company might be very specific on technical issues, outlining a tool-heavy site complete with user accounts, credit card processing, and real-time mapping. That specificity gives a slightly clearer picture of the eventual interface. (See Fig. 1.1)

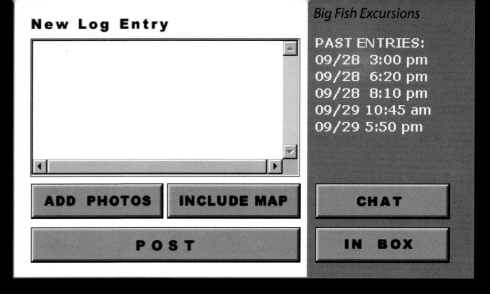

FIGURE 1.2

One of the differentiating factors of this site is that excursionists can communicate with other excursionists and on-lookers while in the field. Therefore, this interface will be used outside, possibly in the rain, on a portable computer. The buttons and type sizes may larger than one might expect in a Web site, and require an alternate version for an excursionist who is using a Palm device.

New Log Entry

Big Fish Excursions

PAST ENTRIES:
09/28 3:00 pm
09/28 6:20 pm
09/28 8:10 pm
09/29 10:45 am
09/29 5:50 pm

ADD PHOTOS   INCLUDE MAP   CHAT

POST   IN BOX

It's common for technical decisions made in the initial development phases to have an effect on the final interface. For budgetary and other reasons, certain technologies may be chosen that come with interface requirements.

Let's say Big Trout Excursions decides to use a third-party, credit-card-processing package that requires the user to create a unique name and password. What seems to be an economic issue or technical detail will have an effect on the interface's usability: will users sign on to the site with one name and password, then create a second identity to make a reservation with their credit cards? To enable users to set up a name and password just once, the designer will need to work with a programmer to craft a behind-the-scenes technical solution.

Strategic Goals

Usability issues can arise in the strategic phase as well. Most strategic goals have to do with the market niche a product is expected to fill. Where online products are concerned, market niches are often characterized by the way an interface works.

Big Trout Excursions' first strategic goal is to provide its clientele with the ability to quickly make decisions about booking a fishing expedition. Its second goal is to create customer loyalty by supporting a community of enthusiasts through the nightly logs and diaries. In practice, customer loyalty will be affected by ease-of-use. If usability is identified as a primary goal at the strategic phase, Big Trout can rule out certain technologies or interface solutions based on the technological capabilities of the user population. (See Fig. 1.2)

Technical Specifications

The specifications document is a working guide for the design and production team. Though it doesn't have to be written by the same people who draft the scope and the strategic goals, its author should be intimate with both. The project scope may mention technology generally, and the strategic

FIGURE 1.3

Technical considerations always have a bearing on design. Here, the original design rendered the excursionist's name and personal statistics over the lower portion of the image. Since the images and personal statistics reside on separate servers, this wouldn't work. The designer had to alter the design.

goals may mention relevant technological issues. Starting with that information, the technical specifications will go on to define the exact software and hardware that will run the site, which in turn will determine which interface conventions will work and which and will not.

The designer will have to invest significant time and energy deciphering these specs before he'll fully grasp the issues, but it's an investment worth making. Specifications are not just details for software engineers. They are the underlying framework of every interface.

Much of the material in the technical draft will be outside your area of expertise. You won't need to know the difference between an NT and Apache server, for example. It may be enough simply to know that there is a difference—ask the engineer or Webmaster what the difference means to the interface.

Say the front-end, or interface, is run by a server that is physically separated from the database server: that would indicate design limits on the interface. For the Big Trout site, if the design requires that every excursionist's diary entry (which resides on a user database server) be accompanied by a photo (which is kept on a front-end server), it may be technically difficult to load the photo to the diary interface. Issues like these must be hammered out between the engineer and the designer as time and scope permit. (See Fig. 1.3)

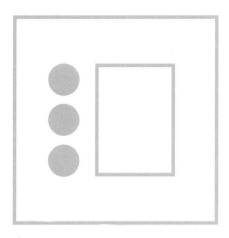

Appearance and Layout

While it's important to approach interface design pragmatically, a successful site is rarely just the sum of technological responses to usability issues. The utility of any interface is only as good as the design that enables its use. Layout, color, position, and the proximity of one element to another all facilitate usability. Web design is therefore a unique hybrid of traditional page design and interface architecture, compounded by hidden variables that make it difficult for users to know exactly what their options are (flexible window size, font scaling, etc.). In the end, good usability design starts with good layout, and especially with a visual hierarchy, based on sound aesthetics, that will guide the eye through the interface.

Beyond this, there is something to be said for visual style—uniqueness. A person may use four or five application interfaces daily, but since all are running on the same operating system, they start to look the same. In Web design, this is not good. Each site has to create an identity of its own, and the competition is intense. A Web user can easily see twenty interfaces online one day, twenty others the next. Each has to be grounded in conventional schemes and familiar models to minimize her learning curve, but that familiarity should not leave them bland and indistinguishable. A tool that offers a balance between usability and aesthetics is more likely to evoke affinity than a similarly functional, but less attractive, interface.

FIGURE 1.4

As is often the case with portal sites, this interface was supplied by a company other than Aarachne. Users are unlikely to attribute any benefits of using the site to Aarachne because the disconnect between the interface and the brand is so obvious.

By using the visual language of the brand on the interface and arranging the elements on a grid that relates to the logo, the user gets the feeling that the utility of the site is fully attributable to Aarachne.

Branding

In the crowded world of the Web, communications must be effectively branded to be remembered. An interface presented by a trusted company with a recognized brand has an initial advantage, because it draws upon the user's positive brand experience. But, unlike lawnmowers and cell phones, if an online brand doesn't deliver convenience with its interface, a user can switch brands in seconds. This explains how a company like Amazon rose to prominence so fast, while its more established brick-and-mortar competition struggled to gain online market share: Amazon built its brand on convenience and good usability.

Like any product, an interface has to create trust and recognition. Online brands have the potential to be more powerful than their offline counterparts. First, the customer has chosen to spend time with the brand. Second, the Web provides better tools: animation, video, audio, and most of all, customizable interactivity. The user can choose what to look at, how much to look at, and how much time to spend. Based on his input, the site can provide just the material he wants— unlike a billboard or brochure.

If the company has both a real-world and an online presence, the interface designer will have to decide whether or not to base the visual language on the existing identity.

Either way, the design communicates something profound. An interface that is tightly connected to the identity will convey a sense of longevity, telling the user the good old company is totally behind the new interface. An interface that evolves the parent brand tells the user that the company is staying abreast of changing times. An interface that gives an old brand an online face that's in deliberate contrast to a major Web competitor announces the brand's entry to a new market niche. To find the right solution, start by asking whether the online and offline goals, customers, and competitors are the same.

Unfortunately, in order to create an online presence fast, some large companies buy pre-packaged interfaces and slap their branding across the top of the page. In these cases the brand design has no relationship to the interface design, with the result that the site feels ephemeral, as if its contents could be replaced from one day to next. This shows a lack of commitment that users will sense. (See Fig. 1.4)

Some interfaces are meant to be specialized marketing tools—one of a suite of brand communications for the organization. Just as a company may occasionally combine a consistent identity with a trendy, stylish, ad campaign, some interfaces are visual counterpoints to the brand, and use a visual style of a different ilk. But even if this is the desired effect, the page elements still have to have a purposeful relationship to each other in order for the online brand to succeed. (See Fig. 1.5)

Look & Feel

In print design, style and appearance factor into the process early on. The details of readability and production are hammered out over the remaining phases. Interface design, as I've pointed out, often begins with non-visual considerations.

Some in the computer science community believe that look-and-feel has no place in interface design: that visual properties should contribute only to usability, not attractiveness. But Web users frequently demonstrate in interviews, focus groups and user tests, that appearance does matter—probably because interfaces serve some of the same strategic purposes as product design. A user likes to identify with her favorite tool on the abstract level of appearance as well as function.

Take a walk through the tool section of a hardware store. Three brands stand out: Makita blue, DeWalt yellow, and Hitachi green. Each company designs their line of tools in a distinct visual style that largely depends on color. Their success in the market is still based on their dependability, durability, and such features as weight and balance, which appeal to professionals. But the look-and-feel is what makes the brand stick in the minds of buyers.

Though interface elements are just one aspect of the overall interface, they are far more important than they might seem to be. They are more closely scrutinized than any other aspect of a site. Their design and performance is analogous to the power, weight, and balance of a good hand tool. These little widgets definitely limit design options—their appearance is necessarily based on established usability models—but they also set a creative challenge that will stretch your skills and talents to their limits.

FIGURE 1.5

When Al Gore was "inventing" the Web, he probably never expected to see a marriage of form and content as unlikely as this. The soft, friendly Cottenelle brand meets the edgy, rave-inspired Web aesthetic—the kind of juxtaposition mainstay brands often use when they feel the urge to update. In this case, the two styles are reconciled by continuity of color, and flat, cartoony icons that are somewhat related to the Cottonelle logo.

chapter 2

WEB SITE INTERFACE DESIGN

An interface provides a person with access to the literal and virtual parts of a machine that allow him to control the mechanism. These days, when we think "interface" we think of computers, but in fact we have been interfacing with machines for many years. To fully appreciate the importance of a successful interface design, look at the automobile. In a car, the consequences of an unclear or dysfunctional interface would be disastrous. Fortunately, automobile interface design has been refined over years of use to the point that any driver can hop into any car and make it work. The interface is deceptively simple—a wheel, a few levers and switches, a couple of pedals—but it gives us control of a very complex machine.

It isn't necessary or practical for the driver to understand exactly what transpires in the bowels of a car when the shifter is moved from forward to reverse—in fact, the task of navigating a car through busy streets would be impossible if the driver were also responsible for synchronizing the flywheels within the gearbox to mesh with the transmission. A shift lever with a few letters stamped on it is a perfect interface: it gives only the essential information, and allows only the pertinent actions required to shift

into one of 6 gears. If automobile interfaces were prone to breakdowns, (as Web interfaces often are)—if R sometimes meant 2nd gear, and shifting into neutral just played a message about the benefits of Neutral—most users would abandon driving in a hurry. (See Fig. 2.1)

There are numerous interfaces between the driver and the inner workings of the car, but they seems intuitive because the entire body is used for different functions. A person can steer, shift, signal and sometimes tune the radio simultaneously.

When a computer application replaces a real-world task with virtual tools and representations, the interface can seem uncomfortable and awkward. (See Fig. 2.2) Like driving a car, numerous complex tasks can be accomplished, but only through the mouse and a couple of other keys. Operations or events must happen one at a time, not simultaneously.

Computers provide convenience, flexibility and power. But interface designers should be aware of how a user's frustration can build as the result of minor annoyances and awkward interactions that accumulate over the course of a day.

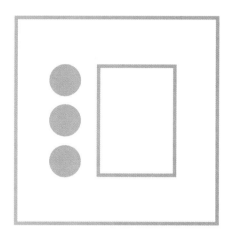

Communication with Target Audience

Today's Web users regularly see and use dozens of interfaces each week. In many cases, they revisit particular sites regularly, once a week, or once a month. Some larger sites—especially portals like Yahoo, Lycos, and MSN—seek to attract regular visits by offering nearly everything imaginable in one place. Intended for everyone, targeted for no one, loyalty to these monolithic sites is often low.

Most people develop an affinity for a site because they want, need, or relate to the content. In successful site design, this content is inextricably entwined with the form of the interface. Though text may be the most engaging element for most people, the surface quality of an interface is the first thing they encounter. Therefore, the site should both *look* obviously crafted to its intended audience and then actually *be* crafted to them, to ensure they move quickly from the veneer to the content.

Metaphors

Most Web interfaces bring users on a journey from the general to the specific using a handful of interface conventions. Even cleverly-integrated scripts that tie user input and preferences to databases and display engines are essentially means to a similar end: they allow the user to forge a path through irrelevant material to a desired outcome.

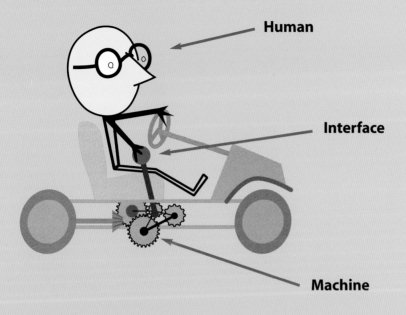

Human

Interface

Machine

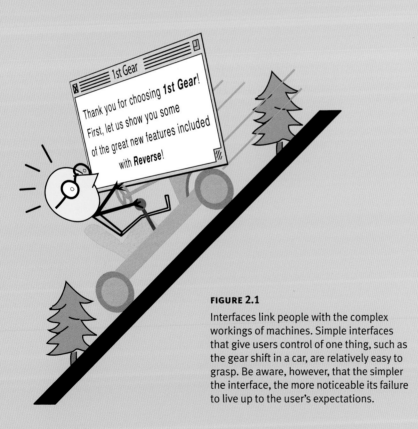

1st Gear

Thank you for choosing **1st Gear**! First, let us show you some of the great new features included with **Reverse**!

FIGURE 2.1

Interfaces link people with the complex workings of machines. Simple interfaces that give users control of one thing, such as the gear shift in a car, are relatively easy to grasp. Be aware, however, that the simpler the interface, the more noticeable its failure to live up to the user's expectations.

A designer must rely on conceptual tricks that help users see past the interface's buttons and menus to focus on the desired outcome. Metaphors are one of the best tricks we have. They are so important that I've devoted Chapter 7 to discussing the theory behind them and the way they work.

There are four reasons to use metaphors in interface design. First, a metaphor can create a sense of familiarity that will help users encounter a new and unproven interface. Second, metaphors can help introduce new concepts in familiar terms. Third, they are useful positioning tools: a good metaphorical interface can help distinguish a site from its competitors. Last, metaphorical thinking can help the designer clarify which interface elements should be interactive, and give him a yardstick to measure the design's success.

Entertainment vs. Interface

Interfaces break down for a number of reasons, and breakdowns can take many forms. A common breakdown results when the line between functional tools and entertaining interactivity is so blurred that the user becomes distracted or annoyed. This problem is especially prevalent in Flash interfaces, where elements are ushered onto the screen in a kinetic play, like clowns promenading around the ring at a circus opening. While animation effects are impressive to designers and geeks, they are invariably regarded as unnecessary by users.

Scalability of Design

I'll say this a hundred times in one way or another: An interface designer must keep the needs of the user in mind, always. Behind the scenes is another, equally important, contingency—the client. That is the organization, the site administrator, or any other body with a vested interest in the ongoing health and evolution of a site. This body is different in every case. People responsible for adding or subtracting content and features need to be empowered by flexibility in the interface design. An online community must be able to add posts to a bulletin board without breaking the interface. A commerce organization must be able to add product images and information of varying sizes to pages on an ongoing basis. Unlike brochures and print ads, the design of a Web interface is never locked down.

Though sites are inherently living, growing, things, every site has a critical mass; a point beyond which adding or subtracting material renders the design inappropriate. Some designers seem to think a scalable Website can go on forever. But in practice, there is a range within which each design functions best, and beyond which the site degrades to "adequate." Therefore, the goal of the designer isn't to make a super-elastic interface that can withstand any amount of modification. The appropriate range of flexibility and scale should be identified in the early stages of design, and the interface should be built to handle it.

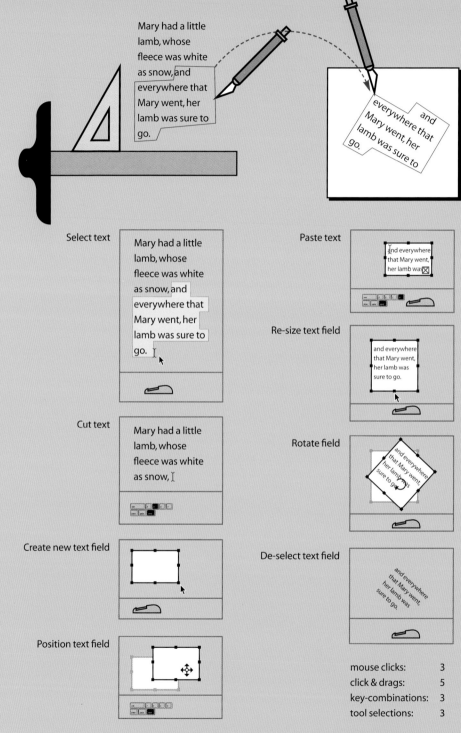

FIGURE 2.2

In the interest of usability—or, at least, familiarity—many computer interfaces are designed to resemble real-world tools and processes. But to the user, even an elegant metaphorical interface can seem tedious, compared to its real-world counterpart.

Structure vs. Flexibility

The other side of design flexibility is the interface's ability to stand up to user customization. An interface should accommodate some degree of user tweaking: altering background and link colors, setting styles for HTML text and interface elements, and changing the size and aspect ratio of the browser window.

Despite some users' desire to control the appearance of everything on their computer screens, effective communication is facilitated by designed systems and perceivable structures. This doesn't mean that the designer can force his or her personal system and structure on the communication. To communicate effectively, two people must speak the same language, even the same dialect, and follow mutually understood forms. With one-way media such as newspapers and television, the success of the communication is often dependent on the structural integrity of the medium—if the format of your morning paper changed every day, how would you know you were reading the same paper, let alone find a particular section?

Structure is the fundamental concern of the interface designer. The Web is essentially an abstract visual environment. Progressing through a site is often described as moving through a physical space, like a building,

but in actual experience the user suffers from a myopia unique to multimedia: she is unable to look around her or to look back at where she came from: she is only able to see where she is. To keep her bearings, the user must rely on ever-present, unchanging navigational elements and a solid mental map of the site, both of which are key ingredients of any interface structure. For a user to confidently embark on a journey through a Web site, the interface has to be tantamount to a diagram of functionality.

This is not as contrary to the idea of flexibility as it sounds. For the designer who swears by grid-design, a structure that evolves in a static preliminary layout can be made into an adaptable grid to suit both the communicator's need for structure and the user's need for flexibility. To do this, some aspects of the grid can remain static while others can be elastic: text can be formatted to wrap and unwrap at the user's will with a minimum and maximum line length, for instance. Other elements that must maintain a close proximity to each other for usability's sake can be anchored to a shared axis. (See Fig. 2.3)

The structure of individual pages within a site may have similar needs for flexibility, as different contents and contexts require different grids. For instance, a boutique site may use some pages to display new fashions, which the layout will accommodate in a right-hand

column that is not used anywhere else. This contextual structure becomes part of the user's understanding of the site. If applied consistently, the right column becomes a signal for fashion. If non-fashion ads were to occasionally appear in a right column, the user's sense of contextual structure would be lost, even though the grid had not changed.

Accessibility

Flexibility is not just about the average user's desire to control the appearance of the screen—it's about accessibility, the potential for an interface to easily adapt itself for an audience with special needs. An interface accessible to a colorblind person requires that red and green not be used together; a site accessible to a blind person would have to dovetail with a speaking interface. Different clients have different needs, and since Website designers can't anticipate them all, browsers allow users to customize site appearance.

Originally, HTML was structured as a formless hierarchy of mark-up tags. The way each tag was rendered would be up to the client. When HTML is written with tags that the client can interpret, the accessibility of the interface is potentially high. Navigation links, for instance, if tagged as such, could be read by the voice synthesizer. In theory, a browser for the blind

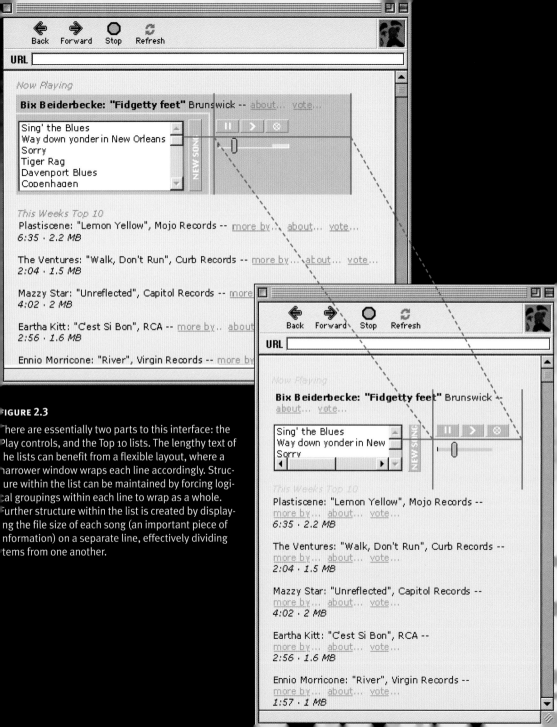

FIGURE 2.3

There are essentially two parts to this interface: the Play controls, and the Top 10 lists. The lengthy text of the lists can benefit from a flexible layout, where a narrower window wraps each line accordingly. Structure within the list can be maintained by forcing logical groupings within each line to wrap as a whole. Further structure within the list is created by displaying the file size of each song (an important piece of information) on a separate line, effectively dividing items from one another.

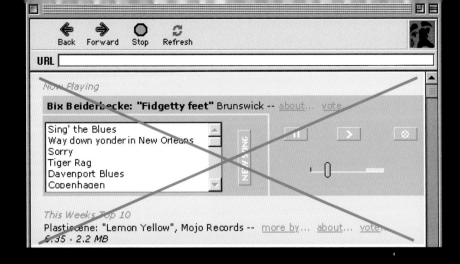

FIGURE 2.3 *CONTINUED*

Elements in this interface should adhere to a grid, even if some of the gridlines are movable. The Play controls work best when grouped together. Too much flexibility would be inconvenient, as the buttons would be increasingly disassociated from the song list.

should be able to read through an HTML document, interpret each tag, and use voice and emphasis to give the listener added insight to the content.

Unfortunately, most of the techniques we use to compose Web pages for the sighted ruin any chance that the HTML tags will be accessible to those with special needs. So much markup and HTML hackery is necessary to build a successful visual interface that it is unrealistic to expect the same code to be useful to people who need to use the site in different ways. It's easier to build an agnostic version of the interface, using only HTML-compliant tags (so that the top of an interface appears at the top of the code, and so forth), which users can translate into the form they need with their own technology. (See Fig. 2.4)

Internationalization

Internationalization is the term for designing for cultural differences among audiences. Consider an email interface, which might need a mailbox icon. The symbol is not universal. The arched aluminum container with a little red flag says "mailbox" in the United States, but in Britain, a vertical red box is the standard receptacle for "post."

The problem is severe in Web design because an interface on the World Wide Web can be seen anywhere in the world—from China to Arizona. It should follow that Web interface designers would be particularly concerned with internationalization. However, even if you were able to come up with a set of icons that would mean the same thing to every audience, you still wouldn't have internationalized your design. Web interfaces are built with interface elements that incorporate text, like button labels. There is no way to make a single version of a site work for all audiences. The only solution is to translate the text, and create a different version of the site for each language.

The Picayune Picayuné

Today's Headlines: Aug. 25, 2002

Thumbscrews Upheld by Supreme Court

With only 2 dissenting votes, the Supreme Court today upheld a lower court ruling that thumbscrews are a valid form of corporal punishment in schools.

Corporal Punishment Archaic

Advocates for overturning corporal punishment dismissed the ruling as irrelevant. Legislation has been introduced in the house to ban all forms of corporal punishment in public schools.

Road to Hell, Paved with Lead

Linotype-Hell announced today that it will be accepting designs for its new corporate typeface, to be issued in standard sizes for hand setting, and as Monotype matrices. The new fonts will not be issued in digital form, because there's no future in that sort of thing.

Coffee, It's Not Just for Breakfast, Lunch and Dinner Anymore

A recent study shows coffee is the preferred dessert drink among 18- to 30-year-olds. A survey funded by the Council for Consumable Caffeine Products (CCCP), sites a 200% increase in 10 years of coffee consumption after 7:00 pm. Late-night diner coffee, of the green variety, is the prefered vintage for 20% of all dessert imbibers.

HTML Code

```
<html>
<head><title>all the news that's legible</title></head>
<body>
<H3>The Picayune Picayuné</H3>
<H4>Today's Headlines: Aug. 25, 2002</H4>
<H1>Thumbscrews Upheld by Supreme Court</H1>
<p>With only 2 dissenting votes, the Supreme Court today
upheld a lower court ruling that thumb screws are a valid
form of corporal punishment in schools.</p>
```

FIGURE 2.4

Basic HTML is an elegant mark-up system, because it builds upon a natural hierarchy. Emphasis and structure are added to text with tags. In the case on the left, the designer has given emphasis to the top header, by using an H1 tag, the largest headline tag. Some browsers may display the headline with 24 point type, others may use something slightly larger or smaller, but the user will understand the page hierarchy based on the relative sizes of heads and text.

A voice synthesizer can easily interpret this page, reading headlines in a slow, loud voice, pausing, and continuing to read the text in a natural tone. The sight-impaired user could even tab through the page, jumping from headline to headline.

THE PICAYUNE PICAYUNÉ

To (3) Headlines: Aug. 25, 2002

Breaking (1)

T(4)mbscrews Upheld by Supreme Court

With only 2 dissenting votes, the Supreme Court today upheld a

Cor(5)al Punishment Archaic
Ad( )s for overturning corporal punishment dismissed the ( ) as irrelevant. Legislation has been introduced in the house to ban all forms of corporal punishment in public schools.

lo(8)court ruling that th( )screws are a valid form of corporal punishment in schools.

Top Stories (2)

Road to Hell, Paved with Lead
Li(6)Hell announced today that it will be accepting designs for its new corporate typeface, to be issued in standard sizes for hand setting, and as Monotype matrices. The new fonts will not be issued in digital form, because there's no future in that sort of thing.

Coffee, It's Not Just for Breakfast, Lunch an(7)ner Anymore
A recent study shows coffee is the preferred dessert drink among 18- to 30-year-olds. A survey funded by the Council for Consumable Caffeine Products (CCCP), sites a 200% increase in 10 years of coffee consumption after 7:00 pm. Late-night diner coffee, of the green variety, is the prefered vintage for 20% of all dessert imbibers.

Get This Delivered, Daily

Typically, advanced grids, which give pages a more sophisticated appearance, are often the result of tables and GIFs used to contain and arrange chunks of text. The page above gets its structure from four tables. What appears early on in the reading order in the browser view may actually be the last thing on the page. If this same page were read by a voice synthesizer, the order would be confusing. Part of the top story would end abruptly, its remaining text being read last. The masthead and information about subscribing would be missed completely, because they are GIFs.

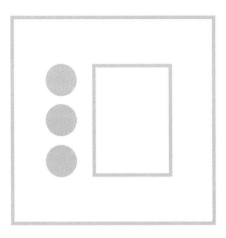

Layout and Organization

The structure of an interface or Web page is more than an expression of a company's personality or a vehicle for its brand. It's the equivalent of the floor plan of a building. A home page can be likened to a lobby with a directory and a clear line of sight to elevators, doors, and stairways. That's good navigation. There are logical and established ways of organizing the contents of a site. Revealing that structure to the user through a logical layout can make the difference between a decision to continue toward the elevator, or turn around and walk back out the door.

Information Visualization

Most interfaces, be they search tools, gateways to content, or even games, are built on a framework of information. In content gateways and portals, the architecture is obvious, and is usually displayed as a list of categorized links/directory. The taxonomy—system of categorization—the directory uses reveals much about the character of the site. A category titled Technology, with sub-categories of "Internet" and "ISPs" would have a different "feel" than a directory that presented "Internet" and "ISPs" under the heading of "Communities." In this way, simple, text-based displays of information can help the user interpret the value of a site. (See Fig. 2.5)

FIGURE 2.5

Configurations of disparate interface elements, however necessary and useful, present a dilemma for the user, who might just be looking for the easiest way to get through the sign-up process. This little cluster is easy enough to use because the sameness of the menus is broken up by the single type-in box, and each element relates logically to the type of information that the user is expected to enter.

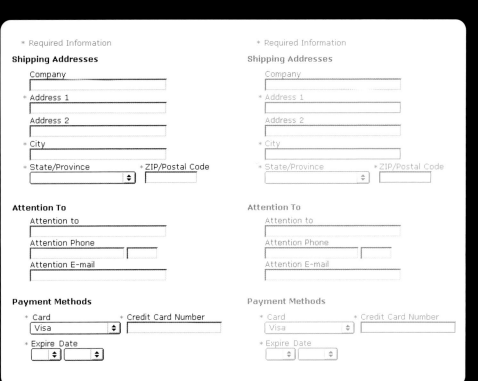

A large collection of elements with a repetitive appearance leaves little opportunity for the information itself to clarify the interface. The user just sees "a bunch of hazardous stuff" (hazardous because of how difficult it will be to avoid mistakes). Making visual distinctions among fields with different purposes can help. If you mark required fields with red asterisks, for instance, the user who is in a hurry can easily see which fields to fill out, and which to skip.

It's always better to minimize the variables in a complex interface by grouping similar material. In this case, the user can more easily visualize the information because required fields are kept completely separate from optional ones. The user can then see the page as functional sections, rather than having to find functional parts within each section.

Organization of Content and Categorization

A ground-up, information-up, approach to design will naturally lead to visual organization. If possible, identify the single most important thing or purpose in an interface, and design everything to serve it. A search site should have a prominent text-input field and submit button (see Google.com). An online pet store should have obvious links to dog, cat, and aquarium items.

However, most Web interfaces are much more complex, requiring patrons to sign up or log in, while offering important messages or news items as well as presenting links to all the content. The competing bits

of information on the average Web page are often at odds with the user's purposes. The task of organizing the information becomes more challenging with each new competing element. (See Fig. 2.6)

Categorization can be used both to display content to the user, and to guide the designer in structuring the interface. The first point has its obvious manifestation in directories and site maps, where the exact relationship between the sections of a site is displayed as a list of links. Regardless of the fluid nature of hypertext—where any page can be accessed from any other page—creating an appearance of organization helps the user understand the intentions of the site's designers. A site

where the "Contact Us" link is visible at the top of every page tells the user that communication with the audience is important to the owners of the site. Burying the same link at the bottom of an obscure credits and contacts page gives a very different message.

Categorizing every aspect of a site in the first phase of development is a valuable technique for coming up with a design architecture. The categorizing scheme does not have to manifest itself in a way that is obvious to the user, though. In some cases it is enough to allude to categorization, or to suggest a system or structure subtly, over time. (See Fig. 2.7)

FIGURE 2.6

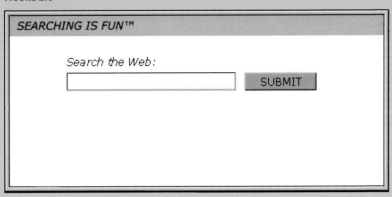

When a site does one thing only, there is little need for visual organization to help the user identify its purposes and value.

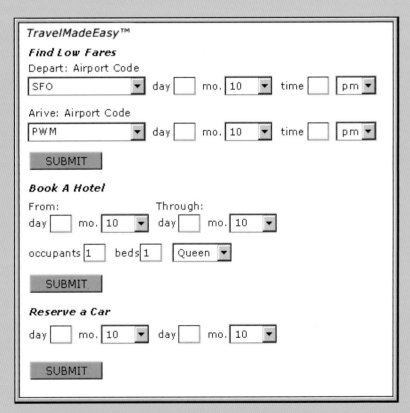

With every additional layer of service, users need more organizational cues to help them zone in on what is important to them at the moment. This interface offers no such guidance.

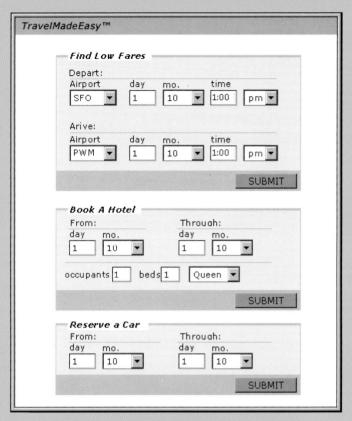

If a site does three things with equal competence, the sum of their functionality becomes the single most important thing—in this case, general travel arrangements. The general utility of the site is indicated in the masthead, and reinforced by the repetition of the Submit buttons. The designer's next concern is to make the interface immediately useful by clearly distinguishing among each task, which occurs naturally in this case because a convenient hierarchy is created by the descending complexity of each tool.

Outline for TravelMadeEasy.com

Page Types:
1. Task Specific (search, results etc.)
2. Information Related (help, FAQ, tips, etc.)
3. Dialogue (errors, confirmations etc.)

Page Map:
Level 1
Index Page/Search Interface   — type 1

Level 2
Search Results   — type 1
Power Search   — type 1
Nil Results   — type 3
Error Dialogue   — type 3
Travel Tips   — type 2
Airport Codes   — type 2

Level 3
Power Search Tips   — type 2

FIGURE 2.7

This outline, used in the early phase of design, shows how the designer went about structuring the site. That structure is not explicitly evident in the page design, but after some time using the site, the user will get a sense for it. Search pages are orange, help pages are blue, and error pages always use a white background with a red key-line. This subtle delineation through color helps the user learn the place each page occupies in the hierarchy. Even though the Airport Code look-up page is a search interface, it is treated like a help page in its design. The user will sense that it is a brief side trip that will loop back to the main search utility, as does the Travel Tips page. If the page were orange, the user might expect it to branch off into a separate search.

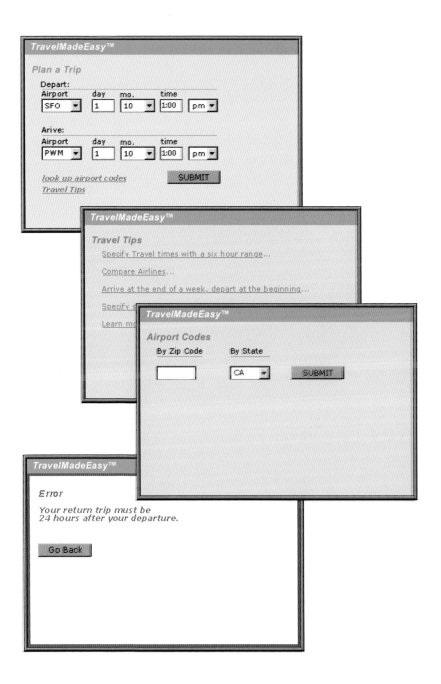

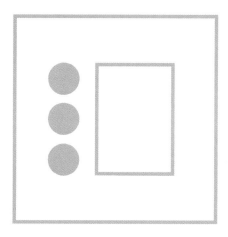

Way Finding

If the process of moving though a site were strictly linear, starting at page one and progressing sequentially through pages two, three, etc, navigation would be easy. But hypertext makes site navigation more like gophering through a vast landscape: the user can pop up in any place without the benefit of watching a sequence of pages that might help him orient himself.

At every turn, every time one page is replaced in the browser by another, the user needs to be made aware of what just happened, why, where they are now, where they can go next, and how to go back where they came from. Think of a site as an oak tree, and every page is a leaf. Each leaf may have a traceable link through many branches back to the trunk, but describing that route, and following it, is impractical. A more manageable solution would be to name each major branch, that is, each section of the site. A user who looked at several pages within one or two sections would have an easy time finding her way back to those pages if all she had to remember was what branch it was on and have an idea of its relative place on the branch. (See Fig. 2.8)

The World of Sugar Home | **Search** | Directory | Help

Your search for "licorice" had 4 matches:

1. Double Salted Licorice, stronger than morphine, and twice as tasty…

2. Red Vines, for those who don't know better…

3. Anise, The impostor licorice…

4. Make Mine Black, 101 uses for licorice jelly beans…

The World of Sugar Home | Search | **Directory** | Help

Top/ Food/ Candies/ Europe/ Holland/ Licorice

Double Salted Licorice

Stronger than morphine, and twice as tasty, this is an original European treat that defies expectations. An old favorite in Holland and Germany, Duble Zout is reviled by Americans, who prefer a tamer, sweeter treat made with anise.

More about Double Salted Licorice…

More Candies from Holland…

USER'S PATH:
Home Page > Search > Search Results >   **Licorice**

SITE'S PATH:
Top > Food > Candies > Europe > Holland >   **Licorice**

PATH IN THE USER'S MIND, NEXT WEEK:
The Wold Of Sugar > Candies of Holland >   **Licorice**

FIGURE 2.8

A user can get to any page in a site from any number of routes, from links on other pages and sites, and through search engines. In this case, a user searched for Licorice, clicked the top result, and jumped from the Search Page to a page deep within the site.

Two paths matter to the user. Most important is the return route. The browser's Back button serves this purpose, but even better are the white navigation links at the top of the page. They tell the user that a significant lateral move was made from search to the directory. Even though the user is deep within the directory, the distinction between the two major branches helps define the function and structure of the site and provides the user a quick way back to search.

The specific path through the directory (which is conveniently located in the string directly under the masthead) is important for context. The user will probably not follow this directly backwards to the Home page. Instead, he may decide to move back a step or two, to see what candies other countries have to offer.

This directory path also provides a strategy for finding the same information again later, without the search engine. The user won't remember how to navigate the directory several weeks later; the string will help the user's recall.

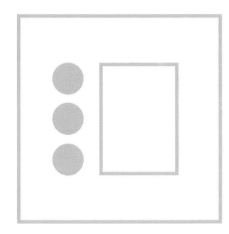

Usability and Experience

The whole of a user's experience with an interface or a site is influenced by how consistently certain design and interface conventions are employed. Some of these conventions are standard, such as listing navigation links across the top of a page or in the upper right corner. Most conventions can be played with or even replaced by a designer as long as the alternative is easy for the user to learn quickly, but both conventional interface techniques and invented ones must be consistently applied to all the pages of a site, or, if need be, evolved from page to page in a meaningful way that is easy to comprehend.

Design Style Standards

An established look-and-feel for all interface elements (type, position, color, etc.) becomes the visual protocol of a site—the style standard. A user of Yahoo, for instance, knows that the style standard for descriptive or running text is unformatted black type on a gray background, and that the navigation is presented as hypertext links in a center-axis format. Every page follows this standard. That consistency helps ground the user, who knows he is at Yahoo even without looking at the branding.

Visual Language

Most users require a moment to get oriented to every page, even if they are familiar with the site. A site with a distinct and consistent visual language can help orient the user, and has a better chance of occupying a place in the user's mind. There are a number of ways to render most interface elements. Buttons can be three-dimensional rectangles, or flat circles with thick borders: menus can be highlighted with a particular color. A site where every interface element is rendered with a drop shadow, submit buttons are always red, and navigation buttons are always blue, will be easy to use because the functionality of each page will be evident on sight from the amount of drop shadows, blue buttons, and red buttons.

Display Text vs. Body Text

Text plays a prominent role in design style standards because it is the easiest part of the document to affect with HTML tags. Many interface elements are rendered by the operating system, and cannot be easily customized to fit a design style—the look and feel of menus and scrolling lists, for instance, will have more in common with the user's operating system than with a site's branding. Text can be scaled and colored, fonts can be specified (with limited reliability): but body text—long or continuous passages—should be formatted in one of the very few comfortably readable screen fonts available (not exactly what most designers like to hear, especially where design style is concerned). Display text, rendered with GIFs or JPEGs, offers greater opportunities to incorporate the design style.

Functional Specifications

Every interface has a purpose—presumably one that was invented by the site's owners, rather than the interface designer. Regardless of who builds the back-end of an interface, its functional specifications should be understood and communicated before design begins. If a search engine has been written to use last names, phone numbers, and email addresses to locate a person's street address, but none of these fields can be used in conjunction with any other, that fact should be written into the design brief. If the designer doesn't know this, she might reasonably create an interface with three adjacent fields for name, phone number and email, giving each one a checkbox. This would work some of the time, but not all of the time. Furthermore, the user would not fully understand the capabilities of the site, since the checkboxes inaccurately suggest that the three fields can be used simultaneously. Errors such as this can easily be avoided by making the functional specs clear from the beginning.

Technical Specifications

There are a number of technical issues that can play a role in the way an interface is programmed, and subsequently in the way it is designed. Bandwidth, or the speed at which the intended audience can access the Internet, is the most common technical variable. If you anticipate a low bandwidth/slow connection environment, you'll want to minimize the K-size of the interface as a whole, as well as the size of pages and files that go into it. Large images, video, animated GIFs, and complicated HTML files will have trouble loading and rendering over low bandwidth connections. But designers should not assume that a high bandwidth audience will have a significantly better experience viewing large files. File transfers, from server to client, are typically fraught with bottlenecks at different points in the 'Net, regardless of the client's connection speed. (See Fig. 2.9)

Wise Web interface designers use self-imposed technical specifications that favor smaller files and the simplest HTML coding. Limiting the number of GIFs on a page goes a long way toward speeding up the page-load (the time it takes to render a page online). Grouping navigation images into a single large image, for instance, is better than posting several small ones, as each of the smaller images will require a unique negotiation between client and server.

FIGURE 2.9

The file transfer issues involved in browsing the Web can make it a frustrating experience for high-bandwidth audiences as well as lower-tech users. One page can have components residing on a dozen different servers a thousand miles apart. The quality of hardware used to serve a site, and the circuitous journey its elements take through routers and ISPs before they reach the clients is always questionable. Prior to clicking a link, there is no inherent way for a user to know how big the requested page will be, or how slowly it will render. Before presenting a large or high bandwidth interface to users, let them know what they are in for.

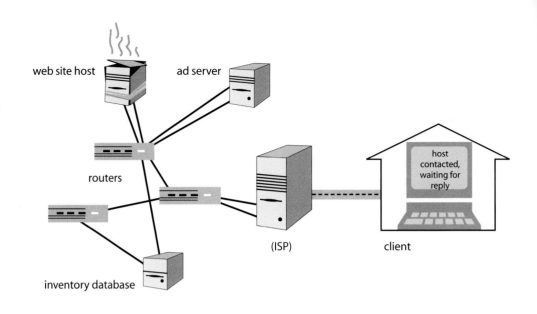

It's bad practice to make the user choose between high and low bandwidth on the home page. Besides, two distinct paths mean more work for the designer and for the production team that has to maintain two versions of a site. Give the user meaningful information early on. Rich media such as QuickTime or Flash can be presented as an option deeper in the site, where the choice will not feel burdensome to the user.

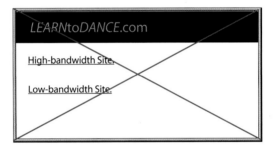

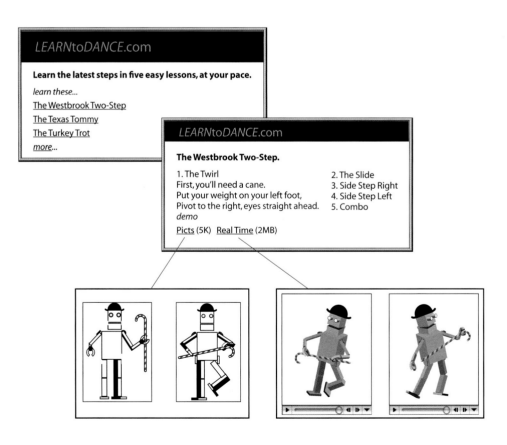

38 DESIGNING WEB SITE INTERFACE ELEMENTS

Most designers welcome firm technical specifications. There are so many ways to build an interface that reducing the options with a technical spec will help simplify both design and production. A technical spec can be as simple as a mandate forbidding the use of JavaScript, or a prescription for maximum file size.

Interaction Paradigms

The appearance of interface elements and their placement on the page are only part of interaction design. Interface designers should be aware of existing interaction paradigms—models of action and reaction between a user and interface elements. Most elements follow certain interaction paradigms on the micro level. A button, for instance, can only be pressed, and that action can only produce one result. On the macro level, more complex paradigms exist for interface systems. For instance: before an interface performs an irreversible task, such as saving a file in a word processing program, it should query the user. That way, the user can confirm irrevocable decisions. This dialogue and response is not only a safeguard, it's an established protocol between human and computer. An interface should never appear to have a mind of its own.

Most users are aware of these interaction paradigms, and are sensitive to interfaces that break them, although they might not be able to articulate their discomfort. Scrutinize your interaction decisions from the point of view of the user to avoid breaking these paradigms.

User Testing

Most designers know what it's like to be so close to their work that they can't judge it effectively, and they start showing it around to get feedback. Enlisting outside perspective is especially helpful where interface design is concerned. Although there is an apparent kinship between two-dimensional interfaces and other flat communications (posters, television commercials, etc.), the subjectivity that drives good design in traditional media is a red herring in interface design. It may be difficult to argue the existence of objectively right or wrong solutions for poster design, but there can be no argument that a given interface solution is wrong when users consistently misunderstand it.

Most problems with interfaces are the result of unclear relationships among interface elements, and confusing labels and instructional text. User testing (a misnomer—the user isn't tested, the interface is) can provide needed reality checks at critical stages. Interfaces should be given a test drive by people who resemble the target audience at least twice: after the initial concept work, and before final production.

Once the obvious strengths and shortcomings of the initial interface design have been revealed, most designers will recognize opportunities to use color, size, typeface and scale, and the rest of a designer's visual tools for creating a visual hierarchy that will guide the reader's eye through the content.

Additional Reading

A few good books have been written on the subject of usability. Steve Krug's *Don't Make Me Think* is a must-read, and Jacob Neilson's *Designing Web Usability* (taken with a few grains of salt), will help with the scientific context. For a good, in-depth discussion of the user-testing process, see *DesignWhys: Designing Web Sites That Sell* by Shayne Bowman and Chris Willis.

For the adventurous designer with an ear for geek speak, The Usability Engineering Lifecycle by Deborah J. Mayhew gives interaction paradigms their due.

SECTION II:
Basic Linear Interface Elements

If the page of text is the most basic HTML document, what is the most basic HTML interface? Consider two separate pages of text, viewable as separate screens in the browser window. There is nothing remarkable or interactive about either one until you put a hypertext link on one page that displays the other when clicked and allows the reader to decide which page to look at and when. That page is no longer an unremarkable block of text. It is a point on a decision tree, and the hypertext link is the interface—the gateway to other branches.

A hypertext link is a word or words that reveals a linked page in the browser window when clicked. It's the simplest (and I think the most elegant) of interface elements because it requires a minimal alteration to the text—just a simple HTML tag that modifies the word. At this point, it also presents virtually no learning curve for users.

From there, interface elements take on increasing complexity, from the button, to the checkbox, to the menu. They all have one thing in common: each is used to advance a user through a task. In the case of the hypertext link, the task is to move from page A to page B. In the case of a button, the task may be the same, or it may be to send a bit of information somewhere. In the case of a checkbox or a menu, the task may be to specify the information that is to be sent. In every case, a single task, or a single facet of a task, is embodied in each element. These kinds of interface elements can be thought of as linear: each can be used as a link between the beginning and end states of a task. (We'll get to multifaceted interfaces in section 3.)

The principles discussed in this section are meant to provide a foundation for anyone designing Web interface elements. Some of the discussion of basic linear elements purposely ignores the advanced capabilities of today's and tomorrow's browsers, disregarding the extended formatting capabilities of Cascading Style Sheets (CSS). We'll focus on default appearances instead. Hypertext links, for instance, are introduced as the blue-underlined text of the bygone Web, even though most interfaces now use formatting to control link color and appearance.

This is useful because the original appearance of HTML elements (gray buttons, blue text links, white checkboxes) is still in the backs of most users' minds—it's their baseline image of Web interfaces. The default appearances also crop back up in the natural degradation of HTML pages in the browser as CSS, font tags, and other display technologies fail. Though unattractive, these reversions in style don't substantially affect usability. The principles that govern usability in basic, linear, interface elements carry over very well to more complex interface systems, and as such, are still worth learning.

We will touch upon more advanced ways of formatting interface elements, but, again, we'll focus on appearances and usability and leave the actual coding techniques needed to implement them to CSS and HTML manuals.

chapter 3

LINK ELEMENTS

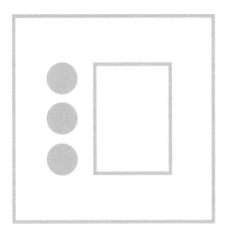

Link elements—blue underlined text or graphics that function as buttons or links—are the first line of interactivity in a Web interface. In particular, the text link serves as the linchpin of HTML navigation and the easiest interactive element to code, making it one of the first casualties to haphazard and inconsistent application. A gap has opened between the designer's need to control the appearance of link elements, and user's expectations of the link.

Most designers see the brightly colored, underscored type in a text block within a browser as an interface convention to avoid, preferring more elegant graphic links. But link elements are some of the most powerful resources in Web interface design, because they are flexible and direct. By simply wrapping an anchor tag around a word or graphic, the content of a page is extended to incorporate the Web. In Figure 3.1, the author of a Web log (blog) has found what looks to be an important part to his car. He is unable to describe it but makes an articulate query for its identification with a single link to a picture.

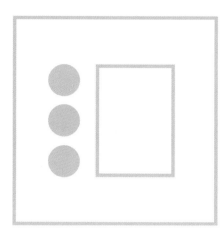

Text Link Styles

There are two variations on the familiar blue-underlined text link: integrated links, which appear within a sentence or paragraph, and nonintegrated, or linked-text, links, which are usually singular and solitary.

Text Links

Text links deserve higher status in the world of link elements. Although they are frequently eliminated in favor of the more malleable GIFs and JPGs, text links are the most versatile method of linking. Easily editable, text can be generated by servers and databases, as is the case with search engine results. Linked text—in the context of explanatory copy or didactic language that explicitly defines the link's purpose—implies an immediacy unavailable to similar graphic links. People with slow connections commonly view Web pages by ignoring images while they load, preferring the immediately available HTML text and links.

once the carburetor was rebuilt, the valve-clatter went away, allowing me to hear a new, even more disturbing sound: *Ave Maria* squealing through a gap in the intake manifold.

On another mechanical note: Can anyone identify **this** for me? I found it under the floormat, and I'm afraid to throw it out.

| last week | just rescued from the scrap heap |

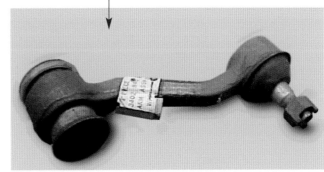

FIGURE 3.1

The author of this Web log has a strange object that he wishes to identify. Rather than describing it, he simply links to it.

"If you can't find what you're looking for here, try looking here."

Taken at face value, this is a confusing statement. Add a single underline, a little color and "here" becomes a common interface element.

If you can't find what you're looking for here, try looking **here.**

"Here" is no longer redundant. It means elsewhere, another page, an alternative location. It represents an option for the user.

On the negative side, misused text links are responsible for the majority of visual noise in Web interfaces. Most e-commerce, search engine, and corporate sites increasingly prefer to display their content as taxonomical lists—directory by category. HTML directories rarely function as well as the kiosks and indexes whose form they borrow. A printed index's high resolution and easy page flipping are more conducive to navigating long lists. Likewise, a building directory is easier to use than its HTML counterpart, because the users already understand the context and know how to reach the floors of a building. The method of movement is separate from the directory—the directory is free to function as a simple list.

On the contrary, it is difficult to present large amounts of hypertext links clearly. An HTML directory must allude to the structure of the site and convey the means of movement using only a few thousand pixels. That's a lot to expect from a low-resolution display environment. The densely packed type of an HTML directory with its multitudinous commas, underlines and ellipses present the user with a Great Blue Wall. (See Fig. 3.2)

Linked text
Essentially the same as a text link, the context and purpose of linked text is different. Links within a body of text are more akin to footnotes than signposts. Linked-text links tend to be more successful because they are buried in places where only an engaged reader is likely to see them. They serve only the reader who wants to know more, so they are less crucial to the overall navigation of a site. In fact, when users see a link within a body of text, they frequently assume the link goes off site.

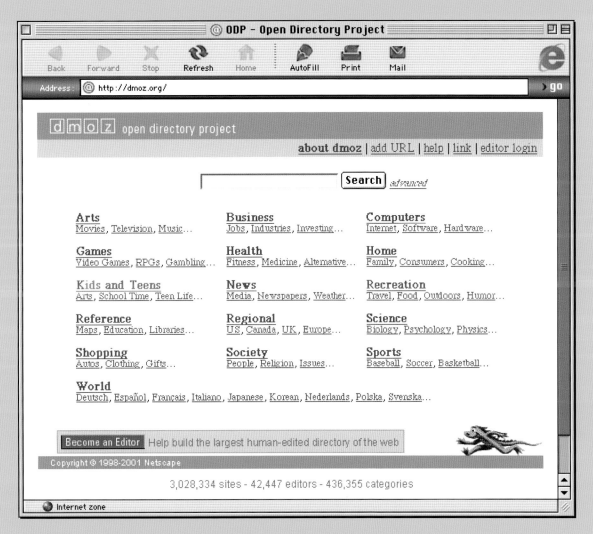

FIGURE 3.2

The Open Directory Project (ODP) uses good, old-fashioned text links for all of its navigation. Everything on the page is universally understood as an entry point into the directory, and is relatively accessible. However, if this weren't a directory, the page might seem too dense.

Nontext Link Types

In addition to standard text links, simple link elements can be made from graphical, rather than HTML text. If used correctly, GIFs fashioned to look like text links can even improve usability.

GIF-Text Links

In the case of HotBot, the developers (and myself as the designer of the team) wanted to give users access to what was essentially a filtered view of the results sorted by a third party. A button presented as an option across the top of the interface made sense to users, but they didn't use it (oddly, users are disinterested in most navigation elements on a results page). Users look closely at the linked headlines that begin each text result. A linked line of type explaining the new feature turned out to be more engaging than a button. However, the link had to be a GIF as it was essentially a submit button that sent the user's query to another database. A GIF appearing as a line of copy with the same typeface, size, and aliasing as the results text allows users to "View the 10 most popular matched for [their query]." (See Figs 3.3 and 3.4)

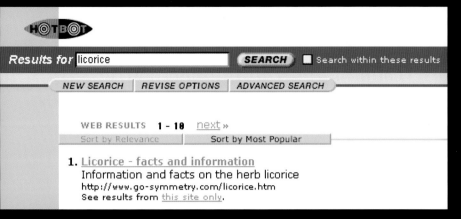

FIGURE 3.3

Users understood that a new button above the results allowed them to filter them by popularity, but only after the option was pointed out.

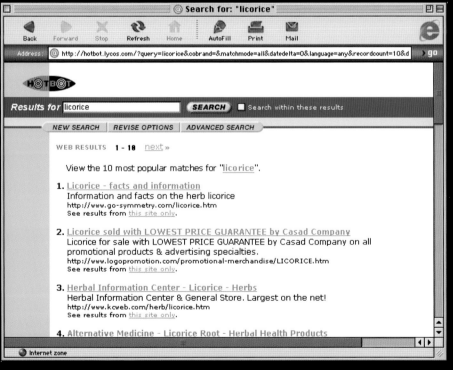

FIGURE 3.4

A line of instructional linked text was the most effective way to break through the user's routine of looking only at the results.

Graphic Links

Images (most of the time, GIFs and JPGs) have the potential for a wider variety of appearance than HTML text. Images can look like buttons, text, pictures, graphs, silhouettes, icons, etc. Any image can be made into a link by wrapping an anchor tag around it. An image can be made into an array of links by using an image map. A linked image can even be an invisible Easter egg, surprising the user who clicks on it.

Clicking a link whose functionality isn't sufficiently communicated can be as jarring as tripping over an Easter egg. Users too frequently discover that an image is a link when they click by mistake. It's too easy to suppress the graphic's blue outline—a linked image's equivalent to a blue underline—without providing any alternative context to identify the graphic and its use.

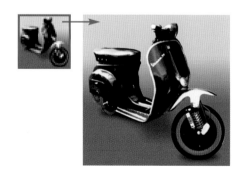

FIGURE 3.5

A small photograph is too complex to represent a single task and too small to be read as content. Its failure as an image provides a clue to its purpose: a gateway to a larger version of itself.

FIGURE 3.6

The size and shape of real-world control points—buttons, switches, even archaic dial holes—are based on the size of a fingertip. This may explain why virtual buttons tend to convey usability best when they adhere to a narrow range of shapes and sizes. Note that fingers have an avatar in the computer: the cursor, which determines the minimum sizes for links and buttons.

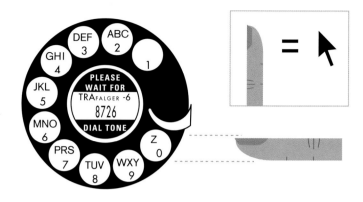

This grid shows the range of shapes that feel best as buttons without the aid of common affordances like beveled edges. The more static obtuse shapes seem to work better than say, a triangle. A hexagon, for instance, relates better to round, real-world buttons such as elevator buttons, whereas triangles have a stronger association with alert symbols and signs.

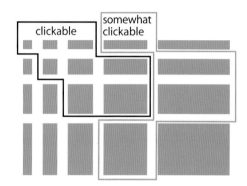
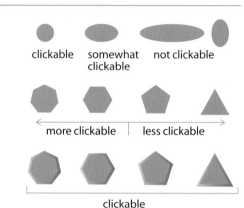

Symmetrical geometric shapes make the best graphic links, but symmetrical shapes that suggest movement are also useful. This diagram illustrates that, the more irregular the shape, the less it feels like a button. On the other hand, adding a bevel to even the oddest shape forces it into the role of button.

Uniformity and symmetry contribute to a shape's interactive appearance, as do affordances like beveled edges. Even a shape that lacks an interactive appearance can be made to look like a button with a slight 3-D beveled edge. The element's purpose is clearer still when it bears a label or instructional text.

FIGURE 3.7

Autonomy is especially important for graphic links. How functional a graphical link appears is somewhat proportional to its size, shape, sharpness, and luminosity. Graphics that seem to pop off the page appear to be naturally functional links.

Even without didactic text, blue outlines, or beveled edges, a user will click on the little colored signs of this example. The large gray image (while linkable) feels like background art, where as the colored signs pop off the page. Each small image has autonomy, which implies functionality.

FIGURE 3.8

Linked images are best used as navigational elements and as representations of functionality. A small image of a printer works as a representation of the "print this page" functionality.

Whether it's a single icon or an image map, the existence and purpose of a link should be apparent to the user before clicking on it.

You can use many methods to convey usability for graphic links that are gateways to other pages (See Fig. 3.5). (Most of these options will be covered in Chapter 4: Button Elements.) Small geometric images in a range of sizes and proportions seem to work best as graphic links (See Figs. 3.6 and 3.7) especially in the context of other similarly designed images. Linked images mimicking the appearance of traditional interactive tools—buttons, levers, and dials—further communicate functionality. Simple representations of functionality, such as a small graphic of a printer for "print," communicate clickability. (See Fig. 3.8)

Link Arrangement

When a designer deals with complex interfaces incorporating several style and link types, arrangement becomes the highest hurdle. How a user's eye moves through an interface can determine how useful the interface is. Users bounce from link to link, sizing up an interface to formulate a plan for how to use it. Categorizing similar functions into element clusters is the basis for complex interface composition. Designers should create pockets of like functionality that are easily

Hypertext Webster Gateway: "licorice"

From Webster's Revised Unabridged Dictionary (1913) (web1913)

Licorice \Lic"o*rice\ (l[i^]k"[-o]*r[i^]s), n. [OE. licoris, through old French, fr. L. liquiritia, corrupted fr. glycyrrhiza, Gr. glyky`rriza; glyky`s sweet + "ri`za root. Cf. {Glycerin}, {Glycyrrhiza}, {Wort}.] [Written also {liquorice}.] 1. (Bot.) A plant of the genus {Glycyrrhiza} ({G. glabra}), the root of which abounds with a sweet juice, and is much used in demulcent compositions.

FIGURE 3.9

The University of California, San Diego hosts a public-domain dictionary online. It renders every word in a definition as a link. The ability to jump directly to a new entry from within the definition may be useful, but it comes at the expense of readability.

FIGURE 3.10

Since it is a given that everything in the ODP interface is a link, the real challenge is to provide easy access to each link's content. Eliminating underlines and decreasing color intensity makes the page easier to read.

identified by the user. Pockets or clusters should contain parseable and autonomous link elements. Several clusters of functionality can coexist in an interface if you make them appear autonomous through the use of dividing space, display text, and color.

Link Density

In body text, articles, Web sites, and companies should be linked when they first occur, making them easier to find when the user is ready to explore. Since new ideas and terms are usually introduced early in an article, the opening two paragraphs are going to contain a high concentration of links. The questions arises: how many links

are acceptable? Unfortunately, there are no hard-and-fast rules about link density. The number of links you place on a given page depends on the type of page.

A news article with linked text in its opening paragraphs is more versatile than the same article with no links or its printed counterpart. Conversely, the same story with too many links—say, one per line—would imply that the author had inadequate content and needed to rely on outside texts. Additionally, excessive links are a distraction, especially when they're underlined. When making links, be selective. If text contains too many links, it will be riddled with little blue holes. (See Fig. 3.9)

Sometimes it isn't possible to limit the amount of text links per line. Under those circumstances, making the interface easy to read should be your primary goal. (See Fig. 3.10)

Autonomy

Autonomy, the condition in which something appears distinct and unique in spite of its similarity to everything around it, is the critical consideration in clearly displaying links. For a link to function well, it should represent a singular action, destination, or concept, and must be distinguishable from the surrounding elements.

Links of uniform length take on an appearance reminiscent of evenly formatted buttons. A group of uniform links is easier to visually parse than multiple links of varying length, which can appear as a single body of linked text. Space and color are essential in defining where one link begins and the other ends. (See Fig. 3.11)

Polarizing

Clustering links of similar function—and polarizing groups of links with differing functions—will further help a user to draw cognitive distinctions between and among link elements. (See Fig. 3.12)

Link Grouping

Links are often cleaner and more useful if you separate them from their text and place them in margins. This allows the content to be free of any distracting decoration. The underline, if used at all, can return to its original function—emphasis. (See Fig. 3.13) Form follows function when links are placed in the margins. The two modes of inter-action (reading and clicking) are polarized and thus easier to access.

A margin of links also helps the user make quick decisions about the content by offer-ing a quick list of scannable topics.

Many search engines attempt to "under-stand" the meaning of a page by parsing links and groups of links, ascribing a higher value to them than other text on the page; the assumption being that if those words are important enough to be linked, they must be keywords for the page. Marginal-ized links can therefore have a positive effect on a page's search-engine ranking.

My favorite sites are:
Antique 78 Digest, The Old Crank, Look For The Dog, Nauks Antique Record Auction, The Shellac Enthusiast, The Victrola Source.

My favorite sites are:
Antique 78 Digest
The Old Crank
Look For The Dog
Nauks Antique Record Auction
The Shellac Enthusiast
The Victrola Source

FIGURE 3.11

In the top list, commas define where one link ends and the next starts. This method is functional but not quickly grasped. The second list makes a clearer distinction between each line. The space between each line clarifies the difference between single and multiple-lined items.

TIP:
Leading is essentially nonexistent in HTML. To control the space between items in a list, use a nonbreaking space ( ) one or two sizes larger than the surrounding text.

Source:

```
<font size=2>
<font size=4> </font>Look For The Dog<BR><BR>
<font size=4> </font>Nauks Antique Record Auction<BR><BR>
<font size=4> </font>The Shellac Enthusiast
</font>
```

Effect:
Look For The Dog
Nauks Antique Record Auction
The Shellac Enthusiast

FIGURE 3.12: CLUSTERING GROUPS OF LINKS

The technique of clustering and polarizing link elements is abundantly evident on the home page of *Wired News*.

Nearly everything on this page is a link, or supports a link. The center of the page is the main column of headlines, which are lengthy text links. The section navigation at the top of the page is rendered as graphic links in an image map. Despite the lack of visual clues (blue outlines, beveled edges) these elements are obviously links. They are short, uniform words, all of the same type face and size with plenty of space around them.

Didactic text, which explicitly tells a user how to use a link or form—like that just below the search box—can incorporate multiple instances of linked text with separate destinations that add value to the single act of signing up for free delivery.

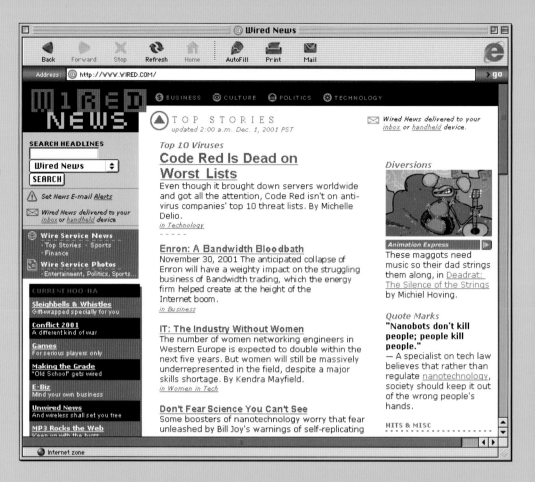

FIGURE 3.13

Rather than integrating the relevant links into the story, they can be collected in one place like a column, where users can easily find them once they've decided to branch out.

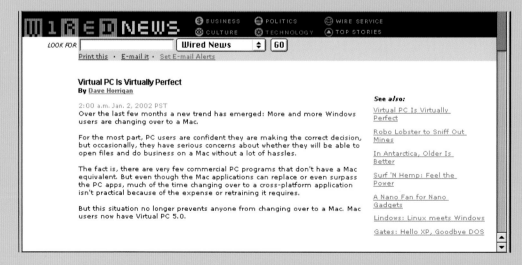

Link Placement

Finding the best placement for a link or group of links can be confounding to a designer. Logic and tradition tell us to place navigation across the top of a page, along with branding, as well as down the left column. Watching many users in front of most Web interfaces demonstrate that this may not always be the best approach.

Colored, underlined hypertext links are an established vernacular and one of the few navigation conventions that all users recognize. Unfortunately, the hyperlink is often usurped by people who want to capitalize on its powerful association. Ad banners often include pseudolinked text to combat banner blindness. As a result, users associate value with the center of the page, disregarding the top as banner land, even when text links are present. Sometimes their attention drifts into the right margins (perhaps because the right edge of a window is dynamic and resizable).

In determining placement, weigh the options of where a link logically belongs versus where will it be noticed. Placing a link in an odd spot may help its visibility but irritate the user who wants the cognitive page map to follow tradition. Conversely, a link that is too important to be ignored may merit the initial confusion of an odd placement. (See Fig. 3.14)

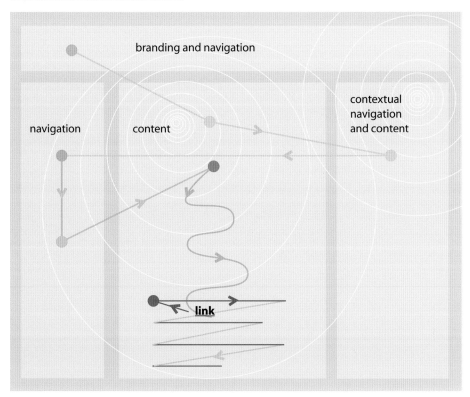

FIGURE 3.14: HOW PEOPLE READ WEB PAGES
After a bit of scanning, a user's eye gravitates toward hyperlinks, virtually skipping over everything else on the page.

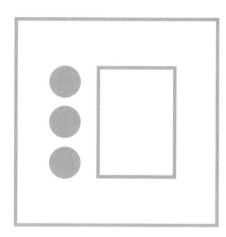

Link Descriptions

There are two ways to approach text link formatting: linking an entire group of words or linking a single word or short phrase within a sentence. The difference between linked text and text links has already been discussed, but the decision on which to use is often based on design rather than language issues.

When didactic text has a specific function encapsulated in it, linking the operative word— the word that bests distinguishes the purpose of the phrase—can be less redundant than linking the object of a phrase. In Figure 3.15 (top), each sentence is about licorice, but the purpose of each line is clearest when the operative word is linked. The text would be redundant and seem less engaging if "licorice" were linked repeatedly. Linking the operative word helps each sentence stand out as a unique option.

This example's drawback is its spotty appearance, which is caused by several links that have no common alignment or axis. Short phrases, each of which is a link, provides a uniform solution as seen in Figure 3.15 (bottom). The linked phrases would seem less descriptive than the earlier version without the aid of the two headings.

Read about licorice's long history.

Try some classic licorice, or have white licorice.

Learn about double salted licorice.

Fealing brave? Take the double salted licorice challenge.

Make your own licorice.

Learn More: Taste Tests:
History of Licorice   Double Salted Licorice
Making Licorice   White Licorice
Double Salted Licorice   Classic Licorice

FIGURE 3.15
Double Salted Licorice appears in both lists. The headings eliminate redundancy
between the lists, and allow the user to zero in on the desired task (reading vs. eating).

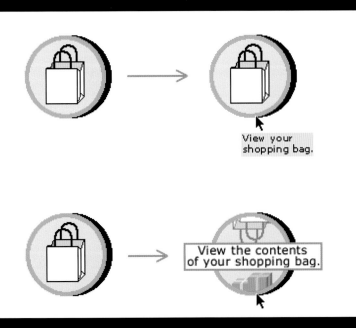

FIGURE 3.16
The rollover and its predecessor the tool tip, are convenient ways to hide lengthy descriptions while making them available when the user needs them. Balance saving space and
creating work. Users shouldn't have to mouse over every element on the page in order to
use an interface.

Users get the most out of interfaces with concise links and buttons. Icons are an excellent
way to represent complex ideas in a limited
space. Users have grown accustomed to
operating systems and applications that use
symbols in conjunction with brief descriptions to represent certain tasks. However,
icons are not always self explanatory. If I see
an icon of a shopping bag, I need to learn
what it means. Most users are uncomfortable
with the time it takes to learn a whole new
iconographic system in a Web interface. You
can provide descriptive text with the icon to
make it usable, but if you do the icon is
hardly a space-saving device. Fortunately,
there is a good alternative. The icon can
appear alone, with explanatory text revealed
when a user mouses over it. (See Fig. 3.16)

Mouseover effects with tool tip text have
become a standard bridge between an icon's
simplified appearance and the complex communication of its function. Tool-tip language
(alt text) can be added to an anchor tag and
can appear when the cursor remains over
the link. Mouse over a link and the URL—or
an email address—appears in the info bar at
the bottom of a browser as well, helping the
user make an informed decision about
where a link will take him.

A user gets frustrated looking all around the browser for hints about a link he's moused over. Don't require this kind of interaction too often. The meaning of a link should be readily apparent without investigative mouseovers. Use mouseover tool-tips for added clarity, not as the primary source of definition.

Presentation

A great deal of consideration should go into the presentation of links. Every aspect of link display has an effect on the compositional hierarchy, color palette, editorial voice, and user perception of an interface's value. The conventions of link presentation and appearance are the legacy of hands-off design, allowing users to define link color, color of visited links (v-link) typeface and size. This should not dissuade designers from subjecting link appearance to the same scrutiny as they would any other aspect of a design. The most significant aspect of link presentation is one of the most cantankerous elements of design—color.

Link Color

Blue was chosen as the default Web link color by the process of elimination. Red, green, and blue each use only one phosphor on a computer monitor's screen, providing a sharp display. However, green is too light and red is both charged with implication and stands out too much. Blue is dark enough for contrast and reads well against black text.

Any color you choose for links should address luminosity, contrast, and any cultural and psychological implications. A white page, dense with red and blue links, can be reminiscent of the American flag, giving an interface an unintended patriotic flavor. Green seems neutral and makes sense as a link color because it is synonymous with "go," but there are a host of other implications to the color. Green often feels earthy, or grassroots; it is also synonymous with money. On black backgrounds, pure green has a low-tech appearance reminiscent of old video games.

Less intense colors tend to be freer of subtext, such as the grayish purple seen on the left side of Figure 3.17. It has enough luminosity to read as a link, without the floral cast that is created when bright purple is used repeatedly on a white background. (For a vivid look into the cultural implications of color, see David Bachelor's *Chromophobia,* 2001.)

Before you plunge in, carefully consider the implication of multiple link colors on a page. A cluster of blue links next to a cluster of green links implies that there is a fundamental difference between the two clusters. Try to render like functionality with similar colors. (See Fig. 3.18)

Visited Links

Visited links are the bane of a designer's existence. A page full of links rendered in blue quickly turns into a menagerie of blue and purple once a user has done some clicking. Although I wish that I could get away with never using them, visited link

Wormwood

(ARTEMISIA ABSINTHIUM)

Use this for disturbances and weakness in the stomach.
A pale green perennial grows to about three feet (90 cm) high. The flowers are a pale olive early on, changing to brownish-yellow.
Locations: garbage pits, ditches and roadsides.
Flowering: Early to midsummer.
Astrology: Governed by <u>Mars</u>.
Medicinal: Leaves and flowers are good for <u>gout</u>.

Uses: <u>Stomach tonic</u>; for expelling worms and reducing fevers.— 1 OZ (28 g) to 1 pt (568 ml) boiling water ; dosage: 2 fl OZ (56 ml) — this is one of the best remedies for <u>poor liver function</u>, <u>dyspepsia</u>, and <u>gastro-intestinal pain</u>. Use as an <u>antiseptic</u> and to promote menstruation. DO NOT USE IN PREGNACY!
Vermouth: A <u>liquor</u> made from <u>Absinthol</u>, (an extract of wormwood) soothing to the <u>nervous system</u>, but damaging if taken to excess.

W: Wallflower · Walnut Tree · Wheat · Willowherb · Rosebay Willowherb · Willow Tree · Wintergreen · Woodruffe · Sweet Woodruffe · **Wormwood**

FIGURE 3.17

Link color defined in the body tag is universally applied to every link on the page. If an interface uses more than one background color, a single link color may not work everywhere on the page. It is possible to get around this limitation by specifying a different color for an individual link.

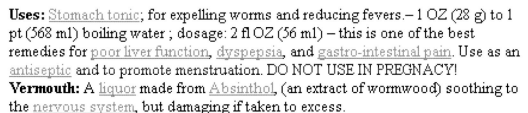

FIGURE 3.18

A dark green link shows up well on white, but over this black background, a lighter, less intense green is used to appear similar to its counterpart on white. The column of red links is obviously addressing a different kind of functionality than the green links.

TIP: A font tag with a new color nested between the anchor tags will give the link a unique color. The body tags' visited and active link colors will also be overridden by the font color in the tag.

```
<a href="x"><font color="red">link</a/font></a>
```

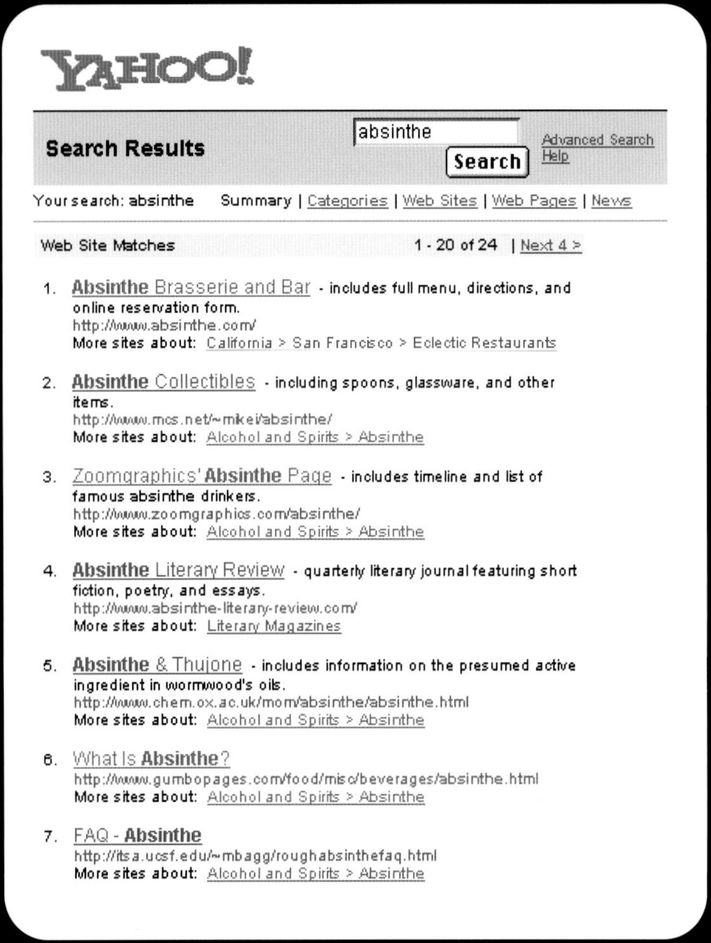

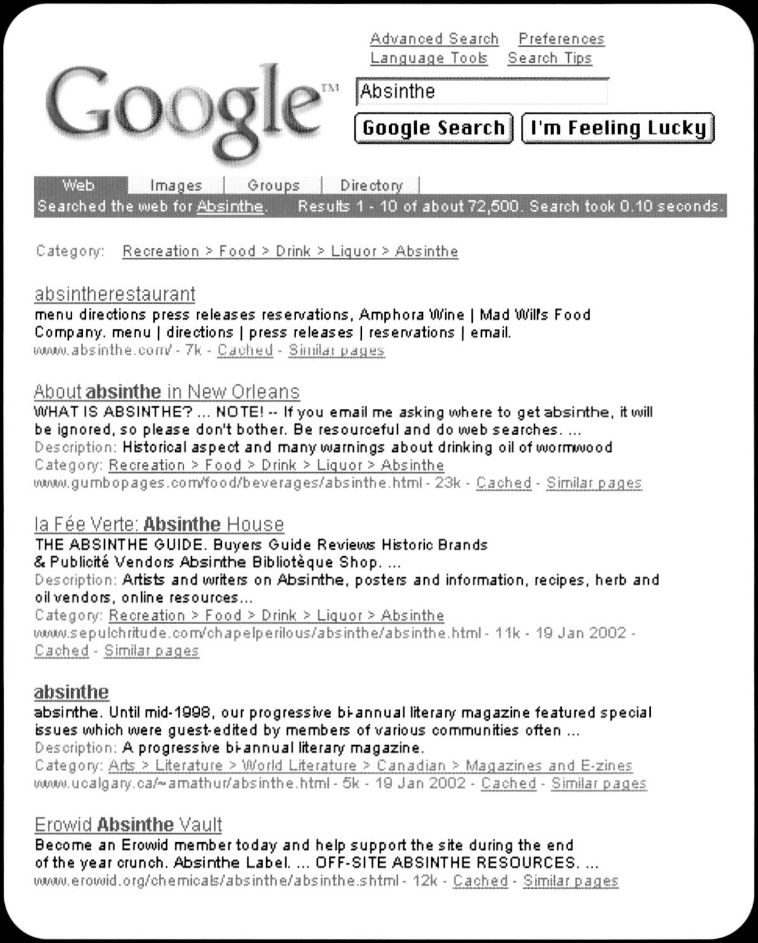

FIGURE 3.19

The convention of using a color complementary to the link color for visited links can have an adverse effect on the cast of a page. The color scheme of an interface will appear to shift as links become visited. The Yahoo interface uses purple as the visited link color. With every click, the page becomes more garish.

Once a user has visited a link, it is probably less important and should recede into the body of the text, rather than draw attention to itself.

colors help users return to links, or avoid them in preference to unexplored ones. For usability's sake, visited links should appear used. In real life, new things are shiny and bright, used things are often dull with a patina. When using a blue link color, a slightly grayer, slightly darker blue works well for the visited link, as if the link has faded closer to the black of the surrounding text. (See Fig. 3.19)

Active Links

Active text link colors occur while the mouse is down when a user clicks a link. In human-computer interface (HCI) terms, this action is called feedback. When a user does something, feedback confirms that the computer has accepted the input. Even if there is a lag while the browser requests the URL from a server, the active link color reassures the user that the click actually happened.

Since most graphic links have no way of providing click feedback when the link outline is set to zero, users have become accustomed to interactive elements that do not feedback on mouse down. Active link colors can now largely be ignored by designers.

Link Typography and Legibility

GIF-text links are prevalent in Web design because most onscreen text is ugly and difficult to read. Most designers prefer anti-aliased typography that accurately embodies the subtleties and character of traditional type design.

Typeface and Type Size

Bad type online started with the first version of Mozilla and Netscape. Times was chosen as the default display font because it's a proportional face that existed on both Macs and PCs. Presumably someone at Netscape was told that serif faces were the most legible types. Ironically, this couldn't be further from the truth for onscreen type. Times, and most other serif faces, are not the best type to use for text or links. The pixel bits that form the serifs of a 10-point letter amount to visual noise and hog more than a quarter of the cap height. Underlines are broken up by descender serifs.

When an interface has so few links that a user can navigate them easily, consider specifying the same color for links and vlinks.

Color and Legibility

The pixels that make up a letter are not as uniform as you might think. On a monitor, three tiny grids of phosphors entwine to form a pixel. Black pixels are easy on the eyes as they use the phosphors at their dimmest, while white is the full force of red, green and blue strobing at fifteen thousand times a second. (See Fig. 3.20) Since color is an inextricable part of text link elements, the bleeding effect of luminous pixels is burdensome.

For this reason, the popular tendency to design interfaces with white type on a black background has the opposite effect on user comfort than does the same color scheme in, say, a car dashboard. White type on black is complex and hard on the eyes. Link elements may take on an attractive vividness on black, but the long-term effects are eye straining.

Link Presentation Effects

As computing power and bandwidth increase, Web clients can display more complex and user-friendly solutions for link elements. Designers should feel comfortable breaking away from blue-underlined text. The legacy of the blue underline continues to be the baseline for link elements, so any deviation from tradition should reference the old form to some degree. Users understand that a word within a text with a unique color or subtle type treatment probably means link.

Mousing over the text in question should provide immediate reinforcement to this expectation. As long as every link of that type is treated the same way, the user has effortlessly learned the page's visual language, and can get down to the business of using the interface.

There are as many solutions to the problem of creative link presentation as there are variations on basic type display. Cascading Style Sheets (CSS) allow a designer to easily define static and active characteristics of anchored type. The most common solution has been mentioned already—suppressing the underline until the cursor is over a link. On mouseover, a text link can change face to bold or italic and even become larger. Be careful in your choice of visual cue. Any type alteration that increases the size of the link may have a rippling effect on the surrounding text, causing it to rerender, wrap or push adjacent page elements around. Limit the use of type resizing to links that have a substantial buffer of space around them. (See Fig. 3.21)

Most type effects initiated on mouseover work fine as feedback behaviors. Since the effect occurs only on user initiation, even ugly effects are frequently forgiven. They have no adverse effect on the static read of a page. Avoid multiple mouseover effects in a small space. They can look like a spinning disco ball, and are worthless considering the effort and extra code that goes into them.

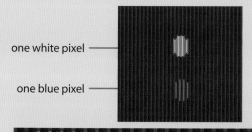

one white pixel

one blue pixel

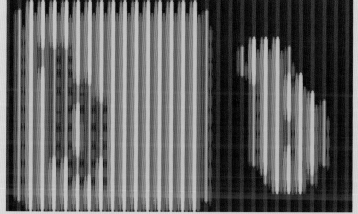

12-point Times "b" bold,
white on black @ 1200%

12-point Times "b" bold,
black on white @ 1200%

FIGURE 3.20

Each pixel is actually a mesh of three quickly
flashing colors: red, green, and blue. Since they
are each set off from one another, no pixel is as
sharp and uniform in reality as in theory. Pure red,
green or blue type on a black background is the
cleanest combination of phosphors, while any
color scheme involving combinations of colors
takes on a subtle fuzziness.

FIGURE 3.21

Reinforcing behavior by brightening the link color
and displaying an underline on mouseover helps
users feel comfortable with this slight shift in
paradigm, away from the old convention of omni-
present blue lines. Other effects that don't cause
the adjacent text or page elements to move—
such as reversing and knocking-out type, or
enlarging the link on mouseover—are also useful
and become part of the overall style of an interface.

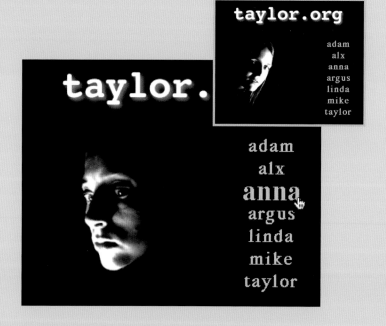

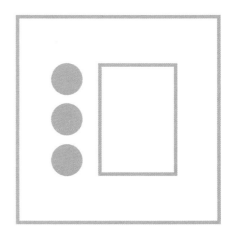

Cross-Browser and Platform Link Presentation

Different browsers, platforms, and clients handle type differently, depending on the settings of their display preferences. HTML was originally intended to be free of absolute type formatting (relative formatting such as H1, H2, etc. is part of the original HTML spec) so users could specify size. Leaving type size to be specified by the client runs contrary to what designers know about page composition. Controlling the appearance of type is necessary in creating visual hierarchy. Over time, font tags and CSS were introduced to HTML to address the needs of design, but the programming world has never fully turned over type control to designers. Text link elements have unpredictable appearance on the client side, despite our best efforts and intentions.

FIGURE 3.22

For our friends with Macs and a modicum of good taste, the text will look like this:

Eric Gill is rolling over in his grave

The rest of the Mac world, and some of the PCs out there will see this:

Eric Gill is rolling over in his grave

The remaining PCs, and the Unix boxes that have no decent fonts, will see something like this:

Eric Gill is rolling over in his grave

Eric Gill is rolling over in his grave

```
<font face="gill, helvetica, arial, sans-serif" style="font-size 24px>Eric Gill is
rolling over in his grave</font>
```

FIGURE 3.23

The *Wired News* list of stories ports easily to a Palm because the linked headlines translate well into the PDA's narrow display environment. A top story is emphasized by its size and boldness, while still functioning as a link.

Seeing and selecting link elements is especially difficult on phones. Links should be distant from one another and as short as possible.

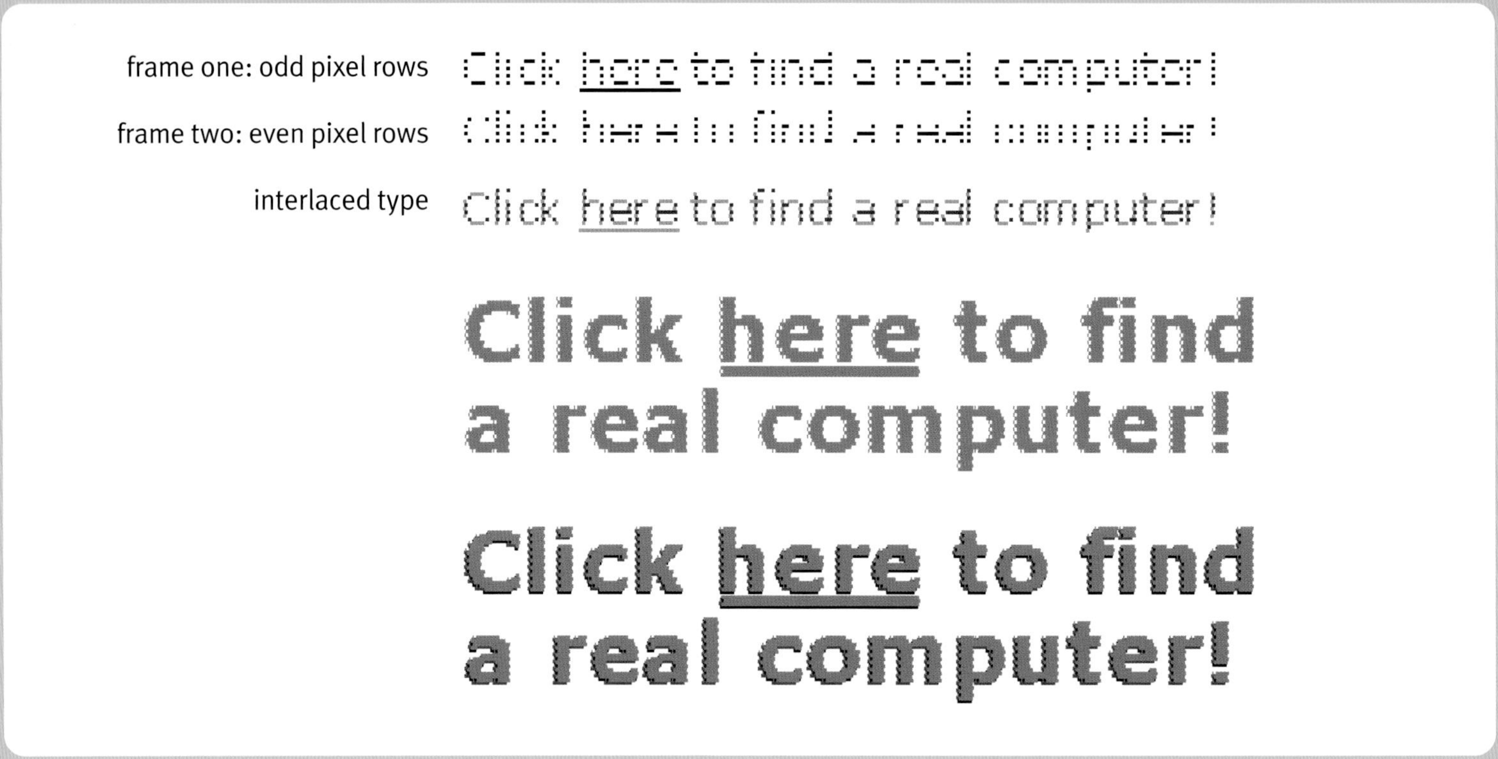

frame one: odd pixel rows   Click here to find a real computer!

frame two: even pixel rows   Click here to find a real computer!

interlaced type   Click here to find a real computer!

Click here to find a real computer!

Click here to find a real computer!

FIGURE 3.24

Thick strokes and drop shadows help to ease the strobe effect caused by interlacing and the misaligned phosphors of television screens.

Always view your work on both the Mac and PC. Microsoft Internet Explorer (IE) and Netscape (NS) are the two browsers to look at on each platform—a minimum of four views to consider. The difference in type rendering between versions of a given browser is relatively consistent, so don't worry too much about Netscape 5 vs. 6, for instance. The main issue is size, which tends to effect line measure and text wrapping. In general, Macs render type a bit smaller than PCs.

When specifying a typeface in HTML, you are limited to the fonts residing on the viewer's machine. There's no telling what fonts are installed, so it is best to focus on the typefaces that come free with all computers. The two platforms have few fonts in common. Times and Courier exist in both platforms, but Helvetica seems to be a mystery to PCs, which instead provide Arial (a Helvetica knockoff). PCs ship with Verdana and Georgia, which are also included as part of the IE download package for Macintosh. To hedge your bets, font specifications can be written like a wish list, in descending order of importance. (See Fig. 3.22)

Multiple Delivery Channels: Browsers and Handhelds

What linked text lacks in design possibilities, it makes up for in versatility. Since an underline is a simple modification to the appearance of a word, traditional hypertext links are easily ported into the PDA environment. In the colorless world of one-bit, 175 X 150–pixel handheld devices and even smaller phone interfaces, underlined links work better than graphics. (See Fig. 3.23)

Link Elements on WebTV

WebTV is the ugly stepchild of the browser. Designed to accommodate an audience about as Web-savvy as the Druids, and stymied by the superbly bad display quality of television, link elements in this environment are a bear. Briefly, the big issues to consider if you must design for WebTV are:

Interlacing: A standard TV renders its image one line at a time. Every image is divided into two consecutive frames that display every other row of pixels. Frame one will render the odd rows and as that frame is half-finished painting, the second frame of even rows is filling in the gaps, or interlacing. Each frame is rendered fifteen times per second. Since every pixel row is constantly appearing and disappearing, link underlines appear to fade in and out, as does just about every other part of small type. The remedy is to use very large type (24-point Helvetica Bold, for instance) so that each horizontal stroke and underline is three pixels high, or more. (See Fig. 3.24)

Pixel Bleed: TVs are not precision monitors. The phosphor bleeding that surrounds a pixel, is so pronounced that small elements are too fuzzy to be used. Drop shadows give enough girth to type to keep it from getting lost in fuzz, without appearing significantly bolder than originally intended.

NTSC Color Palette: When color TV was invented, transmitting color images on radio waves called for a limited range of color frequencies. Bright colors that were considered unrealistic or unpleasant (reds and magentas especially) were dropped from the transmittable spectrum. So, most TVs before the advent of high-definition television were not built to adequately render intense colors, limiting the palette of colors available to designers of WebTV interfaces. Colors that fall outside of the NTSC palette (most of the bright reds that are common in Web design) bleed and vibrate significantly. Even the more stable blues and yellows are fairly unpredictable. Yellows easily become white, and blues can become much darker than intended.

chapter 4

BUTTON ELEMENTS

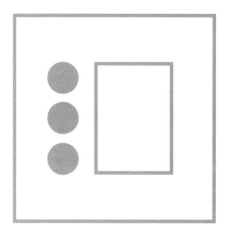

Buttons are the most significant elements of interfaces. Nearly every important communication between human and computer is initiated, verified, or executed through a button. We use buttons when responding to dialog boxes, sending messages, and moving about the Web. For most people, buttons are the primary means of interacting with computers.

On the Web, interface conventions are stretched to the breaking point. Nowhere is that more apparent than in the employment of buttons. For every rule about button design and usage that I discuss in this chapter, there is a contradiction on the Web that verges on becoming a new convention. Though the original theories behind buttons may seem antiquated, Web designers should understand them, since most users first experience computing in an environment that still strictly adheres to conventional interface theory, the desktop. (See Fig. 4.1)

In essence, a button is a shortcut. (See Fig. 4.2) Originally, buttons served as shortcuts to executing scripts or performing a set of functions that would otherwise require programming knowledge.

Designers tend not to think of buttons as programming shortcuts. We think of buttons visually: as rectangular, shaded items with a single centered label, perhaps with a 3-D beveled edge, or a rounded outline. We make a distinction between icons and buttons, and we vaguely acknowledge a difference between iconic buttons, and iconic labels. We can draw a button in Photoshop and save it as a GIF; define it in HTML and render it from the collection of system level forms; or we can build it with table cells and HTML links, or with CSS. To a user, however, neither appearance nor technology define a button. For a user, a button is any concise, regular shape that responds to a mouse-click by consistently performing a single action. As long as a user thinks it appears and functions like a button, it is a button.

FIGURE 4.1

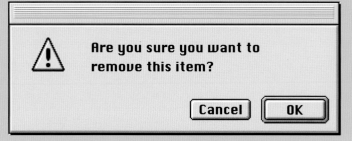

This dialog box shows the purest use of buttons. There are two possible outcomes represented by buttons in this dialog box. The purpose of the buttons, as well as their consequences, are clearly communicated through their design.

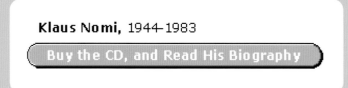

This is a common sight in Web interfaces—a button that seemingly has more than one purpose. It is not difficult to guess what will happen when this button is pressed—a page will appear with ways to buy a CD and a book—but the conventional simplicity of buttons is replaced by something ambiguous.

FIGURE 4.2: HOW A BUTTON EXECUTES A SCRIPT

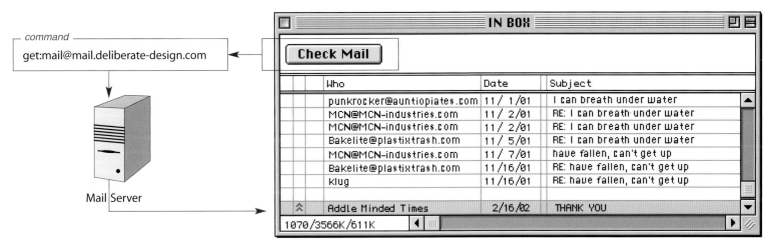

command

get:mail@mail.deliberate-design.com

IN BOX

Check Mail

		Who	Date	Subject	
		punkrocker@auntiopiates.com	11/ 1/01	I can breath under water	▲
		MCN@MCN-industries.com	11/ 2/01	RE: I can breath under water	
		MCN@MCN-industries.com	11/ 2/01	RE: I can breath under water	
		Bakelite@plastixtrash.com	11/ 5/01	RE: I can breath under water	
		MCN@MCN-industries.com	11/ 7/01	have fallen, can't get up	
		Bakelite@plastixtrash.com	11/16/01	RE: have fallen, can't get up	
		klug	11/16/01	RE: have fallen, can't get up	
☆		Addle Minded Times	2/16/02	THANK YOU	▼

1070/3566K/611K

Mail Server

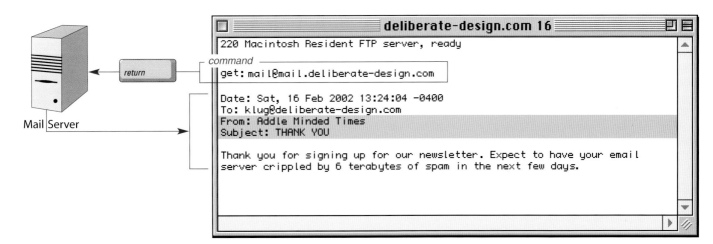

deliberate-design.com 16

220 Macintosh Resident FTP server, ready

command

get: mail@mail.deliberate-design.com

return

Date: Sat, 16 Feb 2002 13:24:04 -0400
To: klug@deliberate-design.com
From: Addle Minded Times
Subject: THANK YOU

Thank you for signing up for our newsletter. Expect to have your email
server crippled by 6 terabytes of spam in the next few days.

Mail Server

Buttons generally execute a script command. Pressing the Send button on an email client is nothing more than using a shortcut. The action sends a preformatted command to a mail server. A nongraphical mail client, such as Pine, issues the same instructions to the mail server but without buttons. The user must type the script commands by hand. From the mail server's point of view, there is no difference. The button is a convenient shortcut only the user sees.

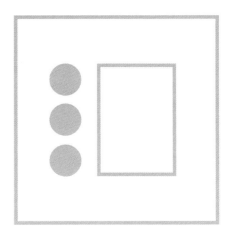

Buttons vs. Links

Buttons should be visually unique, autonomous agents of a specific task. They function best when the essence of that task can be communicated with a single word or a single symbol. A text link may incorporate many of the same characteristics as a button, but it is just as likely to be the hot spot in a longer phrase. (See Fig. 4.3) To use the right one, you need to understand their different purposes. A button accomplishes something, while a link references something.

Clicking on a button should result in an expected progression through a task, or the initiation of a process that is directly related to the interface. In most cases, if it simply results in jumping to a new piece of content, it should not be a button. It should be a link.

While it may be difficult to draw a sharp line between buttons and links, the best way to identify what makes a successful button is by recognizing what makes an unsuccessful one and avoiding it. It is easy to tell when a button does not work. From the user's perspective, if it doesn't act like a button, regardless of what it looks like, it isn't a button. (See Fig. 4.4) The degree to which a button is perceived as such by the user is largely based on context. (See Fig. 4.5)

Although Web designers don't think of menu items as buttons, that is, in fact, exactly what they are.

FIGURE 4.3

While there is no doubt that the underlined words are links, it's a little murky as to which geometric elements are buttons in 2 and 3. Examples 2, 3, and 4 show that there is a large gray area between what qualifies as a graphical link and what is clearly a graphical button. In theory, you should try not to design interface elements that reside in the gray area between button and link. In practice, getting people to identify many navigational elements means bending the rules a little. This example would fare better if the designer eliminated the ambiguity of example 2.

Q:	**Which elements are links?**		**Q:**	**Which elements are buttons?**
A:	1. obviously links		**A:**	4. obviously a button
	2. a link			3. these are buttons
	3. these are links, or are they buttons?			2. not sure if this is a button or a link?

Got a story we should know about? **Send it.**

Got a story we should know about? **SEND IT**

Got a story we should know about? <u>Send it.</u>

FIGURE 4.4

The top example is too ambiguous. Is Send it a button or a link? The border coupled with the underlined text draws attention to the element, but it is unclear what result clicking will have. Will it act like a button and bring you to a form to be filled out or like a link and bring you to a new page?

The second example is visually clearer, but when you read the text, it is difficult to imagine how Send it is a progression through a task, since no task has been initiated.

The third example is the best marriage of form and perceived function. It is not in the ambiguous gray area between link and button of the first two examples.

FIGURE 4.5: IS IT A LINK OR A BUTTON?

Clicking an interface element to go to a URL is usually the mark of a link. From the user's perspective, however, the More Power button enables an advancement in task. Despite the button being only an image linking two pages, the user progresses through the interface. The linked image truly is a button.

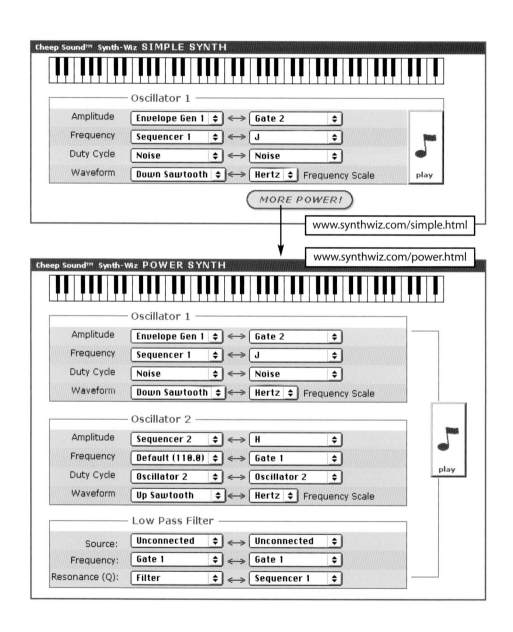

Boxed Light
Alternative Photography made easy (sort of)

PINHOLE focal lengths, diameters, thickness...
MULTIHOLE overlapping, separated, effects
ZONEPLATE defined
HYPERFOCAL examples, methods
CONSTRUCTION wood, paper, brass...
LINKS
SUPPLIERS

This site is part of the Rebel Art Foundation.
Breaking the Rules in Photography, Video, Design,
and multi-media since 1994.

see more of the **Rebel Art Foundation**

FIGURE 4.5: IS IT A LINK OR A BUTTON? *CONTINUED*

When two unrelated interfaces are linked by a buttonlike graphic, the graphic is just a link. No advancement in task has taken place. In fact, the task has changed.

figure it out (taglinebroughttoyouby robots)

flat 3-d kenetik

new, less new, near dead

grant writer needed

System Buttons

A button succeeds if it references the convention of system buttons well. A system button is one that is defined by an operating system. When you specify a Submit button in HTML, you are telling the browser to use the look of the standard button of the operating system in use by the user's computer, whether it be Mac, PC, or something else.

System buttons are the most widely recognized button style, the very appearance of which seems to shout "do something here." Users are already acquainted with their appearance, behavior, and function. Despite users growing familiarity with different button behaviors, the System button is still the most effective model. Its behavior best addresses the user's need for feedback from interface elements. (See Fig. 4.6)

Each operating system has a visual button style. However, this isn't only because the makers of an operating system want to distinguish their product from the competition. A group of virtual tools should have a unique overall appearance to reinforce the user's sense of place. All the widgets that make up Windows have a specific design sensibility. The proportions of the window controls, the shape of the buttons and menus have a unified look that differs from the corresponding elements of the Macintosh OS. These differences tell the user that he is in a specific computing environment. Web interface designers attempt to do exactly the

System buttons are easy

to apply because they are

created with a simple tag:

`<input type="submit" value="SUBMIT">`

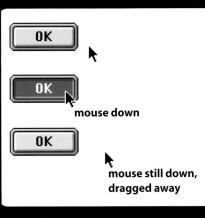

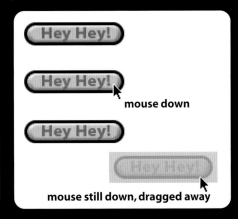

mouse down

mouse still down, dragged away

mouse down

mouse still down, dragged away

FIGURE 4.6: SYSTEM BUTTONS VS. GIF BUTTONS

System buttons have been designed with great attention to how people best interact with virtual tools. They respond to user interaction by changing color or displaying a depressed state on click.

Like most system-level tools, the button has a built-in forgiveness for user uncertainty. Pressing a system button can be interrupted by moving the cursor away from the button before releasing the mouse. This behavior makes it easy for users to change their minds midclick.

The same scenario using a GIF button results in no feedback. The only way to know for sure that you've clicked this GIF button is to wait and see what happens. Given the lag time with many browsers and server responses, clicking often provides no immediate result. Users tend to click the same button repeatedly while they wait. Backing out in midclick results in the unexpected result of the image being dragged along by the mouse.

FIGURE 4.7

Clicking buttons that are stylistically related to the rest of the interface will probably have a result that is consistent with the purpose of the site. Your guess is as good as mine as to what would happen if you click Zoom. The button name gives no clue to its function. The user can't draw any conclusions about its purpose based on the theme of the interface, because it has no visual relationship to the interface.

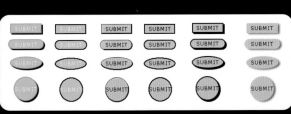

FIGURE 4.8

The closer a GIF button is to a system button, the more reliable it appears to a user.

same thing when we design buttons that are visually related to the look of the interface or to the identity of the organization that created the interface, rather than to a specific operating system.

Users are generally comfortable with elements that are stylistically related to their interface, as long as the basic behaviors and interaction models are consistent with their system buttons. On the Web, where a person can jump effortlessly from one product and its unique identity to another, it can be reassuring to see interface elements that are firmly grounded in the page's look and feel. This seems to contradict user affinity for the tried-and-true System button, but in fact only reinforces users' needing the sense of a familiar place. Custom-rendered interface elements can provide the same reliable results as system elements. (See Fig. 4.7)

Because of the haphazard adherence to interface conventions online, many users are skeptical about uniquely designed buttons. A user practically sighs with relief when presented with the gray system button in a Web interface, because it looks like a direct link to functionality, rather than a gimmick concocted by a novice Photoshop jockey. (See Fig. 4.8)

Emphasis

Curiously, one of the more useful conventions of the System button is not available to buttons in browser windows—emphasis. In a modal dialog box (one where a user must respond to the options before continuing) there are typically two choices: commitment or withdrawal. Both options are rendered as buttons. To reduce anxiety (do I cut the red wire or the green one?) the least dangerous option, representing the action least likely to result in irreparable harm, is recommended to the user by its thicker border. There is no way, using traditional HTML, to evoke this kind of button.

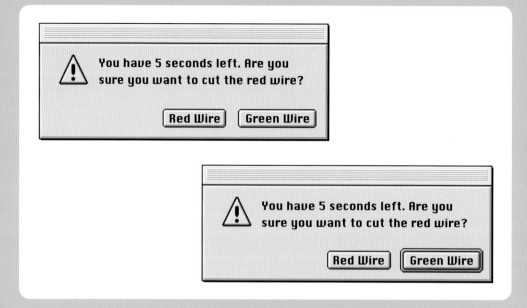

Cross-Platform Rendering

Buttons can be rendered differently by different clients (browsers, Flash, or Java interfaces, etc.). Buttons tend to appear larger in Netscape and the type within the button can be affected by font tags used to format the surrounding type. It's little wonder that designers prefer GIF or JPEG buttons, despite their larger file sizes, slow rendering speed, and loss of interactive feedback behavior. They render more reliably.

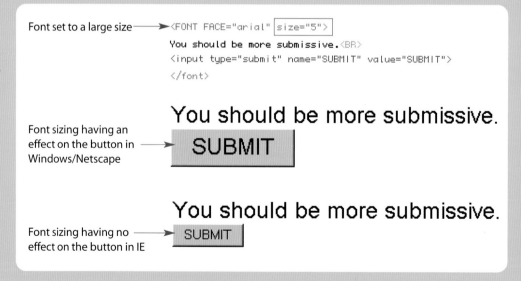

GIF Buttons

Both GIFs and JPEGs can be used as buttons. However, they are not equally effective. Since all buttons are measured against the system ones, clear, sharp, image-based buttons make the best presentation. Overly modeled buttons with multiple colors and shadows appear overworked. Most users don't know the particulars of compression, but they do identify crisp, flat GIF images with few colors as more bandwidth friendly, and equate them with value in an interface. From the user's point of view, the most task-specific items must be quick-loading elements.

GIF buttons allow for a greater range of color and style than the gray rectangular buttons of an operating system. With control over type style and face, border width, bevel sizes, shadows, and color, a designer has more opportunity to link a GIF button visually to other elements of an interface. A GIF button can reference the editorial voice of a Web page better as well, a marked improvement over the institutional-looking system button. (See Fig. 4.9)

Text Buttons

GIF buttons fall into two categories; text and iconic. Text buttons are similar to system buttons—their function is expressed though language on the button face. Unlike system buttons, text buttons can have more than one line of text and they can be typographically sophisticated. Keep in mind the text button's place on the usability continuum compared with the system button. Some typographic treatments work within the continuum, while others, like multilined labels, are less effective. (See Fig. 4.10)

Iconic Buttons

Most people are familiar with iconic buttons that represent task, places, and functions pictorially, making their functions easier to identify in a group than the same number of text buttons. Labels must be read to be identified, while icons can be recognized even from the corner of your eye.

Quick identification is not the sole measure of a virtual tool's success. Since icons are simplified pictorial representations, they can sometimes be ambiguous. Iconic buttons benefit from labeling. Simple text labels can clarify an icon until the user has learned its meaning. (See Fig. 4.11)

There are a myriad ways to combine icons and labels. Each combination will affect how well the icon is read as a link/button. (See Fig. 4.12)

Designing Icon Graphics

Effectively representing a task or destination in the few pixels of a small low-resolution illustration is an art form. You can present tasks and destinations to users as objects, actions, and places. The simpler the representation, the easier it is for users to quickly grasp the icons' meanings. The frequently asked questions section of a site might be called Help Desk; a simple metaphor to describe the single facet of asking questions and receiving answers. The name magic 8 ball, for instance, is too

FIGURE 4.9
The whimsical nature of this button is consistent with the editorial voice and reinforces the user's sense of place.

FIGURE 4.10
While there is no doubt that both of these graphics are buttons, the message of the lengthy paragraphlike button is less direct. The simple label of the smaller button is more easily read, while the italic type gives the buttons a dynamism unavailable in system elements.

FIGURE 4.11
A picture of a printer could mean either "print this" or "printer." An e-commerce interface that sells printers and also has a "print this page" function needs to reduce the potential confusion. Labeling the icons helps, as does changing the illustration style. A user is more likely to assume that a photorealistic rendering represents the actual printer for sale. An iconic representation of a printer does not reference a specific printer directly, so it makes a better link to print functionality.

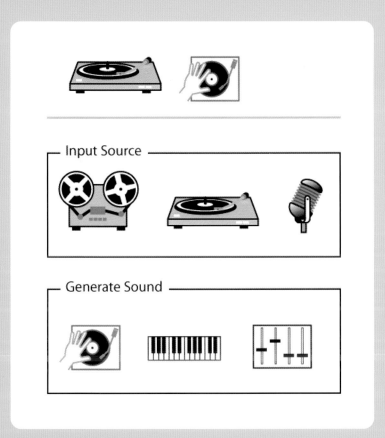

Style and Content

There are no rules about illustrative style and functionality. This interface for mixing audio files uses several icons, some of which are redundant. A flat representation of a turntable next to a more realistic representation implies that separate functions are associated with each icon. A user familiar with these options will quickly discern the difference between the two tasks if you provide a context for the tools.

The context for selecting hardware input sources, which are rendered here with some perspective and varying shades of gray, helps the user quickly differentiate between the two turntable icons. Rather than asking "which of these turntables is the button I want?" the user is drawn to the group of input icons to select a music source. Within that group of tasks, the turntable is easily distinguishable. The same is true when the user wants to generate sound. The second turntable icon is far enough away from the one in the other cluster not to be confused with it.

esoteric, and conjures up too many individual interpretations. Illustrating concepts in a limited space at 72 dpi is difficult but is made easier when the concept is simple. See Chapter 10 for more about metaphors.

When a destination is synonymous with an object, that object will lend itself to an iconic solution. For example, some tasks that have no object related to their task can elude iconic representation. Actions, which don't often have a physical incarnations, can be represented iconically with an object metaphor. (See Fig. 4.13)

Icons are most successful when their shape is discernable at a glance. Realism is less important than representing the essence of something, or using a shape with plenty of contour. (See Fig. 4.14)

When designing icons, be mindful of the phases of visual cognition. People first recognize an object's basic geometry. Then they take in its subtler shapes, shadows and details. Finally, they recognize its unique and defining characteristics. Facial characteristics, for example, are registered most quickly when they are more geometric. People notice eyes quickly because they are round, whereas the more complex mouth shape is recognized later. (See Fig. 4.15) An icon's essential characteristics should be rendered as simply and geometrically as possible to help the user quickly recognize it.

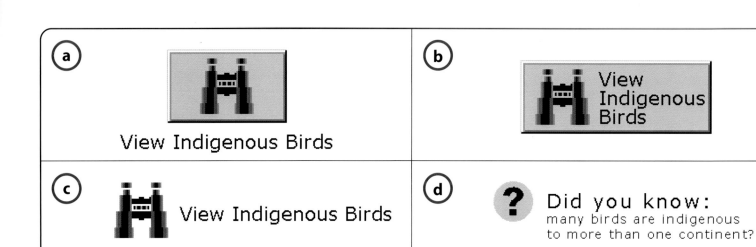

FIGURE 4.12

A designer can combine icon and labels into one graphic (a); associate the label with an iconic button (b); or position the icon and label as adjacent, related representations of functionality, without using visual clues to clickability like beveled edges. In this example, the icon without extra visual clues (c) naturally implies clickability, but the text seems static. Rarely do designers present small images or illustrative representations of objects without associating functionality or clickability with them. Nonrepresentational icons, such as punctuation marks (d), can work as visual anchors without associated functionality.

FIGURE 4.13

Adobe chose a rubber stamp as the metaphor for Photoshop's cloning tool, because the physical gesture of using it is similar to that of a rubber stamp. The functions of the two tools are quite different, but the rubber stamp metaphor still works well as an introduction to the cloning tool.

FIGURE 4.14

Although not many people own a rotary phone anymore, its contour is much easier to recognize at a glance than the modern-day cordless or cell phone. At a glance, a realistic representation of modern phones just looks like a rectangle.

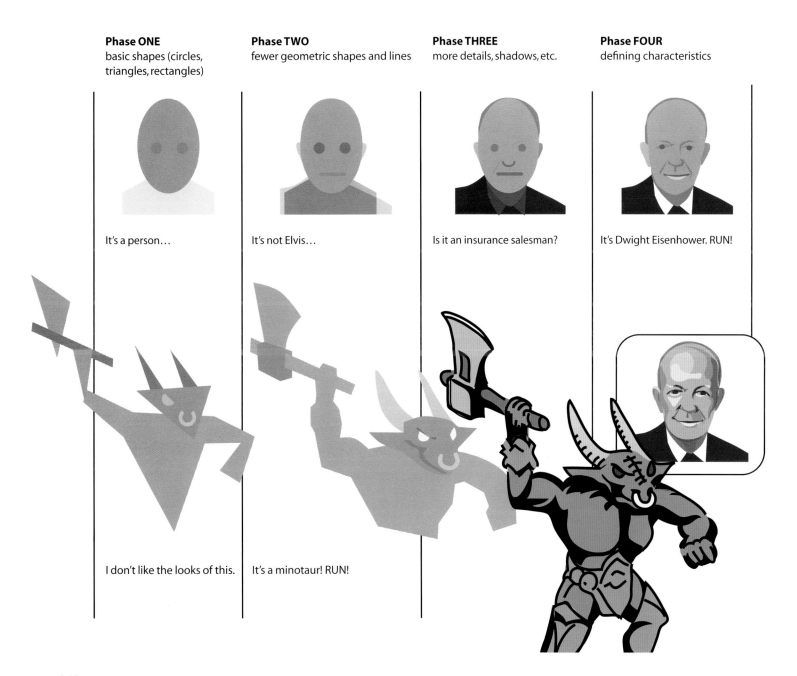

Phase ONE
basic shapes (circles, triangles, rectangles)

Phase TWO
fewer geometric shapes and lines

Phase THREE
more details, shadows, etc.

Phase FOUR
defining characteristics

It's a person…

It's not Elvis…

Is it an insurance salesman?

It's Dwight Eisenhower. RUN!

I don't like the looks of this.

It's a minotaur! RUN!

FIGURE 4.15: PHASES OF VISUAL COGNITION

Part of Dwight Eisenhower's appeal to the electorate of the '50s was his resemblance to Everyman. If I was confronted in a dark alley by the ghost of Dwight Eisenhower, I would turn and run after maybe three seconds—the amount of time it would take me recognize him. But I'd turn and run in a nanosecond of seeing the Minotaur, whom I would never mistake for Dwight Everyman.

Button Affordance Methods

Interfaces generally have two parts, the work space (or reading space) and the tools. Both tools and work spaces very often incorporate text, so some visual language is necessary to differentiate between the two. Encircling text that is a tool (such as a button or menu) with a border or color, is the minimum requirement to differentiate it as a clickable item. Usually something more is needed. That's where affordances come in.

An affordance is a visual clue that helps a user understand that something is an active interface element and what its function might be. A button's beveled edge and its shadows are affordances, telling a user that the shape is meant to be clicked by reminding them of keys on a keyboard, or buttons in an elevator.

Once you establish a visual language for affordances, maintain its consistency throughout all the elements. Mixing affordance styles is confusing.

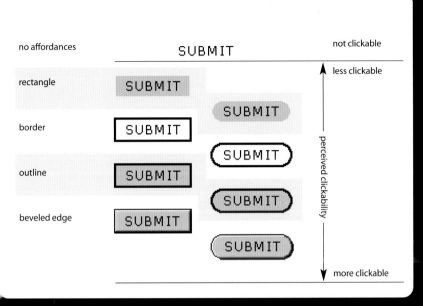

Buttons that have a realistic feel are more obviously clickable than those that remain flat on the page.

FIGURE 4.17
Affordances that are native to the computer still draw upon real-world experience, but more abstractly than 3-D modeling does.

Obvious visual clues help to reinforce an element's usability. (See Fig. 4.16) Such affordances tend to fall into two categories: those that mimic real life and those that build upon a visual language unique to computers. The former generally involves 3-D modeling (like beveled edges) on button elements. Microsoft Windows uses 3-D modeling as an affordance for most of its elements.

While size is not literally an affordance, the shape and proportion of a button can affect the perceived importance of an element. Very small buttons—say, smaller than 15 pixels square—are often missed entirely, while extremely large ones—larger than 100 pixels square—start to look like static graphics, even with affordances.

The rounded corner keyline border in the Macintosh style conveys usability abstractly by referencing a user's tactile sense (consider the cursor a virtual finger). The curved handle of the tool on the left looks more user friendly than its hard-edged counterpart on the right. (See Fig. 4.17)

FIGURE 4.18: LIGHT SOURCES

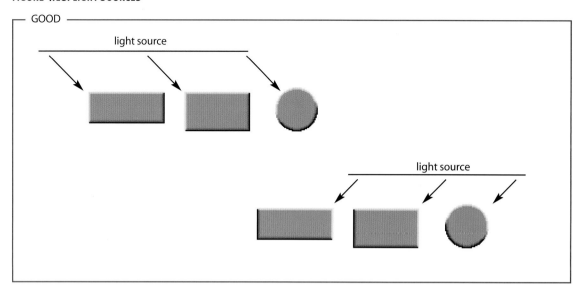

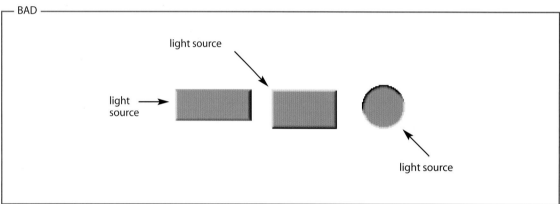

Light and shading are what communicate three-dimensionality on a surface. Maintaining a consistent light angle is critical when rendering 3-D interface elements. When buttons have inconsistent light sources, it is hard to tell whether a button is concave or convex.

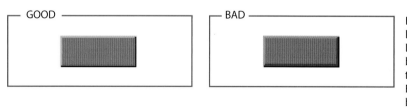

It has become a convention that light sources originate from the top left. In addition, the color of the bevel should be a shade of the button's color, not a new color entirely. Buttons with different surface and bevel colors hinder the 3-D effect.

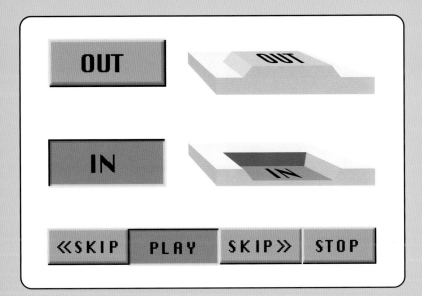

FIGURE 4.19: DESIGNING BEVELS

The 3-D appearance of buttons is not only a useful way of communicating clickability, it is also a means to creating a system of button states (active, inactive, pressed, etc.). Shadows on the outside of a beveled button indicate an inactive state. Inverted shadows on 3-D buttons convey an active state. This visual clue can be used as a feedback behavior on mouse-down (difficult to do with HTML but easy with Flash) or to indicate the state of an interface. In this case, the interface is in the "play mode" state.

FIGURE 4.20

When you want to design a group of buttons with three possible states—in use, not in use, and not usable—you can create enough variety by combining embossed/debossed labels and pressed/depressed buttons to effectively convey the system of button states.

These buttons all have beveled edges, so it is obvious each is usable. The debossed labels look usable because they mimic the look and feel of a raised edge. In contrast, the Animate GIF button appears to be in use, rather than unusable the way the Back button does. It is easy to imagine pressing this button to disable the Animation feature.

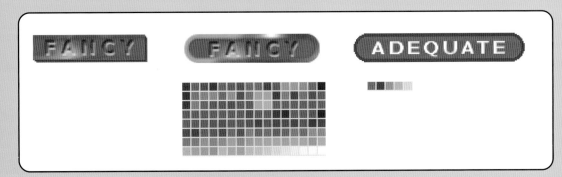

FIGURE 4.21

The first object tempts you to interact with it. It is textured and interesting, especially so in the typically flat world of computer interfaces. However, the object is not obviously a button without the common affordances of beveled edges and rounded corners.

Although seductive, the GIF in the center takes three times the memory to render as its flat counterpart. At 15KB, using 128 colors, the differences may seem insignificant, but a page full of such elements would be noticeably slower to load.

FIGURE 4.22

Color and geometry are a potent combination. The red round button at the top may effectively draw the user's attention, but it also looks like a drop of blood. The appearance of the second button is really disconcerting. Its shape and color say "stop" while the beveled clickability and the label literally say "go."

Borders

We don't know when the rectangular border became part of our collective understanding of what a button is. Today, a single word with a thick border seems to naturally imply that the word is usable. A simple outlined rectangle makes an okay button, but the tactile appearance of a rounded rectangle works better.

Effective sizes and shapes of buttons, as discussed in Chapter 3, depend largely on how affordances such as borders and beveled edges are used. Rectangles with a greater width-to-height ratio tend to work best. Small geometric shapes tend to look like bullets without the aid of affordances.

3-D

Three-dimensional button rendering has long been a convention for conveying usability. In the ultraflat world of computer screens, 3-D affordances provide an immediate link to real-world buttons like keypads. Three-dimensional affordances are convenient design tools because they can be used simultaneously as a system for communicating the state of a button as well as contributing to the overall hierarchy of elements. A combination of rules and conventions now governs the use of 3-D interface elements. Although most designers adhere to them, there is plenty of room for variation within these rules. (See Fig. 4.18)

The most common affordance method for buttons is three-dimensional rendering with beveled edges. (See Fig. 4.19) There are a host of other affordance methods that use 3-D appearance to convey usability; drop shadows, highlights, and embossing. Drop shadows can give the appearance that a rectangle is hovering over the page, giving it plenty of autonomy. Autonomy can help an element appear separate from surrounding elements and page content, but is not necessarily synonymous with clickability.

Embossing and Debossing

Conventions for using embossed type are related to those of 3-D element rendering. One advantage to embossed button labels is that they seem to telegraph interactivity to the user starved for a tactile experience on the computer. Embossed labels are another desktop application convention that help users read a button's state in context with buttons that surround it. A button will appear pressed if its label is embossed, or unpressed if the label is debossed. (See Fig. 4.20)

Embossed labels and reflective highlights have the same effect as drop shadows, but neither of these affordances clearly communicates clickability by itself. When used in conjunction with other, proven button affordances, such as rounded corners, techniques of 3-D rendering can give an attractive sheen to an element. You will, however, pay a price in bandwidth. (See Fig. 4.21)

Color

Color has a threefold effect on the appearance of buttons: First, any color applied to a button puts it further away from the simple system button. Second, color has an effect on the button's autonomy, depending on its contrast with the interface background. Third, the meaning of a button is affected by color.

Color can negatively affect a user's interpretation of a button's role in an interface. Since the trusted system button is usually gray, colored buttons are often seen by users as less important. As a result, designers often discard subtlety for the exaggerated importance of bright colors like red.

As discussed in Chapter 3, color has broad and varied cultural and emotional significance. Buttons, more than hyperlinks, can capitalize on or fall prey to this fact, since there is more space in a button for its color to become a focal point. Geometry, in combination with color, can conjure up images of signs and symbols and affect the meaning of a button. (See Fig. 4.22)

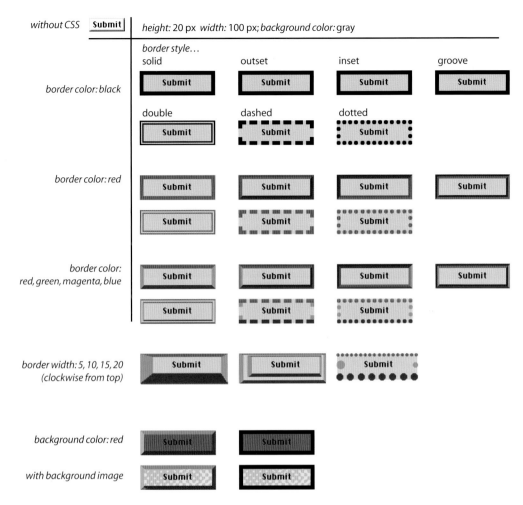

without CSS Submit | *height:* 20 px *width:* 100 px; *background color:* gray

border style…

solid   outset   inset   groove

border color: black

double   dashed   dotted

border color: red

*border color:
red, green, magenta, blue*

*border width: 5, 10, 15, 20
(clockwise from top)*

background color: red

with background image

FIGURE 4.23: CASCADING STYLE SHEETS

Borders range from solid to modeled (outset, inset, grooved), to patterned (dotted, dashed). Modeled borders apply shading to a specified border color. Each side of a button can have an individual border color and width.

A FEW DISCLAIMERS

These examples use a button that is not specific to either the Mac or Windows operating systems. To help illustrate the behavior of patterned borders, I've added a light gray background to these button examples.

Black borders in CSS are different from those specified with border color. Modeling has no effect on black borders.

Buttons and Cascading Style Sheets

System buttons are conveniently easy to code with HTML and have immediate user recognition. But even designers committed to system buttons' quick rendering and low bandwidth want an easy way to control basic button characteristics. Cascading Style Sheets (CSS) are a code-oriented way to alter button appearance without resorting to GIFs. Specifying dimensions, color, border width and color, and typeface are easy with CSS. Style sheets also allow the designer to create a specific appearance for a button's active states. (See Fig. 4.23)

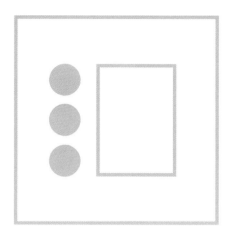

Labels

Labeling is the holy grail of button design. Usually a user is led to a button by a series of interactions or through a form. The user may have some idea of what the button is for prior to reading its label. The label either confirms the user's expectations or alerts him to a different purpose. Since the button represents a decision point in a process, the true value of an interface is determined by what happens after the button is clicked. The button itself should take the least amount of time and effort to understand, as it is merely a step on the way to something more important. The label should be as clear and concise as possible—one word that succinctly identifies the purpose of the button or the surrounding interface. A button that advances a task should have an active label, rather than a place name or object name. (See Fig. 4.24)

A button has a dual purpose. It acts as the facilitator of action, as well as a label. In essence, a button is the last part of a process, the punctuation mark. Even though there is no technical reason a button must appear at the end of a form, it makes the most sense there. (See Fig. 4.25)

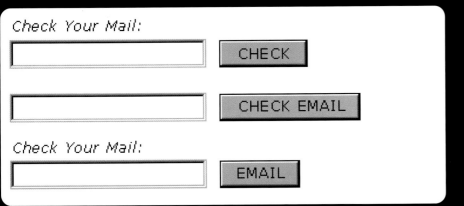

FIGURE 4.24

A form for checking an email account should have a button whose label indicates the active part of the process, as does this first example.

In lieu of display text, the button can be used to identify the purpose of the form, as well as represent the punctuating action. This button is not read as quickly but the form is simpler. These two examples, while different in a approach, address the same need well.

If the button is labeled as an object, as it is in the third example, a user will probably click it, but he will likely pause for a second before doing so.

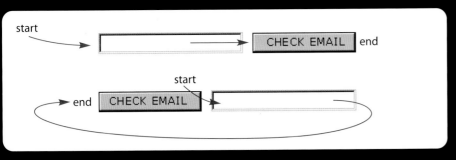

FIGURE 4.25

The button preceding the form will still function but it feels wrong.

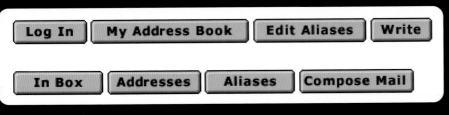

FIGURE 4.26

The top row of buttons does not appear as a cohesive system. The buttons have inconsistent sizes, and their labels are a mix of actions and objects. My Address Book is probably no more important than the others, but it stands out because it is significantly longer.

In the bottom row of buttons each label is a destination relating to the task of using email. While every label is succinct, one is significantly longer than others. Because the relative size of each rectangle is similar, this longer label does not dominate the group.

Group Hierarchy and Button Labels

When buttons are used in groups, their labels have a slightly different effect than when a single button is the sole punctuation of a form. Since all buttons in a group will share aspects of their appearance (color, edges, borders) they will appear related to some extent, even though by definition, each button will produce a different result when clicked. If you assume that each button addresses a single aspect of a task, each label must relate each button to the task, as well as differentiate each button from one another.

The buttons should comprise a system whose typeface and language is consistent in voice, length, and form. If one button is an action, every button should be an action. Unfortunately, buttons that are text labels only (as opposed to icons) will have varying lengths depending on the language used. A button with a longer label will be bigger and appear to have a more prominent place in the hierarchy, even if it is no more important than the surrounding buttons. The relative size of each button can be made consistent, even if the labels aren't, making for flat hierarchy where everything appears to have equal importance. (See Fig. 4.26)

Captions

Whenever possible, a button and its label should be consolidated. A rectangular button with a word or phrase in the middle should be direct and easy to understand. If a button can't be understood without a caption, better labeling is probably in order. A caption accompanying a labeled button is so far from the system button ideal that the caption probably does more harm than good. (See Fig. 4.27)

People use iconic buttons differently than they use text buttons. You should design an iconic button when the task or destination it will represent will be encountered repeatedly, and in the context of many other buttons and graphics.

Iconic buttons benefit greatly from captions. Captions are necessary to teach the user what the icons mean and to affirm their meaning later. It is tempting to consolidate the caption and icon as you would for a labeled button, but icons work best when the label is separate from the graphic. The two elements should be separated so the user will recognize the icon independent of the label. (See Fig. 4.28)

FIGURE 4.27

A complex idea is better represented with a verbose button label than in an adjacent caption. The caption dilutes the button's autonomy.

FIGURE 4.28

This icon is easy to see and identify but, like most icons, by itself it is ambiguous. The caption helps confirm the meaning suggested by the graphic, but it can be easily ignored once the user learns the icon. The position of the caption is important for understanding. If the caption is too far from the graphic, the association is unclear. If the caption is too close to the icon, it appears a part of the graphic, making the icon complex and difficult to read.

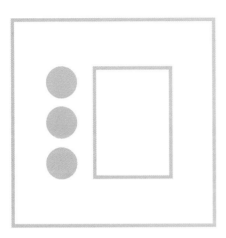

Typography

Text buttons should not be seen as vehicles for your typographic expression. Successful interaction is dependent in part on clear, easy-to-read labels that don't challenge the user's aesthetic sensibilities.

You might have heard that all buttons should be as quickly readable as system buttons are. You may have also been told that serif type set in initial caps makes for the quickest read. Both assumptions are incorrect. But even if they were right, the difference in readability and legibility between, say Helvetica and Times, is negligible. Many other interface design factors can help or hinder readability more profoundly, like the choice of a typeface to match the look-and-feel of the interface. In some cases, it is the designer's job to slow the pace of reading to emphasize a word or button. (See Fig. 4.29)

Readability

System buttons allow little typographic formatting. You can only specify uppercase, lowercase, initial caps, or—if you're feeling tricky—you can extend the width of a word by adding a space between each letter. An advantage to GIF buttons is the level of control a designer has over typographic spacing and rendering. When space is limited, as with a long button bar that takes up the entire width of a screen, each element's readability and size depends on the designer's typographic control.

With all the composition options that are available to a designer, it is surprising how difficult it is to create readable type for small buttons that will aptly capture the importance of the element. To maintain readability when using type smaller than 24 points, you need a hard baseline to ground the sometimes fuzzy or jagged online type.

Character width is equally important. Wide letters with plenty of white space make for better screen readability. The space between letters should be consistent. A word should have either one pixel between each letter, or two. There is no point in worrying about subtle kerning when a computer is incapable of putting two letters closer than one pixel. (See Fig. 4.30).

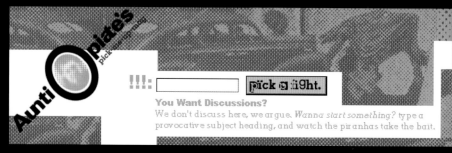

Although an unconventional typeface choice may enforce the stylistic voice of an interface, expressive typography makes buttons look less like utilities and more like gimmicks.

There is room for expressive type in interface elements, especially with elements that relate directly to the personality of the site. This site is has a confrontational slant, so the symbol characters are appropriate for this audience. To the uninitiated, the button may be somewhat cryptic, but that is easily remedied with a mouseover effect. The heavy face and wide kerning distinguished this element from the run-of-the-mill navigational buttons above, which use a traditional type.

FIGURE 4.30: ANTIALIASING AND READABILITY

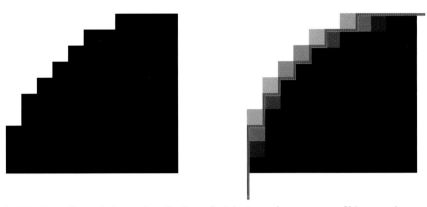

Antialiasing is the technique where the jagged, stair-stepped appearance of bitmapped shapes (especially curves and diagonals) are smoothed by filling in the spaces between steps with pixels whose color is a combination of the foreground and background.

For the sake of simplicity, we'll confine this discussion of antialiasing to black foregrounds (the letters) on a white background. The antialiased pixels will be shades of gray.

S S
8pt (approximate)
at 200%

8pt (approximate)
at 3,500%

Antialiasing helps to preserve the original appearance of typefaces that were designed for print. It helps to approximate the subtle adjustments type designers use in rendering high resolution type, like the bowl of an S that dips slightly below the baseline. It makes letters appear closer than they really can be on a computer screen.

FIGURE 4.30: ANTIALIASING AND READABILITY *CONTINUED*

A letter can't be moved less than the width of one pixel. Antialiasing implies a fraction of a pixel by using a combination of shaded pixels.

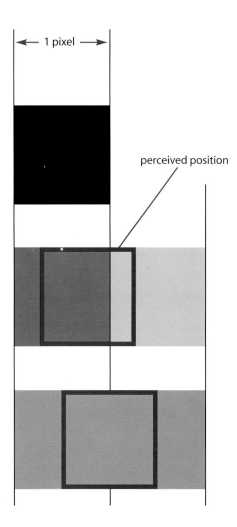

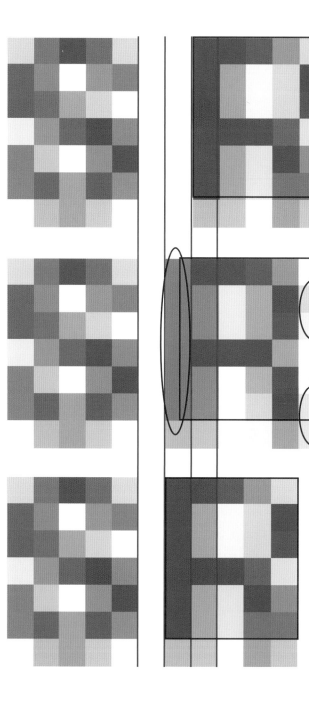

Faithfully approximating a typeface's subtleties is less important than the clear crisp use of vertical symmetry and white space in and around each letter. Return to aliased type, at least as a starting point. Use rectilinear letterforms that take advantage of the computer screen's square and sharp pixel edges to make a simple, clear-looking button label.

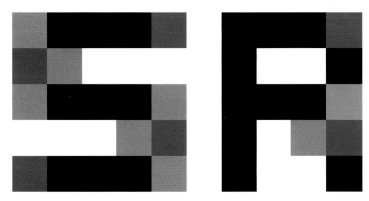

If the letters are too jagged or flat, softening curves and slanted edges with transitional-colored pixels achieves the same end as antialiasing. But by working selectively, a designer can choose only the most important pixels to soften, maintaining a hard baseline and letter spacing.

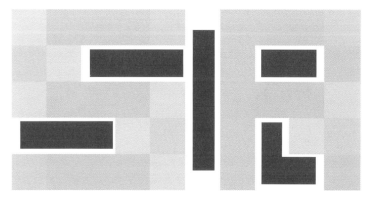

The pixels indicated in red above show an even distribution of white space—critically important for comfortable reading.

FIGURE 4.31

a. This button is part of a system with a predefined width. The label exceeds the available space. Type set small enough to fit the space looks bad. The antialiased version is fuzzy, the jagged aliased type is breaking up.

b. It can be better to start with aliased type, and add antialiasing later as needed. You can add or remove pixels to make letters symmetrical and evenly spaced. Adding a few pixels (here shown in magenta) and deleting a few others (in cyan) cleans up these broken-up letters. Adding space between and within each letter (as in the A and L in EDITORIAL) makes the label read better.

c. The aliased O, which is too close to the surrounding letters, would look better if it was rounder. By adding antialiasing, you soften the corners without changing the width of the character, but the result is an O that takes up less space. The final version benefits from both the crispness of square, aliased type and the fine-tuning of antialiasing, without fuzziness.

FIGURE 4.32

Submit buttons represent the end of a process. Navigation buttons represent the beginning of a new process at the button's destination.

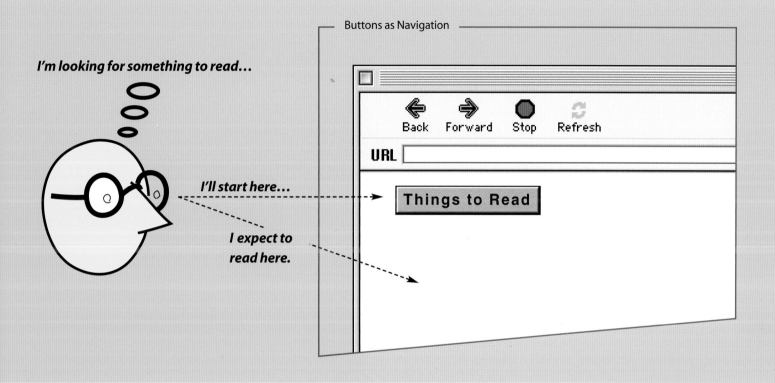

Buttons in Forms

I'm filling out a form...   Now I'm Done

Buttons as Navigation

I'm looking for something to read...

Back   Forward   Stop   Refresh

URL

I'll start here...

Things to Read

I expect to read here.

Most designers have encountered this problem: A very limited space for a very lengthy label. Using a readable type size results in a label too wide for the button. A smaller font size loses its character through missing pixels, or is blurry when antialiased. If the design and layout of an interface lead to a button that is too small to read, either you have to change the button requirements or spend more effort fixing the type. (See Fig. 4.31)

Arranging Buttons in an Interface

In simple configurations a text field is followed by a button. It's the logical order for such elements, but it also presents interface problems.

Most button usage falls into one of two basic categories: 1. as the final act of sending a form option to a script; 2. as a navigational element in a button bar. The second represents a gateway to what the user wants, not

an end in itself. These are two opposite kinds of interaction, and require different placement in the interface. (See Fig. 4.32)

In most computer applications, useful elements are positioned around the outer edge of a work space. Given this familiarity, as well as the top-screen navigation layout of most browsers, Web designers often place navigational elements that represent key decision points at the top of a page. (See Fig. 4.33)

FIGURE 4.33

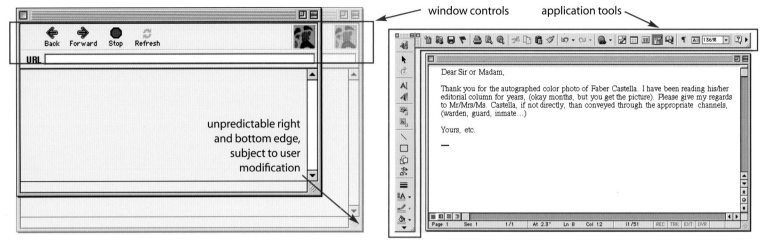

window controls   application tools

The top left is the most stable and reliable part of a browser window, since the right and bottom edges are often adjusted by users.

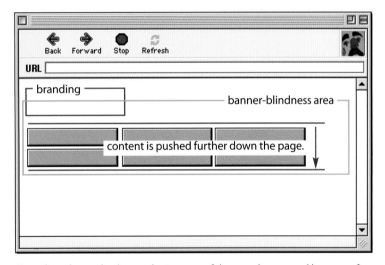

branding

banner-blindness area

content is pushed further down the page.

unpredictable right and bottom edge, subject to user modification

Users have learned to ignore the top area of the page because ad banners often appear there. Another drawback: Buttons at the top of the page use precious vertical space, pushing important content further down.

L STANDARDS | MASTHEAD | AUNTI'S SORDID PAST | SUBSCRIBE | WHC

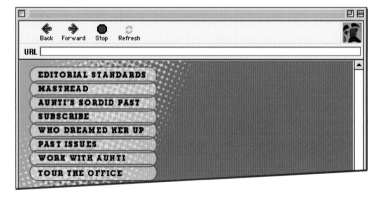

EDITORIAL STANDARDS
MASTHEAD
AUNTI'S SORDID PAST
SUBSCRIBE
WHO DREAMED HER UP
PAST ISSUES
WORK WITH AUNTI
TOUR THE OFFICE

The left edge of a Web page offers a flexible space to stack multiple buttons. While horizontal button bars have a limit of fewer than ten average-sized buttons, a vertical stack can accommodate many more, and functions as a list where new buttons can be easily added. Vertically stacked buttons tend be more uniform than horizontal ones. The letter height doesn't vary, and each label, if written simply, will likely fit a width of, say, 200 pixels, regardless of character count.

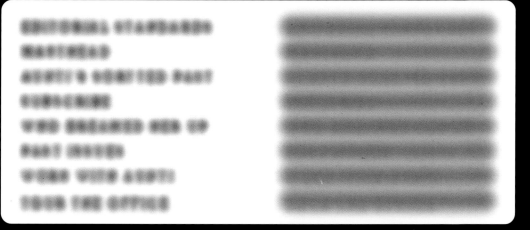

FIGURE 4.34

Without reading this list, you can easily spot the chunks of information, thanks to the differentiation of each line caused by the ragged right edge. This benefit is lost on a list of uniform buttons. The stack of buttons holds together as a group, which helps the user distinguish it from other clusters in the interface. This cohesive unit transforms the ragged, easy-to-parse shape into a single visual blob.

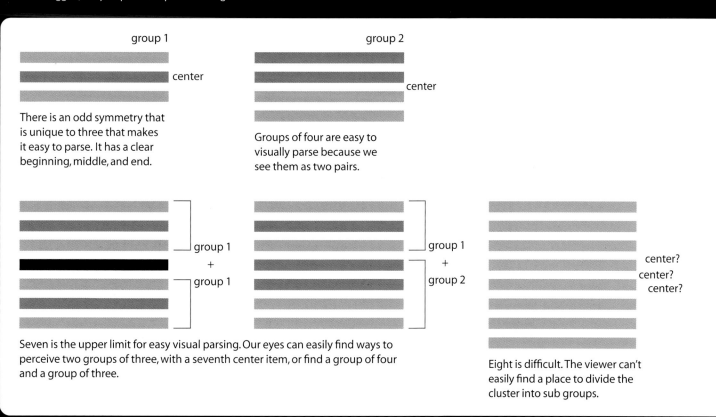

group 1

center

There is an odd symmetry that is unique to three that makes it easy to parse. It has a clear beginning, middle, and end.

group 2

center

Groups of four are easy to visually parse because we see them as two pairs.

group 1
+
group 1

group 1
+
group 2

center?
center?
center?

Seven is the upper limit for easy visual parsing. Our eyes can easily find ways to perceive two groups of three, with a seventh center item, or find a group of four and a group of three.

Eight is difficult. The viewer can't easily find a place to divide the cluster into sub groups.

FIGURE 4.35: THE FIVE TO SEVEN RULE

Visual Parsing

You can make visual parsing easier by using the patterns that are created by a symmetrical text rag. This group of eight is easier to deal with than usual because the rag suggests a convenient place to build a subgroup.

Alas, there is a sensible order to this group of eight, but it does not present a good rag. It's best to keep the subgroupings logical based on content. If these buttons are set in two groups—standard publishing stuff and curios—the list can be separated into two clusters of four.

EDITORIAL STANDARDS
MASTHEAD
AUNTI'S SORDID PAST   center
SUBSCRIBE
WHO DREAMED HER UP

group of 5
+
group of 3

PAST ISSUES
WORK WITH AUNTI
TOUR THE OFFICE

EDITORIAL STANDARDS
MASTHEAD
SUBSCRIBE
PAST ISSUES

AUNTI'S SORDID PAST
WHO DREAMED HER UP
WORK WITH AUNTI
TOUR THE OFFICE

Groups of three are the easiest grouping to remember. Even the color spectrum acronym ROYGBIV, which is already a group of seven, is taught to students as Roy Gee Biv.

An interface that uses many buttons as gateways to many functions or site branches presents a unique usability problem. While users recognize that each button is clickable, finding a specific link amidst many similar looking links can be difficult. The uniformity of buttons makes for sameness. Groups of differing labels aren't as easy to negotiate visually as a similar text list, because the user does not benefit as quickly from typographic differentiation, such as the ragged right edge of a flush-left text list. The obvious difference in each line helps the reader quickly parse the list. (See Fig. 4.34)

Button Grouping

A large group of buttons can be difficult to parse visually. Whenever uniform items are clustered together, the eye looks for ways to segment and categorize the cluster. Small groups of two to five items are relatively easy to digest.

Interface designers often talk about the Rule of Seven, which states that seven is the maximum for grouping like elements. In fact, the ideal is between five and seven. Groups smaller than five lack the mass to appear as a list, and groups larger than seven are just too long to easily parse. (See Fig. 4.35)

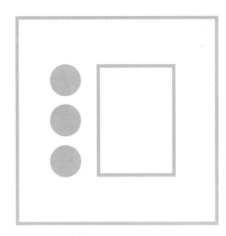

Interactive Buttons

Until recently, the only feedback available with buttons was a depressed appearance of the button on mouse click. Those limitations no longer apply. Between Macromedia's Flash with its easy-to-implement mouseover effects, and the stock JavaScripts included with graphical HTML editors such as Dreamweaver and Fireworks, interactive buttons have become common in Web interfaces. (See Fig. 4.36) In some cases, the interactive effects are a welcome addition to the static pages of most Web interfaces; but when numerous, they can be an annoyance to users, and a strain on bandwidth.

Mouseover Interaction

Perhaps to reinforce which graphics in an interface are buttons, designers have been employing simple mouseover effects on GIF buttons. A mouseover effect is when a simple JavaScript swaps one image for another when the cursor rolls over the button. Mouseovers have become a ubiquitous method of reinforcing clickability, and providing additional information about a link.

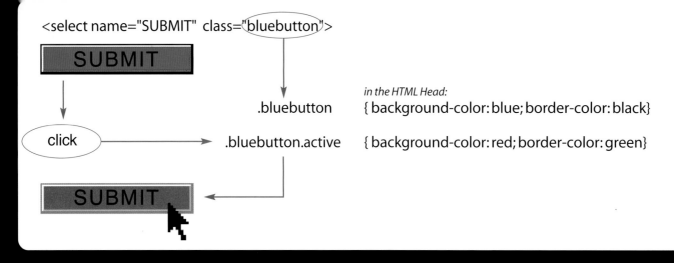

FIGURE 4.36: USING A SUBCLASS TO CREATE A FEEDBACK BEHAVIOR
Any class can be given a subclass called ".active." If I specify a blue button with a black border and refer to it as class="bluebutton," I can then define the sub-class "bluebutton.active" to be red with a green border. When I click any button with the specified class of "bluebutton," it will turn red with a green border, and then return to Blue with a Black border when I release the mouse.

The extent to which a button's appearance can be altered on mouseover is limited only by the imagination of the designer. If the technique for mouseover involves the "swap-image" function of JavaScript, then the dimensions of the GIF are the only content that must be shared between the two images. Of course this can lead to some disorienting mouseovers if the two images are dissimilar. (See Fig. 4.37)

It's possible to create complex interactions on mouseover, revealing a range of interface elements that go far beyond a swapped image. Dynamic HTML (DHTML) layers can be used in conjunction with JavaScript to effect the appearance of a button. Image-swapping requires the new image to fit within the dimensions of the original one. That limitation does not exist in DHTML. A mouse event (such as a mouseover) can trigger a JavaScript to switch the visibility of a layer (specified in CSS) from "hidden" to "visible," extending a button beyond its original size, and, if need be, covering other parts of the interface. (See Fig. 4.38)

Animation

An animated GIF can be an element in a JavaScript image swap on mouseover that a user can initiate. Although an option, it is difficult to imagine how such an effect can be usefully applied to a button. The sudden presence of an animated button, or an animation near a button, would distract the user at a critical decision-making moment.

Of course, animation does not have to mean cartoon characters running around. Effective use of animation can help a user track the movement of interface elements. If a button is used to open a navigation list, for instance, other elements are pushed further down the page. If you animate the movement, the user can see where the pushed elements end up. (See Fig. 4.39)

FIGURE 4.37: MOUSEOVERS

image src="button.gif"

image src="button_red.gif"

Mouseovers may be necessary in an interface where the quantity of graphic elements makes it difficult to see buttons. The highlighting is like Braille to a user blinded by complexity.

image src="bigbutton.gif"

image src="bigbutton_red.gif"

If you click me,
I'll take you to a new page.

A mouseover can also be used to reveal something about the button or its destination.

Swapping images on mouseover does not require visual consistency, and plenty of useful interface effects could be attained by swapping one image with a completely different one. But successful buttons should have a reliable appearance. If a button changes too much when the user interacts with it, the impression is that of a button with an unreliable function.

Audible Feedback

Audible feedback—the triggering of a sound upon mouse click and mouseover—is not part of HTML. But it is easy to do with Flash, and with some effort, can be created with DHTML. Though not yet widely used yet on mouse interactions with buttons, audible feedback represents one of the more useful interface tricks of the last few years. Aside from crafting an extremely simple interface with large text and buttons, there is little a Web designer can do to provide a useful inter-face for users with below-average eyesight. Audible feedback is an elegant way of helping the visually impaired (and the sighted as well) interact better with interface elements.

Many people lack the dexterity to accurately place the cursor over small links and buttons. The extra effort and time wasted as the user tries to line the cursor up with a button can be frustrating. You can eliminate some of the guesswork by playing a simple sound to reinforce a user's successful alignment of cursor and button.

If you use a mouseover sound, you need to also use a click sound. The click is a signifi-cant interaction, while mouseover effects are just precursors to interaction. Otherwise, the natural interaction hierarchy (minor mouseover yields to major mouse click) is thrown out of balance. The mouseover sound becomes artificially significant.

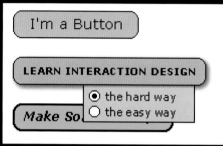

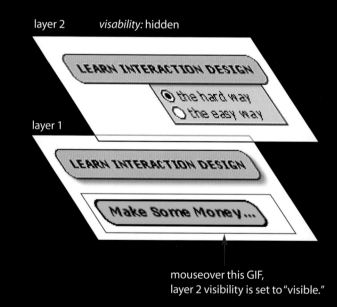

mouseover this GIF,
layer 2 visibility is set to "visible."

FIGURE 4.38

By revealing a previously hidden layer of information on mouseover, you can augment button function-ality without cluttering up the interface. Since the original button (the trigger) is separate from the revealed layer, both elements can have separate sizes and positions. The trigger area can correspond to just the button and does not have to conform to the dimensions of the added information.

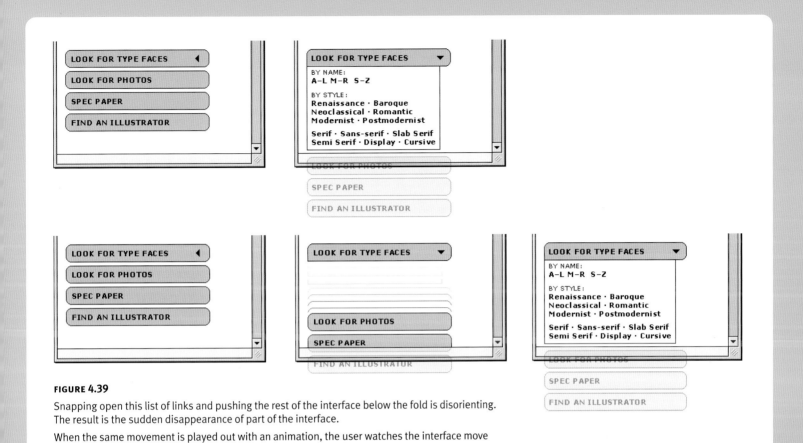

FIGURE 4.39

Snapping open this list of links and pushing the rest of the interface below the fold is disorienting. The result is the sudden disappearance of part of the interface.

When the same movement is played out with an animation, the user watches the interface move below the fold. The elements do not appear to have disappeared.

At this moment in Web interface history, feedback sounds can be a helpful addition to interfaces. Unlike the visual Web landscape, there is essentially a clean background of silence on a Web page. The user can clearly pick out and benefit from the audio feedback. Mouseover effects, such as the ones discussed previously, become necessary in today's Web interfaces because they help to distinguish useful elements from superfluous ones. Audible feedback becomes more difficult to hear in an interface where constant sound, such as a musical loop, is present.

Although sound is both useful and compelling, use it as a user-initiated element. Never play sounds automatically in a Web interface. Every operating system sound is either user initiated (feedback sounds set in preferences, CSS or MP3s played), or a computer alert sound. The clear division between these two types of sounds is necessary to maintain the user's belief that an alert sound is important. If the operating system initiates unimportant sounds from time to time, the alert sound would cease to be effective.

chapter 5

FORM ELEMENTS

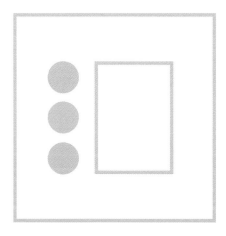

While link elements allow users to move from one part of the Web to another, forms allow them to communicate directly with the site. Forms allow users to input information by typing into a text field, making selections from lists and menus, or clicking checkboxes and radio buttons. Forms are the tools that allow for true interaction between human and computer.

Most form elements are gateways to pre-defined options. When a person selects an option from a form, the input is used by a script which either resides on a server (as in CGI and Perl scripts) or is downloaded to the client machine (as in Java applets and JavaScripts). In essence, the script waits for key instructions from the user, who chooses among the options presented, and submits his or her choices. (Though submit buttons are also form elements, they are discussed in Chapter 4: Button Elements.) Here, we'll limit our discussion of form elements to text fields, lists, menus, checkboxes, and radio buttons. (See Fig. 5.1)

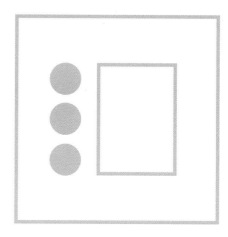

Input Fields

There are two ways to enter information to a form: input fields, which let users type freely, or lists, menus, and buttons that let them select predetermined options from a range of items.

Input fields, where a user types directly into the interface, are vastly different from preformatted lists, because input is the invention of the user and can't be readily handled by pre-programmed scripts. The decision whether and how to use an input field is somewhat affected by this fact, because users, aware of the opportunity for typing errors, naturally approach input fields with a degree of caution. (See Fig. 5.2)

Text Fields

There are two kinds of text input fields; single-line text fields, and multiple-line text fields. They do essentially the same thing—collect typed text from a user—but they address different kinds of interaction. When you type into a single-line text field, striking the return key generally initiates a submit command (as does the Submit button). When you type in a Multiline text field, the return key makes a line break, allowing the user to make paragraphs rather than one long entry.

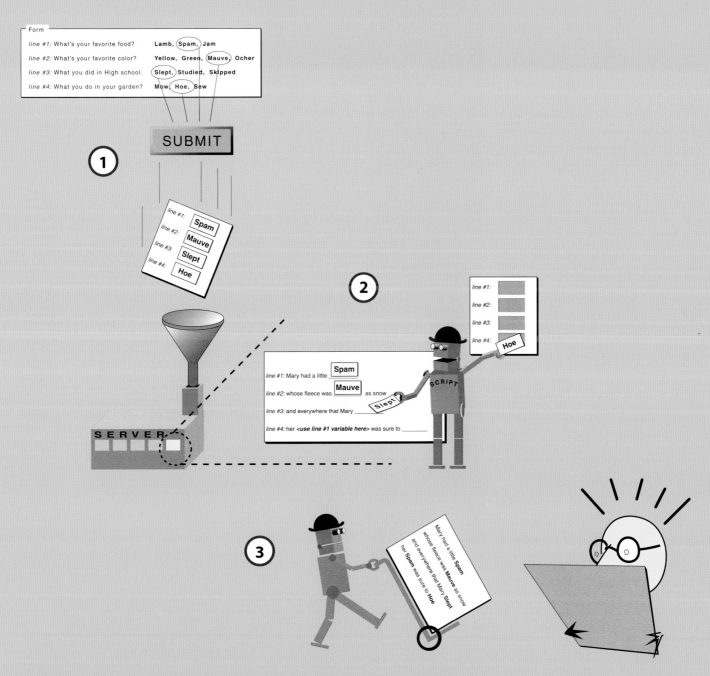

FIGURE 5.1

1. Form elements are essentially lists of options. When the user selects an option and clicks the submit button, the information is sent to a script, which often resides on a server but can also reside on the client side.

2. The script then translates the information into a useful format, and

3. delivers it back to the user.

Though single-line fields may accept an un-
limited amount of text, they limit the number
of characters that can be seen at one time,
which is not conducive to lengthy typing.
Because of this, and because computers tend
to get confused by long strings of language,
single-line fields are usually formatted to limit
the number of characters allowed. This kind
of field is best used for exchanges where
simple input is required. Most people innately
understand this, and assume single-line
text fields are for simple queries or concise
chunks of information, such as email
addresses or zip codes.

Multiline fields are generally used when
large amounts of text will be sent, as in
email messages and chat interfaces. The
computer's role in this kind of interaction
is essentially as delivery agent.

Usually, long text entries are handled by the
script as attached files that have no effect on
the script's inner workings. In these cases,
the email interface handles the short,
specifically formatted information (such as
email addresses) as data. The message just
goes along for the ride. (See Fig. 5.3)

A chat interface typically has a few single-
line fields, followed by a large multiline
field. Even without any clarifying labels,
we recognize this as a discussion format.

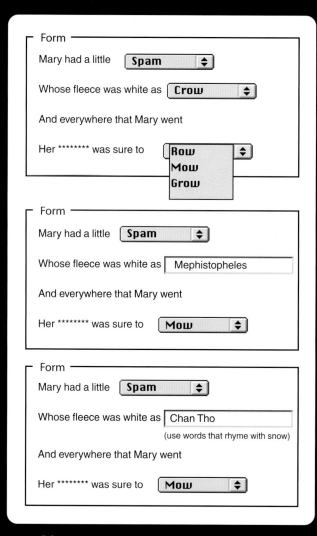

FIGURE 5.2

Each predefined option in these four lists will work with the poem's
original rhyme scheme in such a way that any selection will result in
a rhyming poem. Text input fields offer no such guarantee. Because
there is more room for error, text input fields are often accompanied
by didactic labels.

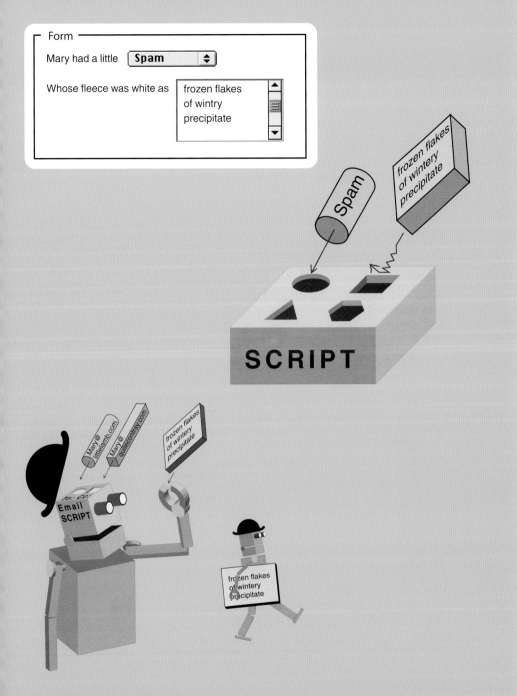

We intuitively understand that the short single-line fields are for precise instructions or addresses, and the multiline field is for free-form messages. Watch people use a chat interface—you will notice that their posture is stiff and attentive as they type addresses and subject lines into the single-line fields. Once they're finished addressing, users sit back and relax into the more natural job of personal communication while they type in the multiline field.

Input fields can be programmed to any size with a few specifications. Width is specified by character count: a specification of forty characters will render wide enough to display forty letters of Courier (or whatever monospaced font is set in the browser preferences). Each browser and platform will render the width a little differently. (See Fig. 5.4) But while extremely wide fields may allow a user to see more of what they are typing, they also exaggerate the variation in rendering from browser to browser.

Different widths also imply different functionalities. A single-line field five characters wide conveys the idea that the field will accept a narrow range of characters and data types—zip codes, but not search queries. A forty-character field is rather wide, and implies that more free-form input is be acceptable.

FIGURE 5.3

A script can easily handle user input when the data is chosen from a list of predefined options. Freely typed information, especially long text messages, are much more difficult to process because they are likely to vary dramatically from the script's preprogrammed abilities, and are often relayed by the script rather than processed as data.

FIGURE 5.4

At best, the way form elements render from browser to browser is haphazard. Text input fields and list windows in most Macintosh browser versions appear smaller than they do in Windows, while Mac menus are significantly wider than Windows ones. The only exception are recent Mac Netscape versions that mimic the appearance of Windows form elements.

These examples show fields with character widths of forty. Note that the number of characters visible does not always strictly match the specification. The Mac Netscape V.4 menu bases the field appearance on forty characters of 12-point Chicago, although it displays a smaller typeface, Geneva.

Another browser inconsistency is that list windows in Netscape on Mac, and Netscape on Windows display horizontal scroll bars even when such scrolling is unnecessary.

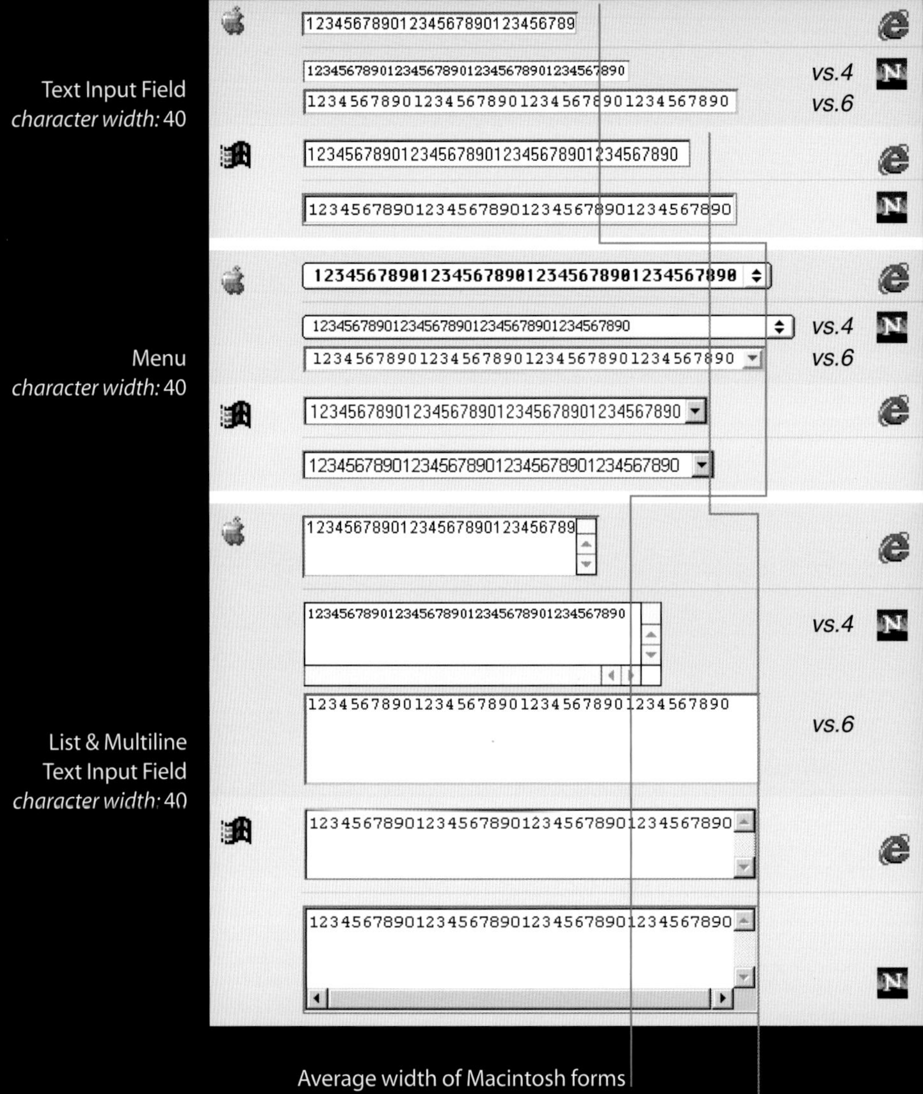

Text Input Field
character width: 40

Menu
character width: 40

List & Multiline
Text Input Field
character width: 40

vs.4
vs.6

Average width of Macintosh forms

Multiline text fields can also be programmed to have a specific height or number of visible rows of text. Like single-line fields, they can accept more text than the visible space seems to allow, but in multiline fields, scroll bars are added to the box to allow users to navigate overflow text.

The width of both kinds of input fields, as well as the height of multiline boxes, should be determined by two factors: visual weight, and browser window size—with consideration given to the premise that the more text is visible, the better. Since it is difficult to know what size a browser window will be, expect the client's real estate to be as small as 600 X 300 pixels (the maximum usable size of a browser window on a 640 X 480-pixel monitor, with all the buttons showing). However, since only a small segment of the Web audience is still using such small monitors, it's okay to assume the next size up: 750 X 430 pixels (the usable area of an 800 X 600-pixel monitor).

Input fields should not extend beyond the visible area of the browser window, for good reason. In a visible area of 400 vertical pixels, a multiline box taller than 400 pixels would require the user to use two scroll bars to see any overflow text: one on the browser window, and one on the input box. (See Fig. 5.5)

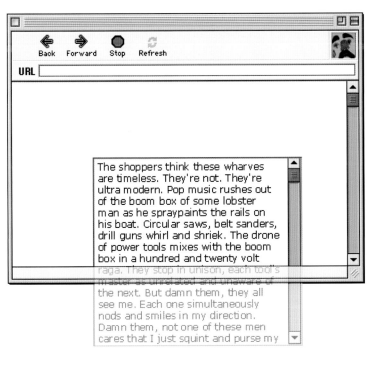

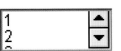

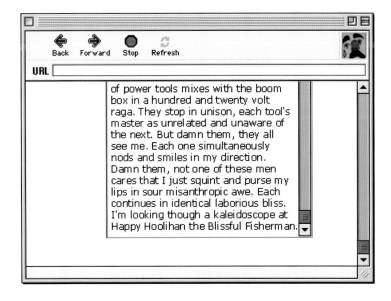

FIGURE 5.5

Since Web interfaces are displayed within browser windows and browser windows vary widely in size, input fields should be designed to safely fit within the smallest screens in common use. If the field is longer or taller than the browser window, users will have to scroll twice, in some cases, to see what they have typed.

Erring on the small side will ensure a box that fits in the browser window. Still, multiline fields should never be less than three rows high, because that's the minimum height at which all of the up and down scroll controls are visible.

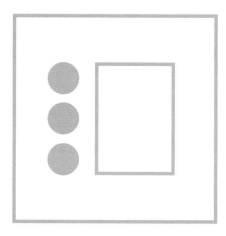

Selection Fields

Lists and menus both serve the same purpose: they allow users to select among a group of predetermined options. A menu is a bar that displays a single option until it is clicked on, at which point it reveals everything available in that category. Lists are scrollable boxes that display multiple options at once. Rather than clicking a header to see its contents, the user scrolls up and down the list to see more options. List windows look much like multiline text input fields, except that the text in a list window does not wrap. Each option is set as one row. Since verbose option labels make for wide list windows, it's best to make them concise.

Despite the difference in appearance and behavior, there is only one functional difference between list and menus: whereas menus only let users select one option at a time, lists allow them to select as many as they like. (See Fig. 5.6)

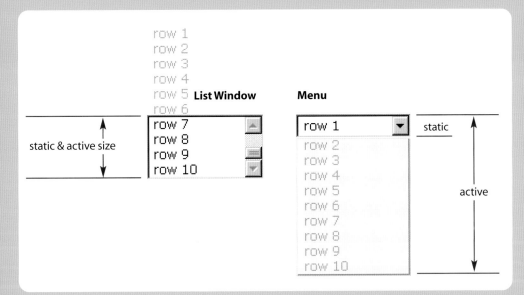

FIGURE 5.6

Menus and list windows allow access to a maximum number of options in a minimum amount of space. Menus require less space when idle, but are as large as lists once they're clicked. List windows take more space than idle menus, but do not change size when clicked.

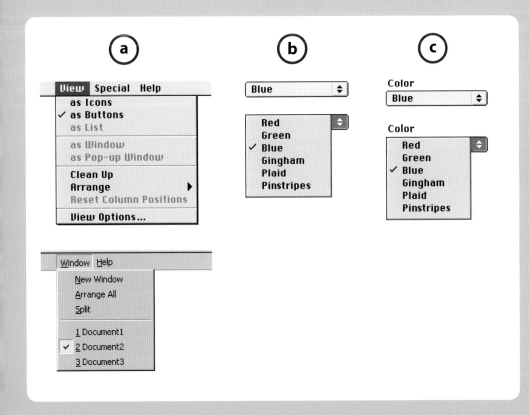

FIGURE 5.7: MENU BARS

a. True menu bars are more complex than their HTML counterparts. Some items are executable commands, while others are states that can be toggled on and off. In menu bars, items can be grouped and separated with rule lines. Menu bars work well because their appearance remains constant—the menu's header is always there. To see the status of items within, users must click on the header. This is slightly inconvenient, because it requires action every time a user wishes to see what options are available and what he has already selected.

b. Menus in Web interfaces don't have constant headers: by default, the selected option is visible. This can be problematic, because the selected item takes on the importance of a header, which might not be appropriate. The upside to this system is that the user does not have to do anything to see which option is active.

c. In some ways, HTML menus accompanied by separate headers function better than either of the other menu styles, because the header and the selected item are visible at the same time. Unfortunately, given the variety of default fonts people set in their browser preferences, it is difficult to guarantee that headers and menu items will have be in the same font family, weakening the visual relationship between header and list.

Menus

Most people are familiar with the menu bar at the top of the Macintosh interface or at the top of a Windows application window. These menu collections follow a slightly different set of guidelines than menu elements used in Web design. (See Fig. 5.7)

Since menu bars are ubiquitous, a user will approach menu elements in Web interfaces with a set of expectations based on repeated interaction with menu bar menus. HTML menu elements can't be programmed to act like menu bars because they lack the means to create external labels, horizontal rules, and grayed-out, inactive options. Nonetheless a designer should keep in mind those factors that make menu bars successful when designing Web menu interfaces, since these factors define how users perceive menus. Successful interaction with the limited implementations of Web interface menus will be measured against system menu bars.

HTML menus have a primal visual quality that draws attention to their obvious functionality. Their main problem lies in the visual weight given to the option that appears by default. Since the visible option acts somewhat like a header, it can give the wrong impression about the value of the element. (See Fig. 5.8)

FIGURE 5.8

When labeled properly with display text, the visible option acts less like a label but still has an appearance of importance that can shortchange the other options in the list. When I see a menu like this, I wonder why the interface is insisting that the chair I buy be red.

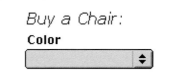

If there is no default option for a list, leaving the option bar blank can be confusing. It looks like something didn't display correctly. I'm left to wonder if I'm required to choose a color, and worry whether leaving the bar blank will result in a random color selection.

It is tempting to use the category label as the default option, but it is not clear if a selection is required, and once a selection is made, the label is no longer visible.

An instructive default option is best, if a bit wordy. If no selection is required, a default option that says so is helpful.

FIGURE 5.9

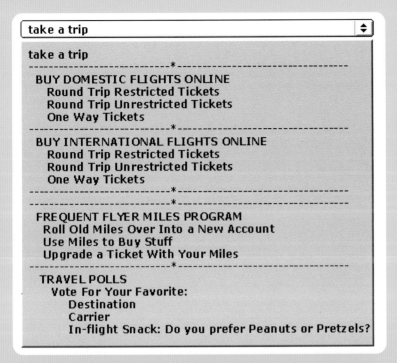

```
┌─────────────────────────────────────────────┬──┐
│ take a trip                                  │ ▲▼│
├──────────────────────────────────────────────┴──┤
│ take a trip                                       │
│ -------------------------*----------------------- │
│    BUY DOMESTIC FLIGHTS ONLINE                    │
│       Round Trip Restricted Tickets               │
│       Round Trip Unrestricted Tickets             │
│       One Way Tickets                             │
│ -------------------------*----------------------- │
│    BUY INTERNATIONAL FLIGHTS ONLINE               │
│       Round Trip Restricted Tickets               │
│       Round Trip Unrestricted Tickets             │
│       One Way Tickets                             │
│ -------------------------*----------------------- │
│ -------------------------*----------------------- │
│    FREQUENT FLYER MILES PROGRAM                   │
│       Roll Old Miles Over Into a New Account      │
│       Use Miles to Buy Stuff                      │
│       Upgrade a Ticket With Your Miles            │
│ -------------------------*----------------------- │
│    TRAVEL POLLS                                   │
│       Vote For Your Favorite:                     │
│          Destination                              │
│          Carrier                                  │
│          In-flight Snack: Do you prefer Peanuts or Pretzels? │
└───────────────────────────────────────────────────┘
```

The effort it takes to distinguish among groups of unrelated information within a single menu makes this element extrawide and hard to use. When closed, there is no way for a user to know all the categories of choices within it. A better solution is to create separate menus, each dedicated to one idea.

Menu options that attempt to engage the user in a dialogue—"peanuts or pretzels, sir?"—are unwieldy. A better solution is to use separate headers and multiple menus.

The menu header, though not explicitly part of the element, is a critical component of its usability. Since HTML menus can't be compartmentalized with rule lines, the options within them should relate logically to each other as well as to the header. Items that fail to address different facets of a single task or define related subcategories within a category might better be placed in separate menus. (See Fig. 5.9) On the other hand, when only one choice is possible within a range of options—even if the options are conceptually unrelated—a single menu is the best solution. (See Fig. 10)

Size is another issue in menu design. Since the number of characters in the longest sub-option determines the width of the menu, concise language will make the menu easier to read and navigate. Likewise, depth becomes an issue of ergonomics. If the list of options is too long, the menu will extend beyond the total height of the screen, making it difficult to move through the options while holding down the mouse. (See Fig. 5.11)

FIGURE 5.10

These options could be split
into two groups (colors and
patterns), but putting them
in separate menus would
require a toggle to prevent
the user from selecting options from both lists when
only one choice is possible.

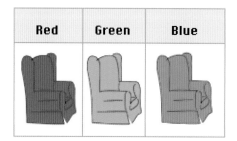

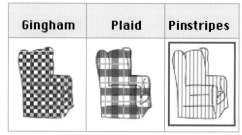

FIGURE 5.10 *CONTINUED*

If colors and patterns can be cross-combined—as in red/plaid, red/gingham, or plaid/red, plaid/green—a single menu is not the best solution. Even if this list of nested options wasn't unwieldy, it would still be problematic, because users might select one of the sub-headings (like Solid), which aren't really options.

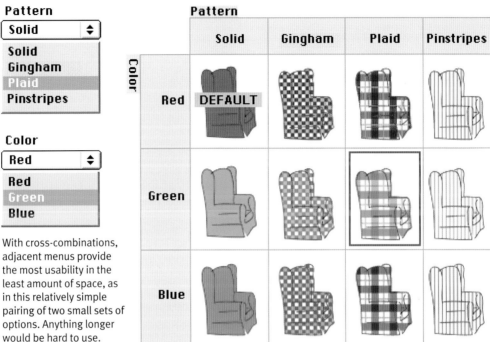

With cross-combinations, adjacent menus provide the most usability in the least amount of space, as in this relatively simple pairing of two small sets of options. Anything longer would be hard to use.

List Fields

Sometimes called *scrolling lists,* scroll bars are how a user accesses the options within a list. A designer can specify as many or as few visible rows of options with any list window, possibly coding the functionality right out of the form. Not only can you specify too many rows, but, specifying fewer than four rows does not allow ample space for scroll bars or the up and down arrows to render effectively.

One advantage to scrolling lists is that multiple options are visible, helping the user better understand the range of an interface. Another feature of the list field is the ability to select more than one option at a time. A user can click and drag to select several options at once or hold the command key (on Macintosh) or option key (in Windows) while selecting options that are not directly above or below each other.

The only other significant difference between list fields and menus, is their effect on an interface. A menu can be used as part of a sentence or string of connected ideas, the visible option bridging two parts of an interface or text. (See Fig. 5.12)

Toggles, Checkboxes, and Radio Buttons

Just as there are similarities between lists and menus and between single-line text fields and multilined text fields, there is one between checkboxes and radio buttons. These two form elements are so much alike that it is often difficult to determine which element to use in certain situations. Both describe binary states: when an option can only be one of two opposite possibilities. But there are subtle differences between them.

If an option's "off" state is implicit in the language of its "on" state, a checkbox is a good solution. (See Fig. 5.13)

Some options have positive and negative states that aren't implicit in their wording. Each state of the option can be displayed with connected radio buttons. Selecting one radio button deselects the other. (See Fig. 5.14)

A list of options, only one of which can be selected at a time, may merit radio buttons. Such a list functions like a menu, but each option is visible. As with menus, a relationship between options should be apparent in the wording. (See Fig. 5.15) If several unrelated options are displayed with connected radio buttons, the radio button behavior doesn't make much sense.

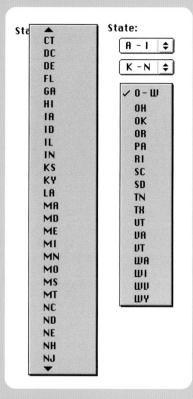

FIGURE 5.11

Most online phone directories ask users to select the state from a single menu. Fifty options is too many. It would be far better to split the list into several menus, either alphabetically or regionally.

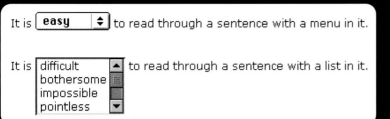

FIGURE 5.12

Lists make a user pause to read them. Lists, with numerous visible options, do not work as well as menus to link groupings that are meant to be read linearly.

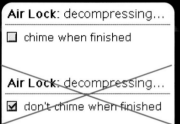

FIGURE 5.13

The chime option can be either on or off. Rather than have a button for each state, it is more concise to have off be the default option and let the user choose to turn the chime on. The opposite wording would technically work, but it would confusingly ask the user to make a positive check on a negative choice.

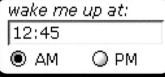

FIGURE 5.14

In essence, this is a binary option, but both options must be visible for the interface to make sense.

Combining Form Elements in an Interface

Form elements facilitate communication between user and computer. There is a fine line between Web page and Web interface. Form elements reside well within the interface realm.

Since lists, menus, toggles, and input fields introduce variable factors to a task, the more form elements you include, the harder it is to maintain clarity in an interface. There is no magic number of form elements that can co-exist in an interface. An interface fails when a user has trouble grasping the relationships between form elements or if he forgets the significance of some form elements when he encounters them. If the purpose of even a single form element is unclear, the interface will fail. The user can't gauge whether the results of a choice match what he was expecting, since he has lost track of the sequence of events in the confusion.

Users get lost easily in lengthy forms. It is difficult to see the relationships between form elements in a long scrolling interface when several different element types are used in the form. Simplicity is always the best policy. (See Fig. 5.16)

A user can easily concentrate on a handful of options as long as the options are in a similar format. Selecting options from many menus is much easier than interacting with multiple types of form elements. Lists, toggles, and input fields are difficult (though not impossible) to combine in an interface.

Refreshing Form Elements with JavaScript

Complex interfaces often involve nested options; sets of variables, each with subsets of variables. The trouble is, users usually don't want to see the options they aren't interested in, and that goes double for the options within the options they aren't interested in. JavaScript can be used to control the display of pertinent options, populating a subset field once a super-set is selected. (See Fig. 5.17)

There are two drawbacks to using JavaScript to update the variables within a form element. When the user selects an option that triggers a JavaScript, the page must refresh, causing the window to go blank for a moment. This may seem like a negligible pause compared to the alternative (submitting each change to a server script and loading an entirely new page) but it is jarring to the user.

Radio buttons are also used in lists of exclusive options, where only a single option can be selected at a time. Options that are grouped with connected radio buttons should be part of a logical set.

When a list of options is inclusive, checkboxes are the logical alternative to radio buttons.

Though not what radio buttons were originally designed for, their exclusivity makes them useful elements in presenting a graded set of options. This is essentially a list of five options, but they are presented as gradations of a single option.

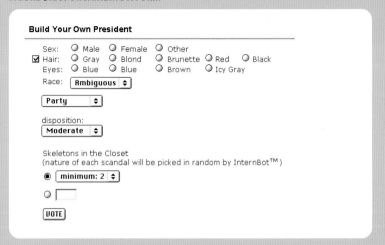

It is initially difficult to comprehend this interface. The multiple element formats are overwhelming.

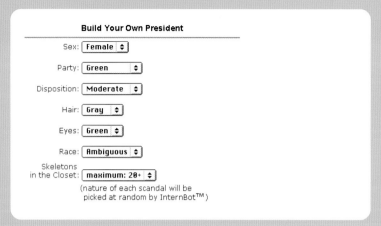

If the same form can be built from one or two element types, a user will only need to keep one mode of usability in mind. In this case, it is selecting menu items. The likeness of each form element tells the user that each set of menus has a similar purpose, thus giving him an instant idea of what to expect from the interface.

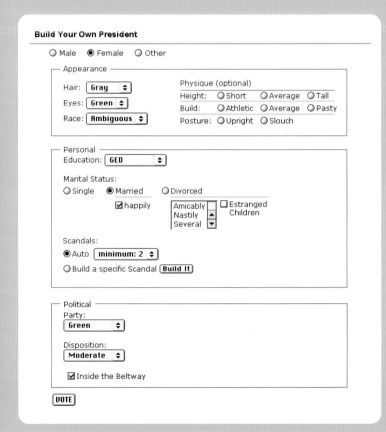

If an interface requires a combination of form types, compartmentalizing the interface by task helps the user understand smaller pieces of the process at the appropriate time.

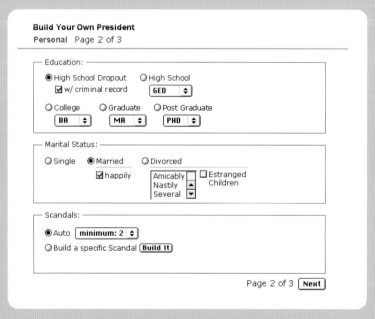

Interfaces that require more than one scroll should be split into steps, by page. A user experiences less anxiety if a simple task is presented, confirmed, and then leads to the next step. As I did in the page header and footer, you should give the user clues about where they are in the process.

FIGURE 5.17

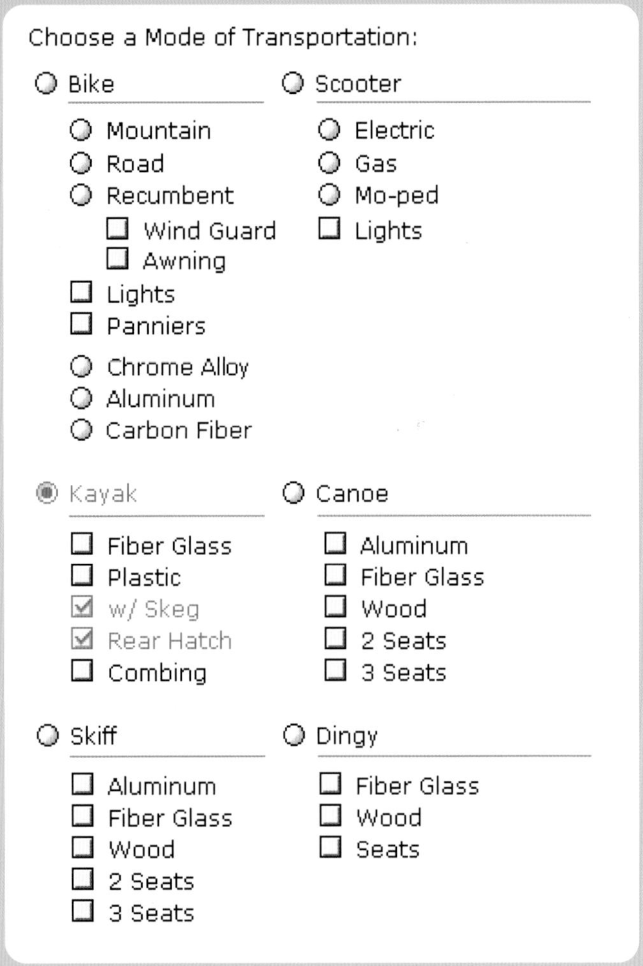

Choose a Mode of Transportation:

○ Bike   ○ Scooter

   ○ Mountain   ○ Electric
   ○ Road   ○ Gas
   ○ Recumbent   ○ Mo-ped
      ☐ Wind Guard ☐ Lights
      ☐ Awning
   ☐ Lights
   ☐ Panniers
   ○ Chrome Alloy
   ○ Aluminum
   ○ Carbon Fiber

◉ Kayak   ○ Canoe

   ☐ Fiber Glass   ☐ Aluminum
   ☐ Plastic   ☐ Fiber Glass
   ☑ w/ Skeg   ☐ Wood
   ☑ Rear Hatch   ☐ 2 Seats
   ☐ Combing   ☐ 3 Seats

○ Skiff   ○ Dingy

   ☐ Aluminum   ☐ Fiber Glass
   ☐ Fiber Glass   ☐ Wood
   ☐ Wood   ☐ Seats
   ☐ 2 Seats
   ☐ 3 Seats

Representing each option in this interface takes up valuable real estate, most of which is successively useless to users the deeper they delve into one path. The checked portion shows the relatively small subset of information that is relevant to this user. The rest of the interface amounts to wasted space from the perspective of, say, a kayaker.

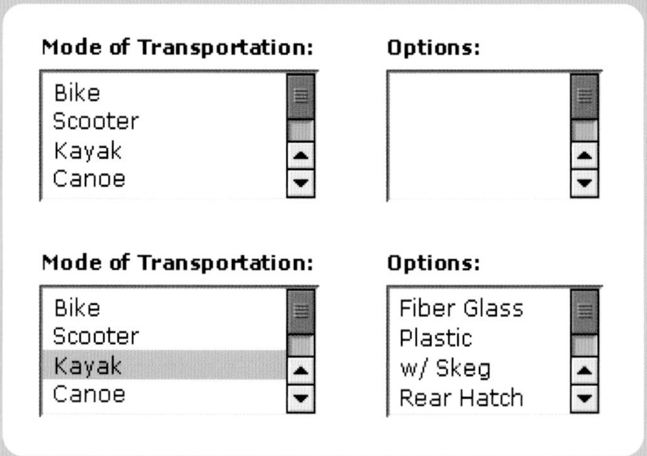

Mode of Transportation:

| Bike |
| Scooter |
| Kayak |
| Canoe |

Options:

| (empty) |

Mode of Transportation:

| Bike |
| Scooter |
| Kayak |
| Canoe |

Options:

| Fiber Glass |
| Plastic |
| w/ Skeg |
| Rear Hatch |

Form elements can be linked by JavaScript. A selected option in one field can update the display of options in another field. Changing the display interactively eliminates form elements that become irrelevant to users once they begin to make decisions.

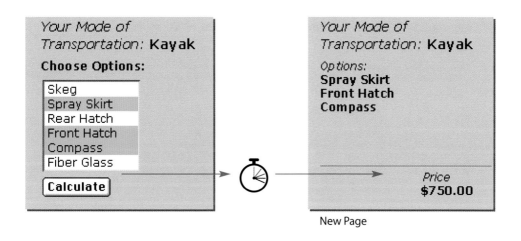

New Page

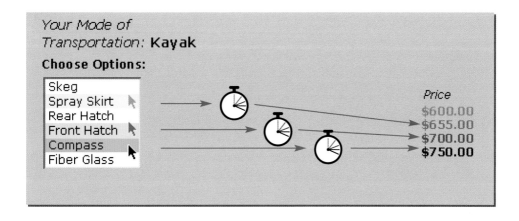

FIGURE 5.18

This interface calculates a new price with every added option. The straightforward pattern of selecting options, then adding them once to determine the new price is replaced with a JavaScript that updates automatically whichever option clicked. The interface does not require a new page for each calculation, but the result may seem like a jarring transition every time the user clicks an option. It is most frustrating for the user who wants to pay for many options.

FIGURE 5.19: CSS AND BROWSER INCONSISTENCIES

CSS can be used to specify height and width of form elements, as well as background colors and images, fonts, and font colors. Unfortunately, many CSS specifications, like height, width, and backgrounds, are applied to form elements inconsistently. Some glaring examples are shown here. The discrepancy between Netscape's and Internet Explorer's implementation of CSS is too broad to illustrate comprehensively here. As always, check your work on several browsers on both platforms.

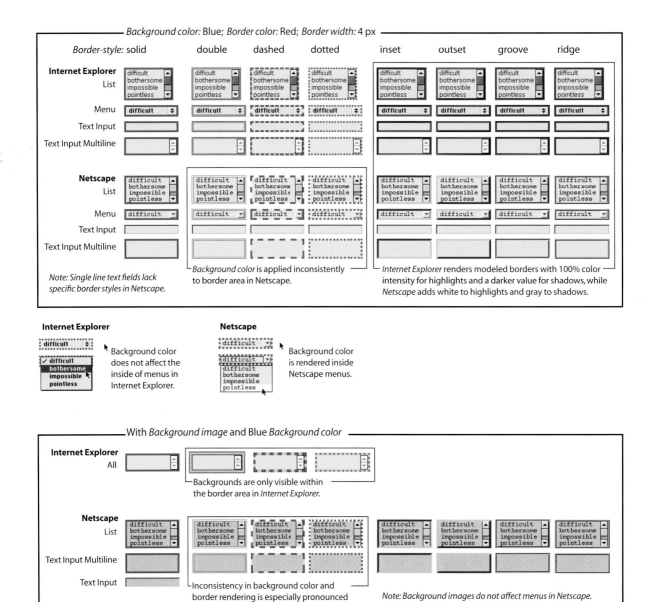

FIGURE 5.19: CSS AND BROWSER INCONSISTENCIES *CONTINUED*

Checkboxes and Radio Buttons
Background color: Blue

Internet Explorer (Borders create a rectangle around the element)	☑ ◉	☑ ◉	☑ ◉	☑ ◎	☑ ◉	☑ ◉	☑ ◉	☑ ◉
Netscape (Borders follow the contour of the element)	▫ ◦	▫ ◦	▫ ◦	⋮⋮ ◦	▗ ◦	◢ ◦	▫ ◦	▫ ◦
	▫ ◦	▫ ◦	▫ ◦	⋮⋮ ◦	▗ ◦	◢ ◦	▫ ◦	▫ ◦
with background color *and background image*	✔ ⊙	✔ ⊙	✔ ⊙	✔ ◯	✔ ◑	✔ ◔	✔ ⊙	✔ ◯
height and width: 50 px								

Height and width affects radio buttons and checkboxes only in Netscape. Check marks are affected by sizing, while the center point of the radio button is not. Background colors are contained within the border until a background image is added. Then the background color extends into the inside of the box or button.

lists & text input boxes

width: 20 px
height: 140 px

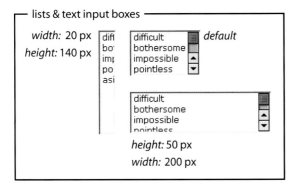

height: 50 px
width: 200 px

menus

width: 20 px
height: 140 px

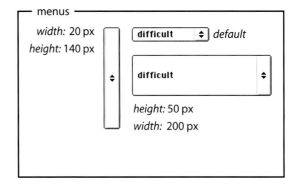

height: 50 px
width: 200 px

HEIGHT AND WIDTH SPECIFICATIONS

Height and width specifications can be taken to extremes, obscuring the element's intended function.

Users are accustomed to pages remaining static until they click a link or press a button. Considering what the average user must go through before arriving at an interface — dozens of pages, scores of broken links, busy servers, broken ISP connections — pages that suddenly refresh upon selecting an option in a list can be quite disturbing.

Users like to poke around a form-based interface; to see the menu and list options before making selection decisions. Java-Script refreshing eliminates this option. Consider the consequences of using JavaScript to manipulate form elements or submit a form automatically. They may take too much control away from the user. (See Fig. 5.18)

CSS and Form Elements

Most users encounter several interfaces every time they use the Web. It can be helpful for an interface to differentiate itself from other interfaces with color and unique type styles. Cascading Style Sheets allow designers to specify some characteristics of any form element: dimensions; border width, style and color; background color; font specifications; and (regrettably) background image. Simplicity is always a virtue, and even more so because many of these elements are not applied consistently by Internet Explorer and Netscape. (See Fig. 5.19)

As attractive as custom form elements can be, most modifications undermine usability. Contrast is a guiding principle in form usability. When an option in a menu has high contrast with the background, the user knows the option is available. Grayed options are not currently available, but they could be under different circumstances.

Grayed options are not part of the HTML form elements feature set, but they are part of the visual language of forms carried over from the desktop. If a user sees low contrast in a menu or list, he might think the options are not available. (See Fig. 5.20)

On the other hand, used appropriately, CSS can be very helpful in differentiating important form elements from others that are less so. You can use CSS to alter a less important element's color, for instance, to give it a lower contrast, effectively "graying down" the element and making it less noticeable without making the mistake of confusing it with an unavailable menu choice. (See Fig. 5.21) As long as the established visual language of usability is still apparent, such a format change can be very effective. (See Fig. 5.22)

Choose One of Your Code Names:

✓ Butch the Bandit
  Mr. I.M.C Moe
  Rex Marshall
  Bab the Impaler

FIGURE 5.20

This menu uses CSS to apply color to the text. Because of the lack of contrast, it is unclear if these options are available.

FIGURE 5.21

Thank you for signing up for our services.
With your permission, we would like to:

Send You Free Money
Ply You With Frankincense
Nominate You For a Nobel Prize
Elevate Your Status to King
Drink to Your Health

[Please Do]

When a user selects an option, the row is highlighted. The color of the highlight can be customized by the user in both the Windows and Mac operating systems.

Thank you for signing up for our services.
With your permission, we would like to:

Bulldoze Your House
Spay Your Pets
Sleep in Your Cupboards
Defile Your Kin
Pimp Your Social Security Number

[Please Do]

This menu has a background applied to it with CSS that is similar to the highlight color. It appears as if every option in the list is selected when, in fact, none are.

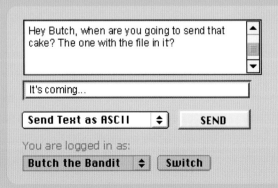

Hey Butch, when are you going to send that cake? The one with the file in it?

It's coming...

[Send Text as ASCII ▲▼]   [SEND]

You are logged in as:

[Butch the Bandit ▲▼]   [Switch]

FIGURE 5.22

This discussion interface uses CSS to create a hierarchy with the form elements. The log-in name menu recedes because it is a similar color to the background, but it is clearly an active menu because the text uses the same font and color as the other forms on the page. The Send button and the text entry field are visually linked with yellow and appropriately come forward in the hierarchy.

SECTION III:
Advanced Interface Elements

Basic HTML interfaces are distinguished from advanced interfaces by the amount of work that can be done within a single browser window, because interfaces, of course, are not just strings of linked pages. In this section, we'll discuss multifaceted interfaces, such as pop-up windows or the controls on a movie player.

The differences between multifaceted interfaces and the linear elements discussed in the previous section reflect developments in site design. In early Web design, interface options or hypertext links served only to connect users to other pages. More recent developments allow Web pages to be self-contained environments. If you think of each Web page as an individual interface, jumping from one to another can be like switching from one application to another. An interface that offers a variety of useful information and tools in a single page provides a streamlined interaction that doesn't make the user wait for a new page to load with every click.

Multifaceted interfaces have their own problems. The amount of space available on most computer screens limits the number of interface elements that can be visible at one time. Most application designers handle this by storing extra tools and functions behind menu items, icons, and standard tool palettes. When a user selects a special function from a menu, a temporary set of tools appears in front of the standard view. A word processor, for instance, devotes most of its screen real estate to the text area and a few crucial formatting tools. To change the margins and font face, you might open a dialogue box while you're doing that task and close it when you're done. Though it's standard in applications, this layering of tools has been slow to find widespread use in Web interfaces.

The powerful technologies of Macromedia Flash, CSS, JavaScript, and Dynamic HTML (DHTML) are changing things. Now that they have become ubiquitous, interface designers can provide many layers of functionality in the limited screen real estate of browsers. Unlike standard HTML devices—menus, buttons, toggles, and links, which are rendered by simple HTML tags—advanced interface devices are made of multiple DHTML and CSS components that can be put together in a variety of ways to mimic layered models of interactivity.

For instance, an HTML-based menu can only present a list of text options. If the designer wants to provide a visual menu, using images instead of words, he can construct the components—the rectangle, the highlight mechanism, the triggers for opening and closing, etc.—using DHTML, CSS, GIFS, and JavaScript (or equivalent objects in Flash).

Custom interface elements like these offer several benefits. First, they make it possible to create tools that have the same look and feel as the rest of the interface. Second, they provide greater usability without making users access new pages. Third, they allow us to design intuitive interfaces that take up less space than conventional interfaces. But they also have some drawbacks. Now that the Web is full of customized interfaces and invented interaction models, using them can be like driving through a tangled interchange crowded with fantastic vehicles out of Dr. Seuss.

The novice interaction designer who desires to avoid common pitfalls while creating new interface elements and systems can acquire perspective from successful usability paradigms. Studying interface elements in desktop operating systems and applications (which inspire many new Web devices), can give designers a foundation in the ways people use interactive tools, and help them understand what people expect when they encounter custom interfaces online.

The following chapters will not discuss DHTML coding syntax or other Web development scripts and languages. There are dozens of ways to code any custom interface element or system and plenty of stock options available. You can find simple JavaScripts for many basic interactions online (see www.webmonkey.com/reference/javascript_code_library/), and in Web design applications like Macromedia DreamWeaver. Flash also comes with plenty of stock scripts to drive custom interactions. This section outlines basic behaviors and alludes to some methodologies you can use with CSS and JavaScript. The goal is to create an overall understanding of the potential of advanced interfaces and leave their code definition to you and your programmer.

chapter 6

CONTROL ELEMENTS

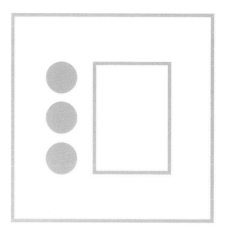

All the interface elements discussed in previous chapters—buttons, radio buttons, checkboxes, etc.—are part of the control family in application design. These elements modify, increase, or decrease some aspect of an interface. The rest of the control family—sliders, up-and-down arrows, and rotating triangles—are conspicuously unavailable in HTML. Web interfaces have not been connected to the browser framework that contains them, so control elements such as buttons and toggles have become associated with navigation and form options, not window functions.

DHTML and Flash have finally made the conventions of application design—small windows and panels contained within a larger interface space—available to Web designers. We can use these new tools to mimic the appearance and behavior of control elements that were long unavailable to us.

Window Controls

Many designers find it valuable to create a dimensional interface in the tradition of application design. In such an interface, many of the tasks once played out over multiple pages are contained within one page. Small windows or panels contained within the browser window allow the user to open and close parts of an interface as they need them, without having to go to a new page.

Once the designer has created layers, panels or windows, the user needs a way to interact with them. The control elements needed for windows in a Web page are not as extensive as are the standard ones in an operating system: resize grippers, scroll bars and arrows, collapse button, maximize buttons, close button, and title bar. (See Fig. 6.1)

To avoid confusion with real windows, we'll call these custom-designed windows "panels." They often take the form of a small layer with a few links in it or a collapsible area with items that extend beyond the panel's boundaries. Each panel requires a set of unique behavior controls. Most of these controls should have some relationship to the familiar operating system window controls. The user will then perceive the Web interface as he does an application. Small panels contained within the browser will have miniature control elements, as will the small palettes contained within the application window. (See Fig. 6.2)

Curiously, windows have no "open" control. From the operating system, windows are always created or launched by an icon or button.

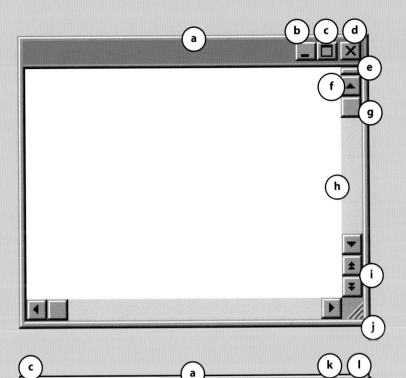

FIGURE 6.1: STANDARD WINDOW CONTROLS

In Microsoft products and other applications, windows have many control buttons that allow the user to navigate very efficiently. Many of these controls can be useful in the space-starved Web environment, specifically jump-buttons, which take the user to the very top or bottom of the window contents, or collapse buttons (Macintosh), which let users collapse the window without losing it entirely.

Windows

a. title bar (window can be repositioned using this)

b. minimize—hides window (Windows)

c. maximize—fills screen with window (Windows)

d. close

e. split window handle

f. scroll button

g. scroll handle

h. scroll bar gap (jumps the content up or down in large increments)

i. jump buttons (jumps content directly to beginning or end)

j. resize gripper

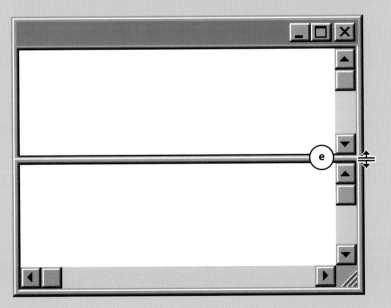

Additional Classic Macintosh Controls

a. title bar uses gripper lines as affordances to convey movability

c. close button is on the left

k. zoom—similar to maximize in Windows, enlarges window to the largest size necessary to display entire contents

l. collapse—hides window, leaves title bar visible

e. split screen handle becomes a movable window border

Anchored Panels
in the Browser

Web interfaces are designed like the "list" view of a window where everything is anchored to the margins, and an item name serves both as gateway to the interface's contents and as a toggle for content visibility.

In the "list" view, you can see folder contents without opening a window. Rotating triangles can be used to open and close a folder in this mode. A control toggling between two states is an efficient use of space. It translates well into Web interfaces when you want to expand the view of an existing element.

As is often the case with Web interfaces, the most useful scheme is a hybrid between a window's scalability and autonomy and the anchored structure of an expandable list. (See Fig. 6.3) The designer may need to be inventive, creating a panel with the controls that best suit the situation. Invention should not contradict established control element behaviors. Flipping arrows, close buttons, and grippers can be combined in unique ways while the established behavior of each is left intact.

FIGURE 6.2: PANEL CONTROLS

Web interface designers quickly outgrow the standard window controls in favor of smaller, more efficient ones. A full-sized window within the browser would confuse the user. Mimicking a specific operating system's control elements only work for users of one platform. Web interface panels should be distinguishable stylistically from operating system windows, and fit within the hierarchical scheme.

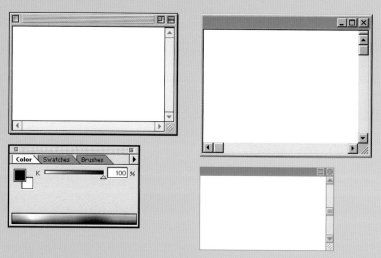

When designing panel controls for the Web, think small. Many applications written for the Mac use smaller control elements for tool panels. The title bar on this color tool, with its tiny zoom and close buttons, fits within the application element hierarchy.

Decreasing control sizes for panels inside the browser window works in Web design, too. Panels that are contained within the interface fit best within the overall hierarchy when their control elements are small.

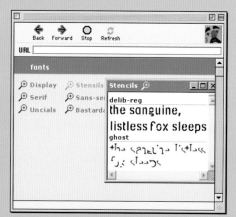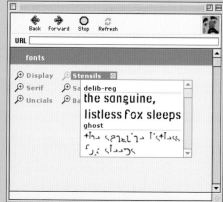

Since most panels are anchored to part of the interface, the title bar, which also allows you to move a window, is not necessary. However, the user may still need to close the panel. Most windows have controls for closing and minimizing, as well as resize grippers for every stage in between. A bar is the clearest place to put a close control, but it is also a waste of space. As long as the close control is clearly marked there should be plenty of options for its placement and design.

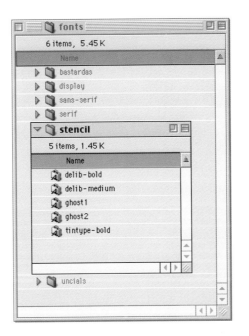

Sometimes you want the user to be unable to open new windows or jump to a new page. Opening a panel anchored to a fixed position can effectively combine the list view and the new window.

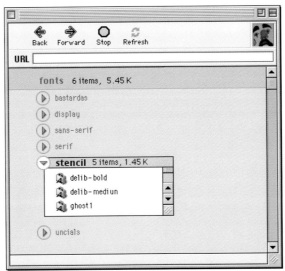

The same information can be viewed through two very different means. The "list" view of a window allows the user to open or close each subsequent folder without opening a new window. The same folder contents can be revealed in a new window, but more controls are needed to navigate this new view.

Scroll Bars

They're difficult to code, and hard to get right, but scroll bars on a panel are the best way to deal with content overflow. In the operating system, scroll bars have the most complicated sets of interactive behaviors. There is no point in reinventing these controls.

If you want people to scroll, stick to the basic structure of the operating system scroll bars. These consist of a slider, a bar for the slider to slide on, and up and down arrows. The appearance of each element can be unique to the interface, as long as the up and down arrows are inversely identical. (See Fig. 6.4)

For some designers and programmers working in DHTML, replicating the functionality and behavior of a scrolling window may be unrealistic. But an up-and-down control can be applied to a panel, without overtly referencing the design of a scroll bar. Arrows instantly explain their functionality, so the designer should have no difficulty providing access to the contents of a panel that extend beyond its visible bounds.

Keep in mind that one of the affordances of the scroll bar is its active/inactive state. It is not always clear that window content continues beyond the bottom edge, like when a paragraph ends above the fold and

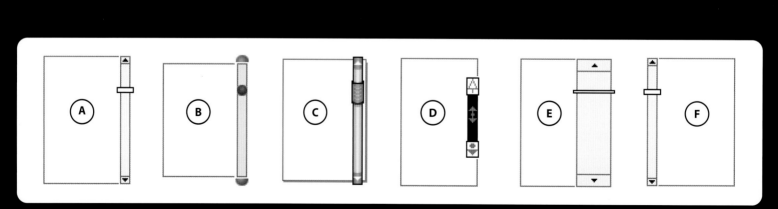

FIGURE 6.4

Scroll bars have such a unique and well-established appearance that even a highly stylized version of the element will work as long as it has a tall thin bar with arrows at the ends and is movable. A and B are true to form. A user might pause before figuring out what C is. The element does not seem to relate to the inside of the window. D and E are too far from the norm. The appearance of F is every bit as clear as A, but using this scroll bar might feel a little bit like writing with your wrong hand.

FIGURE 6.5: SCROLL BAR BEHAVIOR

The behaviors of a scroll bar are complex, because they combine three controls—up and down arrows, the scroll handle, and the gap between the handle and the arrows. This makes it especially difficult to write the code for effective scrolling.

A designer might decide to create a control element that is derived from the scrollbar's up and down arrows. This decision is probably a mistake. Simple up and down arrows are functionally clear, but they don't give the user the same information that a scroll bar does.

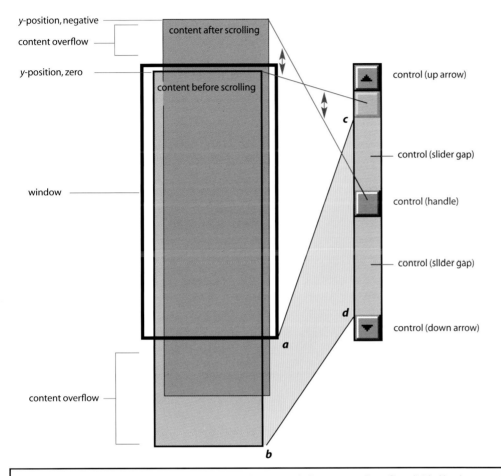

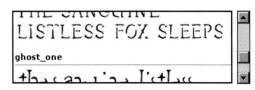

One function of a scroll bar is to provide a key to what part of the content is in view. In this case, the user can tell from the scroll handle which is close to the bottom of the bar, that the end of the content is just below the window.

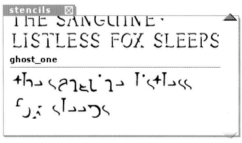

Instead of an entire scroll bar, the designer can use other devices to communicate the up and down arrows' function. In this case, the arrows have active/inactive appearances, telling the user when the beginning and end of the content is in view. The truncated type in the "quink_one" type sample indicates overflowed content.

A designer can decide how much each arrow moves content in the window. Users may find a full jump to the bottom too jarring, but will be impatient with tiny steps. A good rule of thumb for matching content with movement is one text line per click.

The content overflow (a, b) corresponds with the scrollbar gap (c, d). The amount of overflow divided by the amount of gap is used to determine how much the content should move (move amount) when the handle is moved. We'll call the move amount m. $a, b/c, d = m$

In this example a, b is 50 pixels, c, d is 100 pixels. $m = .5$ **(50/100)**

If the handle is moved down 10 pixels, the content is moved up 5 pixels. **10 X .5 = 5**

In the initial appearance of a window with overflowing content, the y-position is zero—the overflow is below the bottom of the window. The distance a scroll handle travels has an inverse effect on the y-position of the content, and that effect is based on the proportion of content overflow to the height of the scroll bar.

The scroll arrows and the scroll bar space on either side of the handle must affect both the position of the content and the handle. How much they affect these positions is determined by the programmer and the designer. One click on an arrow can be one line of text, or one click of the bar gap can be one-fourth of the total overflow area. The space between each scroll arrow and the handle is essentially a control element whose size is liquid. The trigger changes with the position of the handle.

the following paragraph begins below it. An active scroll bar lets the user know there is more content to be seen; the low-contrast inactive scroll bar tells the user all content is visible. A panel that forgoes the full scroll bar looses this important affordance, so the designer must take care to communicate scrollability. (See Fig. 6.5)

There are alternatives to using scroll controls to handle overflow. If there is enough content to conveniently divide the text into two or more equal sections, each section

could be contained on its own layer, with the layers stacked like index cards. If the stack metaphor is obvious in the design, users should understand the navigational method of flipping through the "stacks." Simple sequential controls for flipping replace the up/down arrows, eliminating the need to move the content vertically. (See Fig. 6.6)

Unlike scrollbars, the user will expect this device, as with most controls, to have a limited response—one click yields a new

view, without the transitional views associated with scrolling. You don't have to allow the user to jump around between layers (which would require too many way-finding devices and indicators). They can click sequentially forward, through each virtual card, until they reach the end. Clicking repeatedly backward will return the content to its original position.

Not all content lends itself to modularity or stacking. Large flat areas of content, such as photographs and maps, often require

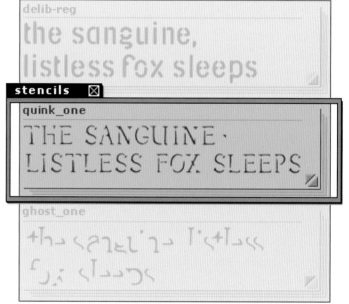

FIGURE 6.6

This panel functions identically to the scrolling example in Figure 6.5, but it looks like a stack of layers. The interaction is simpler than the previous example because the user doesn't need to fine tune the vertical position of the content. A click replaces one visible layer with the next in sequence. This effect can even be achieved using one tall image. Changing the y-coordinate of a single image with each click can create the illusion of flipping. This strategy is particularly useful because it limits the number of GIFs and layers.

FIGURE 6.7: TOGGLES

toggles lower part of panel on and off

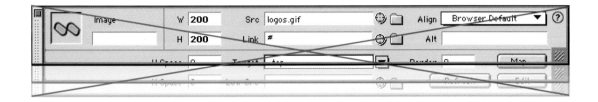

Macromedia Dreamweaver places most image settings into this tool panel. The most common parameters are always visible, while the secondary tier can be seen by clicking the toggle in the bottom right corner.

Would you date this guy?

Mathew	👁		**YES**
Bill	👁		
Judd	👁		**NO**
Thom	⊠		

toggles lower part of panel on and off

Would you date this guy?

This toggle is essentially a resize gripper set at maximum view. There would be no point in displaying every transitional state, since doing so would cut off the view of the secondary parameters.

more screen real estate than this method allows. You can use a small panel to show a portion a photograph, for instance. The user can assess whether they want to see the entire image without relinquishing very much screen real estate. If the user wants to see more of the content, one or two simple controls can offer an expanded view.

Revealing detail in a limited area can take one of two forms. You can show one portion at a fixed resolution, then use a toggle to expand the panel and reveal the rest of the content. Alternatively you can begin with a small version, zooming in to reveal detail, while providing directional controls to pan outside the original visible area.

The first method is used frequently for application tool panels, which may have two tiers of functionality. (See Fig. 6.7) A primary tier, with the most commonly needed tools, makes up the default panel view. A toggle expands the panel to reveal the secondary tools. The second method is used for mapping software, particularly on the Web. (See Fig. 6.8)

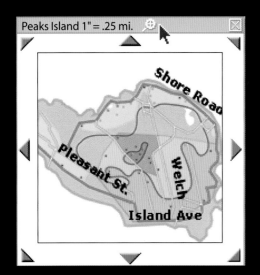
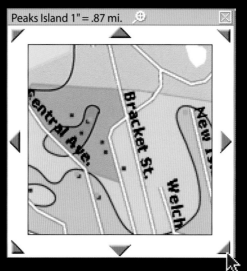
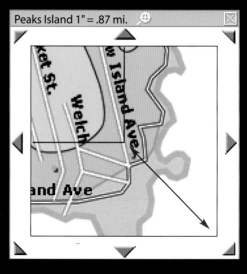

FIGURE 6.8

Since maps must be useful from all vantage points—macro to micro—the computer screen's limited resolution and size necessitates a two-tiered interface. A map can be viewed in a panel with a zoom contro, and with four or eight directional controls that work like the "jump" controls of a page window. Ideally, panning controls would work like up/down scrolling arrows. One click could move the map slightly to minimize each shift of context.

Most maps are so large that the unseen parts must be downloaded only when the client requests them. Without caching the overflow area, there is no way to gradually scroll or pan through a map. For this reason, jump buttons are a map interface convention. A click in any direction will load the next view, keeping the user oriented by including much of what was previously visible.

The controls for this map panel fall into two categories: the panel controls—close button and magnifier button—and the content controls—blue direction arrows.

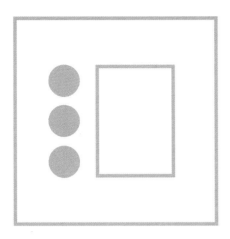

Output Controls

The previous controls are devices for navigating the contents of a browser panel or window, or for modifying the appearance of the panel. These functions are relatively new to Web interfaces, the result of a widespread adoption of DHTML-capable browsers and the Macromedia Flash plug-in. Even later arrivals to Web design are output controls—knobs, sliders, and buttons—controls that manage a variety of actions, from sound output to color balance.

These devices have been around for a long time in the control panels of operating systems. Now that Web interfaces can control sound and motion, output controls are making their way into Flash and DHTML interfaces.

Output controls often look like other navigation interface elements. Play, pause, and stop buttons, for instance, can initially be mistaken for buttons used elsewhere on a site for submitting searches or for navigating. An output control button's state-specific appearance distinguishes it from other interface elements. When users click a button to submit a search or to move to another page, they expect the button they clicked to disappear and the screen to refresh. The essential difference between control buttons and all other buttons is that control buttons remain after they are clicked, even if their appearance is altered to reflect a change of state. All other types of buttons are jumping-off points. (See Fig. 6.9)

FIGURE 6.9

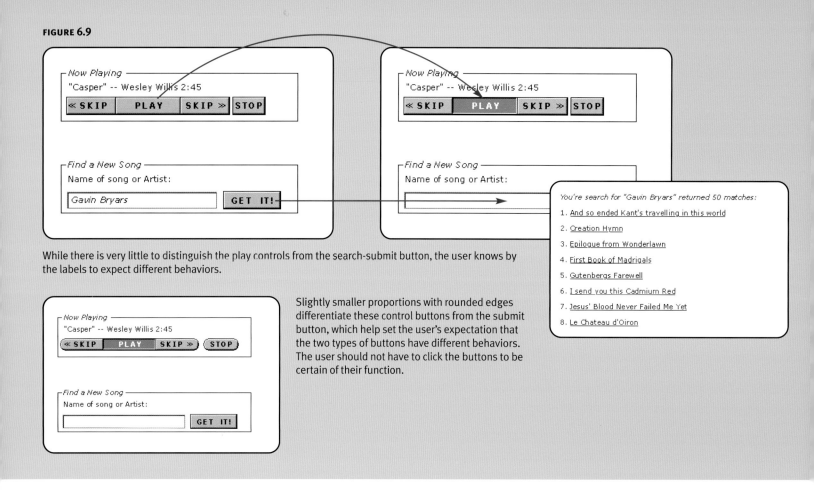

While there is very little to distinguish the play controls from the search-submit button, the user knows by the labels to expect different behaviors.

Slightly smaller proportions with rounded edges differentiate these control buttons from the submit button, which help set the user's expectation that the two types of buttons have different behaviors. The user should not have to click the buttons to be certain of their function.

Sliders and Knobs

Sliders are used to alter things by increments. They provide access to every level between minimum and maximum, as well as display the current level. A slider gives the user a visual key to an object's range of actions, and what part of that range is currently in use.

Since all mouse movement is a combination of vertical and horizontal coordinates, graduated devices like sliders work best if they are confined to one axis or the other. Moving a mouse in a circle is actually quite difficult, making knobs a less viable option for graduated control. (See Fig. 6.10)

A slider's ability to move in one-pixel increments gives it a fluid appearance that often corresponds to the gradual change in an output level. But what effect should motion have on the output level? If a slider controls the volume of a sound file with a maximum potential volume of 60 decibels (dB the standard unit of measurement for sound), how many dBs should one pixel equal? In the case of a slider with a 40-pixel sliding area, one pixel would equal 1.5 dB. However, the human ear can't perceive a change of volume less than 3 dB, so the slider would have to move 2 pixels to perceptibly increase the volume.

Since the jump in volume over 2 pixels is subtle, the user will not notice that the slider is essentially twice the necessary size.

FIGURE 6.10: CONTROL DESIGN CONSIDERATIONS

When you use a graduated control you must consider the increments of the control's movement (how much it moves) and the related increments of output (how much change takes place as a result).

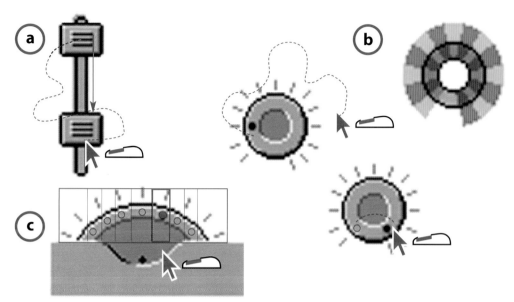

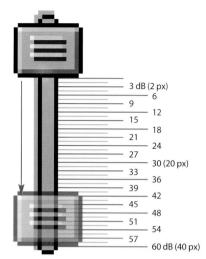

FIGURE 6.11

Fluid movement of the slider (increments of 1 pixel) is even smoother than the corresponding sound output. The slider must move 2 pixels before an increase of sound takes place.

a. Moving a slider in either direction is easy because only the vertical axis of the mouse's movement is registered. The vertical slider here ignores the mouse's horizontal zigzagging.

b. Circular devices are difficult to use. The knob works on a grid of hot spots that corresponds to a knob position. With a small device, the distance between a low position and a high position is too close. As the user tries to move the mouse in a circular motion, the knob must interpret the mouse movement. By inadvertently moving the mouse a few pixels to the left or right, the user can turn the knob from quiet to blaring.

c. An alternative to the fussy knob is a device that combines the action of a slider with the knob's circular appearance. Horizontal mouse movement changes the appearance of the knob to make it look as if it's rotating. This obviously works only when a portion of a circle is used.

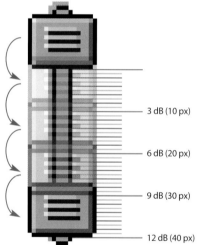

FIGURE 6.12

When a slider controls a quiet sound file with a maximum volume of only 12 dB, the fluid movement of the previous example might be a problem. The user placing the slider between the tenth and twentieth pixel won't perceive an increase in volume. A slider that jumps to each new volume level as its dragged may be more useful, because the jump tells the user that there is no volume level between those increments.

It would be possible to use a slider half the size, one pixel per 3 dB, but it would require great dexterity for the user to fine-tune the device. The 2-pixel/3 dB play in the slider action is comfortable, making it easier to finely adjust the volume. (See Fig. 6.11)

A slider can be programmed to move a distance that corresponds to the output increment. If a 40-pixel slider controls a sound output that has a maximum of 12 dB, the slider may be more useful if it slides in increments of 10 pixels. This would give the control a jumpy appearance, but it is helpful for the user to know there is no increase in output in the increments between 10, 20, 30, and 40 pixels. (See Fig. 6.12)

chapter 7

MENTAL MODELS AND INTERFACE ELEMENTS

When a user first sees an interface, he looks for clues about how it functions and how extensive it is. If all the elements are systematically designed and labeled, the user will create a subconscious mental model of the whole interface to help him grasp its functionality and behavior.

A mental model is both a map of the site and a key to its personality. The model influences the user's expectations, giving him a framework within which to work. We build mental models in both virtual and real-world situations.

We are practiced at building mental models. After all, we require a plan for dealing with every new place or situation. That plan is often shaped by assumptions that we form on first impression. Using a Web site is like navigating an unfamiliar public space: We size up what we can see and compare it to past experiences to determine how best to proceed.

Mental models are especially important in today's computing environment. The average user may use a dozen applications without ever leaving his seat. Many Web interfaces provide much less introduction to their function than do desktop applications.

The power and versatility of most virtual tools can be overwhelming to a first-time user. (Do you remember the first time you used a Web search engine and received twenty-two million matches to your query?) In such a dizzying environment, a user will find it comparatively easy to grasp a well-organized site that addresses a specific set of tasks. But in the initial encounter, functionality and protocol can be confusing unless the user can equate aspects of the interface with something familiar.

One way to transcend software's abstract aspects is to present interfaces metaphorically. Metaphors allow users to equate interface functionality with a familiar real-world state, presenting it in simple rather than technical terms. A tool that allows the user to "globally edit the relative values of any part of a bitmap by initiating a mouse-down state followed by a change in cursor x/y coordinates" is less meaningful to most people than if the same tool is presented as a paintbrush.

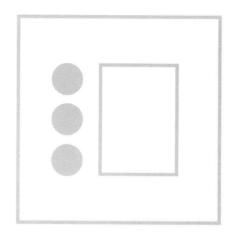

Metaphor Hierarchy

Naming an interface is the first and most effective way to help users build a mental model. A inexperienced user will still immediately grasp the purpose of applications named NotePad, CheckBook, and SketchPad, even if provided with no visual clues about their function.

Each successive level in an interface can validate, contradict, or have no effect on the user's mental model of the interface metaphor, depending on how cohesive the system is. If I open an application named SketchPad and see a blank screen, my mental model is still intact because the blank screen does not actually contradict the notion of sketch paper. However, if I open the CheckBook application and see a blank screen, my mental model, which was built on the idea of tabular accounting grids, is contradicted. I don't necessarily need to see a replica of a checkbook, but I do need interface elements that will obviously allow me to manage check entries and dollar amounts. (See Fig. 7.1)

FIGURE 7.1

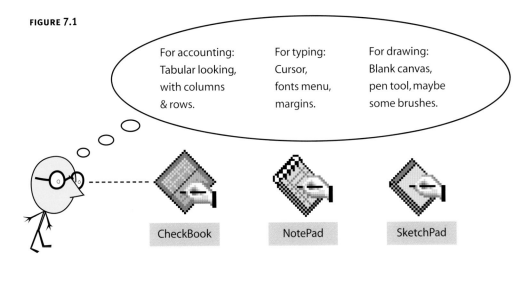

For accounting:
Tabular looking,
with columns
& rows.

For typing:
Cursor,
fonts menu,
margins.

For drawing:
Blank canvas,
pen tool, maybe
some brushes.

CheckBook

NotePad

SketchPad

None of these applications is literally a book or a pad, but each approximates the purpose of their real-world equivalents. A user instinctively assumes that the essential elements of a checkbook will be present in a virtual CheckBook. On the other hand, if the application lacks rule lines, rows, and columns, the user might think he accidentally opened the SketchPad.

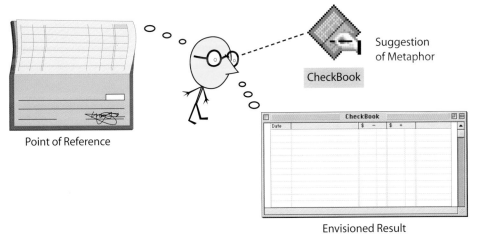

Suggestion
of Metaphor

CheckBook

Point of Reference

Envisioned Result

The checkbook metaphor exists predominantly in the application name, which evokes two mental images: the real-world reference and an imagined interface with the essential characteristics of a personal accounting tool. The application could have been named Virtual Personal Accounting Tool, but then users would not benefit from their mental connections.

Here lies the trick to using metaphors to facilitate usability and mental model building. You create an initial expectation by suggesting a metaphor. However, successful interaction does not require strict adherence to the established metaphor, as long as a tool's function is appropriate and does not contradict the metaphor. A user does not need a computerized spreadsheet to look and act exactly like physical checkbook, but he will be completely confused if it acts like a blender.

Although mental models are built on suggested metaphors, they are continually validated with illustrated metaphors—the interface elements themselves. In the desktop, icons are the interface elements that reinforce the general metaphor. Together, they illustrate a system of containers common to the office environment. The system works because all the elements, have a design consistency which reinforces their relationships to each other. (See Fig. 7.2)

FIGURE 7.2: THE DESKTOP METAPHOR

When the designers of the Macintosh interface described their screen layout as a "desktop," they created a metaphor that allowed users to make sense of the computing environment. "Desktop" was an apt term for a device that would replace much of the paper and bric-a-brac on the user's actual desktop.

The desktop is a successful metaphor because it does not strive to imitate life too closely. We do not literally keep our trash cans and recycling bins on top of our desks, but it doesn't disturb us when we see virtual trash cans atop our virtual desktops.

If computing metaphors functioned exactly like their real-life counterparts, it would be difficult to get anything done. Illustrating the screen exactly like a desktop and imposing the same rules as found in the real world would have put undue limitations on the metaphor. If the metaphor was as strict as this example, we would never have grasped that the computer has a range of behaviors and functions beyond those of desktops, folders, and trash cans.

The initial desktop metaphor is a merely device for framing the more important metaphors for the specific tools—trash can, folder, etc. Once the user learns the specific tool metaphors, the general metaphor is mostly forgotten.

The Macintosh user interface allows people to create documents and to manage the creation, storage, and deletion of those documents. The iconic interface elements are based on a metaphorical system of paper storage. The file is the smallest, most essential element for storing text and images. Files are stored in folders, which may in turn be stored in other folders, all of which may be placed in the trash and deleted.

The operating system would still function if other, equally familiar metaphors were introduced, but the system would cease to be elegant. Documents can be placed on a bulletin board, for instance, and deleted by fire, but mixing concepts makes the relationship between elements more complex and degrades the desktop concept.

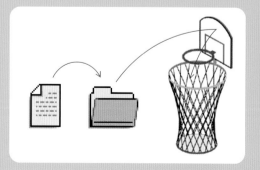

Element design should support the metaphorical system without interfering with the task at hand. Overly illustrative icons draw too much attention to themselves, making it harder for the user to forgive an interface's inability to duplicate reality.

Applying Metaphors to Web Interfaces

Suggesting mental models is especially important in Web design. A user is exposed to significantly more software online than on his computer, and the time available to spend learning each interface is short. To help the user understand a Web interface's functionality more quickly, you can reinforce the metaphor through display text placed beneath the metaphorical name when you introduce it. (See Fig. 7.3)

Web interfaces have a slightly different role in people's lives than do operating system interfaces. The average user interacts with a Web interface at most for a few minutes of a day—even then, the interaction is usually limited to a specific task.

HTML isn't the best interface-building tool, and Web applications have the disadvantage of being nested within the browser interface. Effective use of metaphor can be stymied by a Web designer's inability to create a complete environment, the way you can for desktop applications. As a result, general environmental metaphors are less frequently used on the Web than functional metaphors. Fortunately, users are capable of mentally retrofitting a conceptual environmental metaphor into their mental model. (See Fig. 7.4)

The Page Metaphor

All Web sites inherit the page metaphor, which is now part of our vernacular. The paper metaphor in Web design is so natural, especially where large bodies of text are used, that it is almost unnecessary to illustrate it. However, it is always important to allow users easy access to sequential pages by way of some simple navigational element at the beginning or end of a page. If the user assumes a paper metaphor, rendering interface elements within the paper metaphor can be very comfortable. (See Fig. 7.5)

Directional Signage

Real-world pages lack a common signifier for movement. To move people through a Web site, we often mix other metaphors into the existing Web page metaphor. One of the most prevalent metaphors borrows the appearance of directional devices from signage. By using directional signage associated with highways or airports for navigation, we suggest that users view the site as a dimensional space to move through.

Web designers are frequently tripped up by this metaphor, because the conventions of directional signage do not map directly into flat display. The same arrow is read quite differently in an airport than on a Web page. Figure 7.6 shows how the mixed metaphor of page (which starts in the top left and ends in the bottom right) requires a different interpretation of real-world directional signage.

If one-to-one mapping of metaphors from life to Web was the goal of interface design, anyone using airport signage as a navigation tool would discard the page metaphor in favor of a virtual space. The problems with creating virtual space metaphors are evident in the interface elements. Does navigation happen by "moving" toward the destination as in real life? Moving through a virtual space is difficult when the mouse is only capable of x and y (up and down) movement. If an arrow tells the user where to go, how can it also be the means of transport? Yet that is the dual nature of a clickable arrow. (See Fig. 7.7)

If your sole desire is to move people through an interface, keep your direction elements simple. Any device that implies movement, coupled with explicit text, will suffice.

FIGURE 7.3

This site is dedicated to helping people manage their daily affairs. Each section is named appropriately based on its function. I can tell the basic premise of each section from the metaphorical names (Your-Butler, YourAccountant, etc.). The subtitles give a description of each section's functionality, with more specificity than introductory metaphors can provide. When I read the subtext for Butler, I don't expect the interface to greet visitors at the door—an overly literal read of the metaphor.

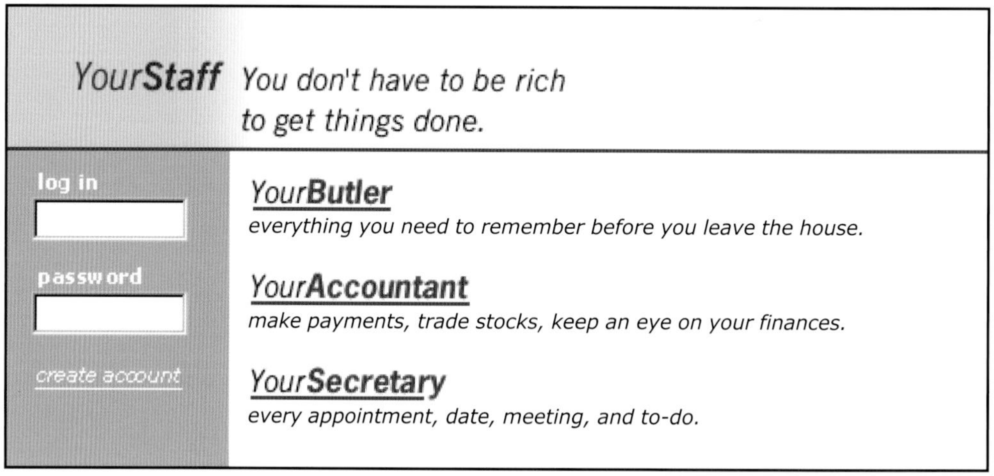

YourStaff You don't have to be rich to get things done.

log in

password

create account

YourButler
everything you need to remember before you leave the house.

YourAccountant
make payments, trade stocks, keep an eye on your finances.

YourSecretary
every appointment, date, meeting, and to-do.

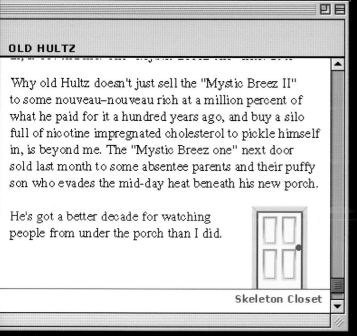

OLD HULTZ

Why old Hultz doesn't just sell the "Mystic Breez II" to some nouveau–nouveau rich at a million percent of what he paid for it a hundred years ago, and buy a silo full of nicotine impregnated cholesterol to pickle himself in, is beyond me. The "Mystic Breez one" next door sold last month to some absentee parents and their puffy son who evades the mid-day heat beneath his new porch.

He's got a better decade for watching people from under the porch than I did.

Skeleton Closet

FIGURE 7.4

Metaphors are most commonly used in Web design to define spaces. If I encounter a door at the end of a page of text, I can immediately assume that the site has an architectural metaphor. My expectations of how the rest of the site is structured will be based on room metaphors. Even though the page isn't called Joe's House, I immediately recognize that the door is a portal—in this case a device for navigating to the next place. I understand each virtual room will have content (text) that is relevant to the room's functions.

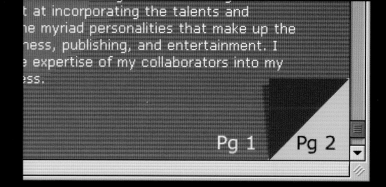

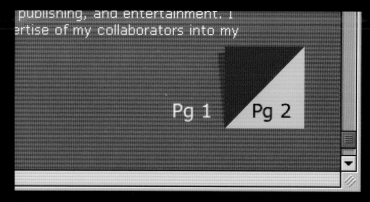

FIGURE 7.5

Once a user is deep into a long page of text, the page's similarity to printed material is undeniable. A turning page as a metaphor for forward navigation is more natural that an arrow; but its success is dependent upon the clear representation of the paper metaphor. A turned page-corner floating free of the page edge looks strange.

In physical space, up arrows mean forward, but down is represented with a diagonal arrow. The same arrows in a Web interface are also recognized as way-finding devices, but are read literally. If the system of real-space directional signage was applied too strictly as a metaphor, on-screen navigation would be very confusing.

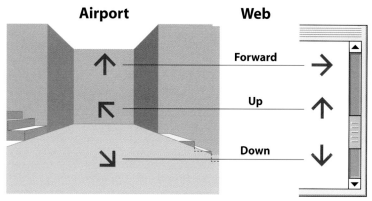

The mere suggestion of a page metaphor is enough to tell us how to interpret directional signage. Given the Western norm of reading from top to bottom, left to right, the right edge—especially the lower right edge—is a natural metaphor for the end of a Web page. An arrow pointing right, in the lower right part of a Web page, implies that clicking it will take you to the next sequential page.

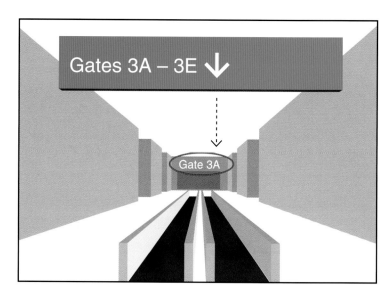

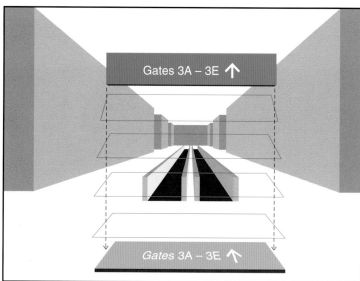

This airport directional sign is literally accurate, as the arrow points to the destination, but it is incorrect in mapping movement in real space. People seem to naturally interpret the sign as if it were lying on the floor.

FIGURE 7.7: DIRECTIONAL DEVICES

 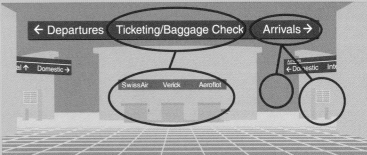

This interface takes the form of a real space, so the directional devices follow the protocol of airport signs. While the metaphor may make for an exciting computing environment, the means of movement aren't clear. The easiest way to navigate is to click on the directional signs or the destination. Either of these solutions negates the metaphor.

The other drawback to this overly specific metaphor is the poor use of space. Each destination requires two space allocations: one for the sign as label and signifier, the other for the mode of transport.

In an early attempt to separate the directional requirements of the *Wired News* interface from the editorial voice of its text, arrows were preferred to hyperlinks as a means of navigation. The format of Wired News was to post a series of breaking headlines, each accompanied by a paragraph of text. The paragraph, which was just an introduction to a longer story, was followed by a green arrow pointing off screen.

Most users were confused by the repetition of the arrow. A page that ends with an arrow as a link to the next page makes sense, but multiple arrows on one page seemed to imply that there should be something adjacent to the paragraph. Users quickly discovered the function of the arrows, but were continually bothered by them. It was discovered that linked headlines worked much better, which destroyed the notion that people navigate through hyperspace the way they read books or newspapers. (Imagine going back to the running title at the top of every page in a book in order to turn the page).

Klug Farm >>

Klug Farm

Directional signage does not have to be explicit. Forward emphasis can be clear with just the suggestion of movement. A roughly cut wooden sign is clear enough—so is the coupling of directional text with the thrust of an italic face.

Environmental Metaphors on the Web

Environmental metaphors give the user a concept of place and function. Call a site The Corner Butcher, and users will expect the interface to explain different cuts of meat. Most environmental metaphors are merely suggested in the name, while most of the metaphor actually happens on the functional level. The ongoing reinforcing of the metaphor through specific tools has the cumulative effect of creating a sense of place. For a user to leave The Corner Butcher site with a lasting impression, the tools and the interface should be presented and labeled in a way that draws upon the vernacular of the local meat market.

When interface elements are used as metaphors, they do double duty as points of interaction and as pillars for mental models. They should be handled delicately by the designer. A rigid system should be employed in the design of metaphorical elements. Consistent size and shape and logical relationships between elements give the impression of reliability. Variation in the size a shopping bag icon, for instance, would call into question the shopping bag's function. The bag might appear to be responding to something beyond the user's control.

From the programmer's perspective, an e-commerce site that sells shirts is no different from one that sells stock photography. The user sees categories (tube-tops or photos of elephants), looks at a thumbnail page (shirts of all colors or photos of clowns), and adds selected items to a list (add to shopping bag or add to light box). From the user's perspective, these T-shirts and photos are unrelated. You must choose the appropriate metaphor to help users trust that each site will meet their needs. (See Fig. 7.8)

FIGURE 7.8: MATCHING METAPHORS TO FUNCTION

The fulfillment of a transaction—acquiring photos or shirts—does not require a metaphor. Disparate items can coexist in an interface if no metaphor is present, although the interface will lack cohesion. The use of metaphorical tools makes the functionality more obvious, but also suggests specificity that does not exist in an interface where you can buy both shirts and photos.

Enlarge Item	Add Item to Purchase List

Enlarge Item	Add Item to Purchase List

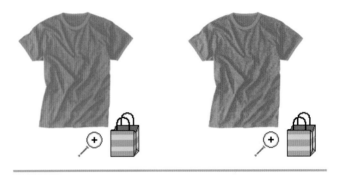

A shirt boutique and a photo archive can have identical structure and functionality.

The shopping bag metaphor is more appropriate to the shirt than the photo. In this case, the metaphor, while roughly functional, does nothing to enhance the user's understanding of the site.

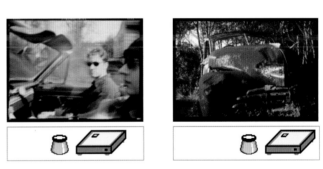

When content is limited to a coherent category and the metaphor is unique to that category, a larger metaphor is suggested (photo-editing studio, versus clothing boutique). When that happens, the entire interface holds together within the framework of the suggested metaphor.

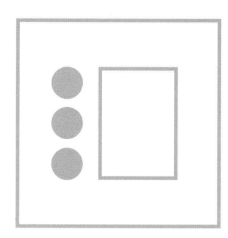

About Tabs

Tabs are both organizational devices and navigational elements. Borrowing their appearance from tabbed file folders, tab labels both communicate organization and provide access to content. When appropriately utilized, tabs are one of the best ways to help a user develop a mental map of content without relying on metaphor. Users instinctively understand how to interact with a tab interface. It borrows its form from a real-world convention that solves the same problem of providing access to hidden contents. The interactive model — selecting a tab to access a collection of related content — is metaphorical, but the metaphor only extends to the organizational superstructure, not necessarily the content.

Tabs on the Web

Tabs have become a Web interface convention. They may be the only widely used interface element that does not have its origins in HTML or the operating system. Any kind of button, menu, or window device will bear a resemblance to the HTML form elements (See Chapter 5), even if rendered with GIFs or colored table cells.

Tabs were introduced to Web design largely as an alternative to GIF buttons, and therein lies the problem with tabs on the Web. They look like an interactive page element that allows you to see hidden content, the way a Windows control panel does, but most Web tabs are nothing more than buttons. (See Fig. 7.9)

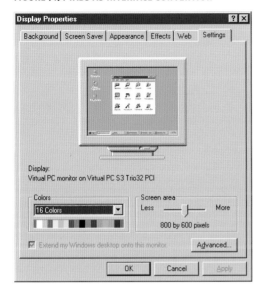

One of the original uses of tabs as an interface convention, and the most successful, is the Windows control panel, where extensive functionality is represented in a small interface.

To avoid dedicating too much real estate to the control panel, the interface designers used tabs as a metaphor for organizing information. In this control panel, they imply a stack of layers, each layer containing related options.

This metaphor is not only a way to help users build a mental model of the contents of the control panel, it is a convenient device for allowing the user access to hidden information.

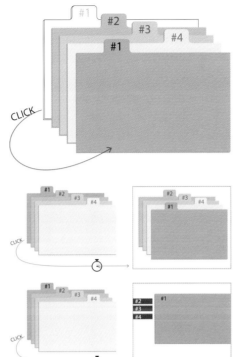

The interactive model of tabs is identical to a real-world stack of file folders. You use the tab to access contents contained within the tab category. The success of this interaction depends on a real-time reenactment of tabbed folders in the real world. Since interacting with tabs is a process of discovery, the content layers must appear to shuffle for the user to get the full benefit of the tab metaphor.

Most Web tab interfaces fall short of this illusion because each tab is either a link to the same interface with a new configuration or a link to a new page.

Even if real-time shuffling is not an option, the tab model can still be a helpful way of organizing information. It provides access to content that will not fit on the screen and communicates the depth and breadth of content to the user.

Task-Based Categorization

The staggered tabs of real file folders identify the contents of a closed folder and make it possible to access every folder when they are stacked. Most people don't care if each folder's contents relate to others in a stack, as long as each is properly labeled. They can contain tax forms, vacation snap-shots and the crust of a long forgotten peanut butter and yam sandwich. There would be no trouble finding any of these items as long as they are properly labeled: taxes, photos, leavings.

Virtual tabs are a little different. They work best when each tab label represents some facet of particular task. An e-commerce site may have multiple categories, all relating to the single task of purchasing. Representing each category on a separate layer (with tabs providing access) is a good way to present numerous items in a manageable interface. The tabs tell the user how the site is categorized, while providing a clear path to specific items. Any task or section of the site that is not a purchase category does not belong in the tab stack. (See Fig. 7.10)

A good way to approach tabs in Web design is to think of them as lenses that filter out irrelevant content. Assuming you've done a good job of organizing content and links into useful groups and clusters, you can gauge when to use a device like tabs by looking at all the groupings together on one page. If it is difficult to find a particular item, ask yourself, "What kind of lens would help in locating the item, and how would it be labeled?"

While none of these four tabs is strictly related to each other, three of the tabs—Books, Music, Electronics—are purchase categories. Even at a glance, Preferences does not belong in a group with Books, Music, and Electronics. Preferences affect all purchases and, thus, arch over every category, so they should be represented in another way. Separate the tasks of defining preferences and profiles (which will affect every purchase) from the actual item categories.

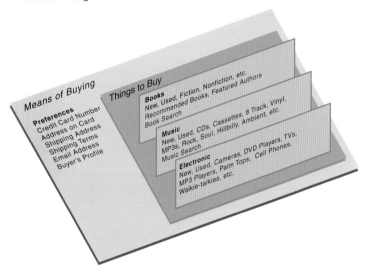

This logical model shows Books, Music, and Electronics (things to purchase) as parallel planes, and Preferences, which affects every purchase, as a plane that touches the others.

Holding a set of magic content lenses up to the page helps illustrate what parts of the interface should be placed behind tabs, and what part should be independent of the tabs. Good lenses exclude everything that is irrelevant to the item you want. Here, a dog lens filters out bird and cat items.

Any links to sections that are relative to all categories should not be filtered out and, therefore, would be accessible with each tab. Links that are not part of any content category should be displayed separate from the tab set because they represent an entirely separate mode of user interaction.

Good Tabs, Bad Tabs

Even if you've done an excellent job of organizing and filtering, sometimes tabs are the wrong metaphor for your information. Tab metaphors fail when the content of each tab serves a radically different purpose from the contents of another tab, or when there is too little screen real estate to maintain the illusion of file folders and how they operate in the real world.

Windows is famous for using the tab metaphor, but sometimes it goes awry. The tools contained within this control panel fit well into a tab scheme based on their content. However, there is simply too little space to make effective use of the tabs.

To attempt to work around this problem, the designers try to keep groups together by moving them around. If a tab in the back row is clicked, it moves to the front row. In fact, all the tabs of that row move to the front. This is disorienting. A user remembers seeing a tab in the back row, and can't find it quickly once it moves.

In contrast, Adobe makes excellent use of tabs within the Photoshop tool palettes. Adobe gathers groups of tools with related functions into panels. When several panels have a similar related applications, they are combined into a multilayered panel with tabs.

For example, the model and appearance of the Layer, Channel, and Path tools are similar, and each tool is used independently of the others. They all address a similar group of tasks: navigating the multiple levels of a Photoshop file. Since none of the three tools is used in conjunction with the other, toggling between them is a convenient way of saving screen real estate and keeping like functionality in one place where it is easily accessible.

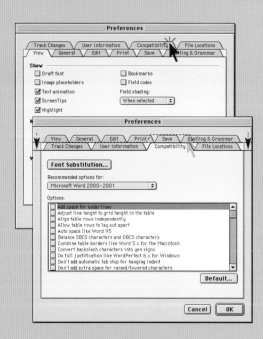

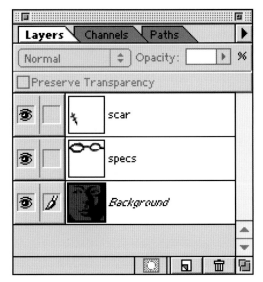

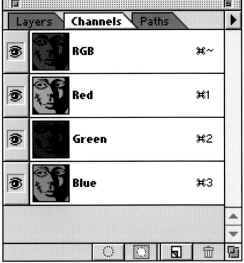

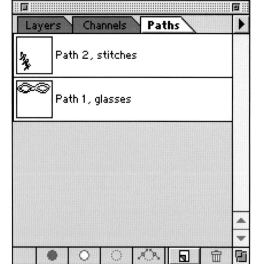

chapter 8

CUSTOM INTERFACE ELEMENTS

There are three tiers of interface elements in the Web designer's toolkit. The first tier consists of hypertext links, along with the relationships among links, didactic text, and structured information displays. The middle tier consists of form elements, such as buttons, pull-down menus, and so on—familiar devices from the earliest generation of HTML browsers. Form elements are always the most effective tools for extending computer functionality to the user.

Custom interface elements are the third and newest tier of interactive tools. While they build upon the success of HTML form elements (and their more powerful counterparts in operating system interfaces) by capitalizing on traditional interactive models, they allow the Web designer to craft a unique experience and appearance that is specific to the interface or product. Custom elements can also be exciting to the user, because they break free of the institutional look-and-feel of standard operating system widgets.

Most custom interface elements are built either on a Flash platform or in Dynamic HTML (DHTML), a marriage of JavaScript, CSS and new HTML objects such as Layers (DIVs, SPANs, etc.). Think of Web sites as theatrical productions: the Browser is the stage; DIVs are the actors or props. They take stage direction from CSS (where to stand, what color to wear, what size to be, etc.). JavaScript is behind the scenes, specifying parameter changes in color or position to CSS in response to events such as mouse clicks, which CSS then conveys to the DIV. (See Fig. 8.1)

DIVs, paragraphs, and hypertext links are all raw material for Dynamic HTML.

Alone, each HTML object's static appearance can be specified either with a traditional HTML tag or through CSS, in which an event such as a mouse click can be used to trigger a JavaScript that tells CSS to change some of the parameters of the HTML object—in this case, the position and color of a DIV.

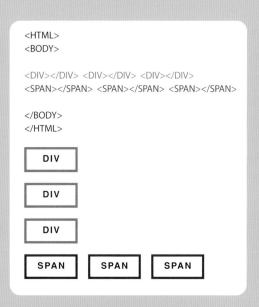

There is little difference between a DIV and a SPAN. Think of them as boxes that can contain HTML images, text, tables, and links—or even nothing at all. Since you can give a DIV box graphic properties using CSS (such as position), its contents can be positioned in the browser window as a group.

The only significant difference between a DIV and a SPAN is that successive DIVs without *x/y* coordinates will act as paragraphs: one will follow the other vertically in the browser window. Successive SPANs can line up horizontally, like text.

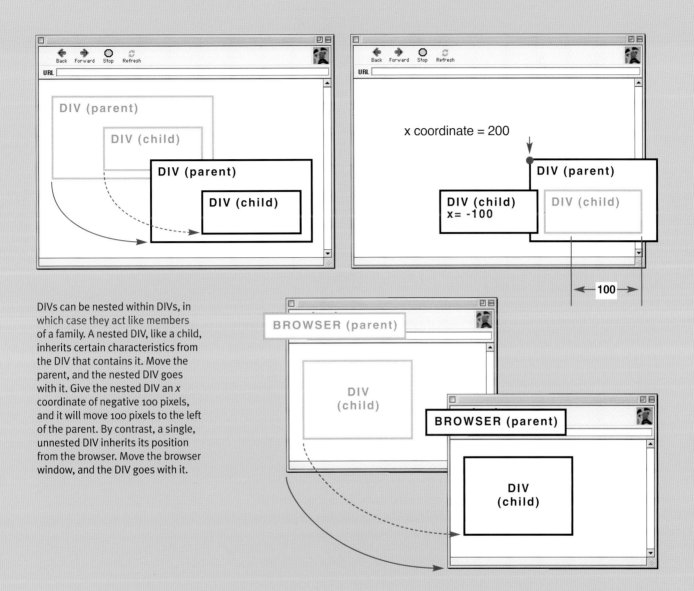

DIVs can be nested within DIVs, in which case they act like members of a family. A nested DIV, like a child, inherits certain characteristics from the DIV that contains it. Move the parent, and the nested DIV goes with it. Give the nested DIV an *x* coordinate of negative 100 pixels, and it will move 100 pixels to the left of the parent. By contrast, a single, unnested DIV inherits its position from the browser. Move the browser window, and the DIV goes with it.

Building Custom DHTML Elements

Since DHTML is built from a fluid set of variables (scripts, parameters, events, etc.), and those parameters can be used in endless combinations, custom interface elements may be designed with few limits apart from the requirements of good usability and established functional models.

Custom interface elements can range from variations on traditional operating system tools to interactive gremlins that border on animated toys. There is a price for this flexibility.

For one thing, it takes more code to create elements using DHTML, and it's often more time consuming than designing with traditional HTML. For another, if you're concerned about browser compatibility, it's twice as hard to develop a parallel low-end interface for a DHTML site. Today, most browsers are DHTML compatible (that is, they can handle CSS and Java-Script), but the finer points of virtual tools—the details that make the difference between good usability and awkward implementation—can be undermined by subtle variations in browsers' interpretations of CSS and JavaScript. If you design a mouse over effect for a button to load a new, highlighted version on top of the static one, the results may look spastic if the browser interprets the CSS positioning code differently than you intended. (See Fig. 8.2) As always, before you decide what tools to use, know your audience and investigate their software situation.

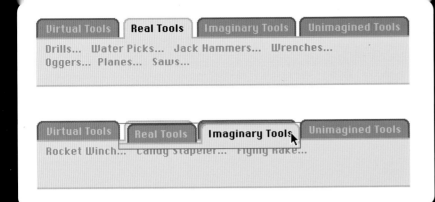

FIGURE 8.2

Even the most straightforward DHTML effects can be negated by slight discrepancies in the ways browsers interpret CSS scripts. This DIV tab is replaced by a highlighted version when clicked. Any slight variation in the positioning will destroy the illusion of flipping tab layers.

Mouseover Effects

In essence, most mouseover effects fall into two categories: those that reveal more information about the object and those that change the nature or appearance of the object.

In 1996, the developers of Webmonkey treated the interface design as an opportunity to use Java to enhance interactivity in what had always been a static environment. At the time, most of the Web audience was using monitors with screen sizes of 800 x 600 pixels or less. In that small space, Webmonkey's interface had to display content from a handful of Web personalities, a week's worth of teaser text, five head shots, and entry points to the seven areas of the site. (See Fig. 8.3)

Over the years, as sites have gotten bigger, browsers' display areas have not. The need

to provide users with scores of hints and options has necessitated more complex interface solutions. Web designers have relied increasingly on DHTML mouseovers to reveal the layers of content behind the headings. This model of interaction— mousing around to collect information before committing to a click—has become the most common interface trick on the Web. It works because it builds upon users' browsing habits. People are accustomed to mousing over the browser's info bar, which displays the URL of a hyperlink, to find out whether the link is within the current site or part of a new domain. Users didn't have much of a learning curve to go through before they understood that they could look before they leapt. For designers, however, perfecting ways to display anything more than tool-tip style information on mouseovers involved a huge learning curve.

Pop-Down Layers

Not to be confused with pop-up windows, pop-down layers borrow their form from menu elements. A word or image can be programmed with an adjacent DIV layer that carries related links or information. The layer can be toggled on (made visible) or off (hidden) with a mouseover or mouse click on the static word or image. You can specify this with CSS—visibility: hidden/visible.

At first glance, the interaction model for pop-down layers is simple: when the cursor moves over a link, the interface displays a rectangle with information in it. Removing the rectangle is a little trickier. With tool-tips, when you mouse off the link, the layer disappears. But if you are trying to click on a link within the revealed layer, you don't want it to disappear when you move the cursor. The designer must allow for an

FIGURE 8.3: REVEALING INFORMATION WITH MOUSEOVERS

 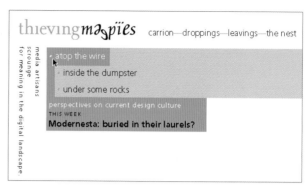

 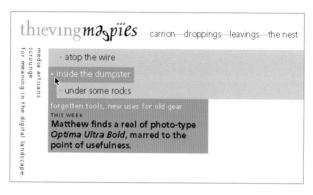

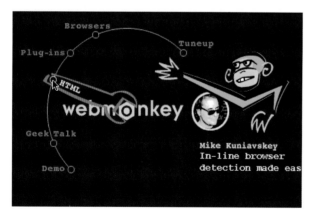 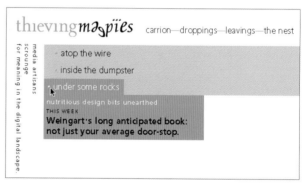

Each section head of the original Webmonkey interface was used not only to link to deeper content but to trigger a Java applet that "rotated" the wrench and displayed the section's author and contents. This design used both types of mouseover effects: revealing new information and altering the appearance of the interface.

Most mouseover interactions reveal more information about a subject to help the users make informed decisions about where to go next. The effect is usually constrained to a portion of the interface, rather than the entire interface—otherwise, the entire window would become one big navigation tool.

interaction where mousing on the rectangle keeps it open, which usually requires the link and the rectangle to overlap a little. Every possible choice thereafter has to be considered. How will users close the rectangle? What happens if the rectangle goes off screen? Will it go away if the user moves his mouse to the browser scroll bars? With every scenario comes several more lines of code, as well as more constraints around initiating and escaping the dynamic layer or HTML object in question. (See Fig. 8.4)

The link and the revealed rectangle must be close to each other so that the revealed information connects visually to the original link. (In fact, they should overlap.) The two elements together should be easy to read as a group when the revealed information is open.

But how should you handle links that are close to the edge of a page or browser window? If the link is near the bottom, the revealed rectangle will be partly below the fold. To see it, the user will go for the scroll bar, mouse off the revealed rectangle, and lose it. With a little bit of extra code the rectangle can position itself in the visible part of the browser window, provided it's no larger than the content area of the window.

If the link is close to one side of the window, the rectangle should be positioned on the opposite side, so it won't run off the page and obscure the link. Barring any lengthy positioning code, the rectangle could remain open until a close button is pressed. (See Fig. 8.5)

It quickly becomes apparent to the DHTML designer that even basic interactive elements have to be given complex sets of responses in order to accommodate variables in the browsing environment. It's little wonder that these elements are generally used in places where users have come to expect navigational devices, either at the top of the page or near navigation elements in a left-hand column.

Custom Windows

The designer bent on using complex interactive elements is often tempted to deal with variations in platforms and behavior by making it impossible for users to alter the browsing environment. Typically, they design sites to spawn pop-up windows without scroll bars or resize grippers, in order to control the appearance of the interface. Custom windows can resolve this conflict. They do focus users' attention, but do not take away their ability to use the browser's navigational tools. As long as the interface in the custom window does not link to outside URLs—as long as you keep all outside links in the larger parent window with its scroll bars, buttons, and grippers— users don't lose usability. They will lose some screen real estate, and every new window will tax the computer's memory slightly, but these losses are less significant with each new generation of hardware.

Regardless of refinements, the user rarely sees any benefit in pop-up windows. Rather than getting a well-composed rectangle with a self-contained interface, he gets a browser on a spree, launching rogue windows at will. Most people think of their browser as a window on the Web, and prefer to focus their attention on a single view. If a user does open multiple windows, it is usually because he or she wants to juggle a couple of sites at one time. From the user's point of view, pop-up windows take control away from him and force his attention on something he may not want.

There is one use for pop-up windows that adds convenience to an interface. A user could be led to a button that launches a new window that functions as a control strip, for instance. As long as he gets full control over launching the window, the user's control is augmented. In this case, the browsing environment hasn't been pinched into a tiny window: instead, the navigational tools have been consolidated in a single palette. (See Fig. 8.6)

FIGURE 8.4: POP-DOWN LAYER BEHAVIOR

The two most essential stages of any DHTML inter-action with hidden layers are the opening and closing events. A mouse interaction with a hot spot can take the form of a mouseover, a sustained click (with the mouse button held down), or a completed mouse click.

Once a layer is open, it must behave in such a way that the user can interact with its content. Leaving the layer open regardless of what the mouse happens to do will give the user ample opportunity to move around without losing the layer.

The layer can be programmed to close when the cursor is moved away from the layer, or when the mouse is clicked again. "Click to close" can be defined as any click, or can be limited to clicks that occur outside of the layer area.

OPEN
Mouseover on link displays layer. Mouseover on visible layer sustains layer visibility.

Hypertext is nice, but DHTML effects are cool.

CLOSE
Mouse out of visible layer resets visibility to "hidden."

OPEN
Click and hold initiates layer, which stays open as long as the mouse button is held down.

Hypertext is nice, but DHTML effects are cool.

CLOSE
Releasing the mouse button resets layer visibility to "hidden."

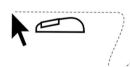

OPEN
Mouse click on link opens layer, which stays open regardless of where the mouse is.

Hypertext is nice, but DHTML effects are cool.

CLOSE
Mouse click anywhere resets layer visibility to "hidden."

Hypertext is stable, while DHTML effects are fussy

- Requires additional behaviors
- Appears to be broken
- Difficult to control

FIGURE 8.4: POP-DOWN LAYER BEHAVIOR *CONTINUED*

Users have varying levels of dexterity. If mouseover/mouse out events are used to control pop-down layers, the area that sustains the layer visibility should be defined with a high degree of tolerance.

Hypertext is stable, while DHTML effects are fussy

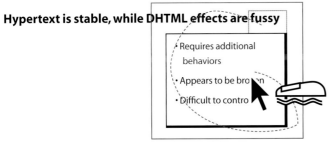

- Requires additional behaviors
- Appears to be broken
- Difficult to control

On the way from the link to the layer, a user can trip over the close without realizing it.

Hypertext is stable, while DHTML effects are fussy

- Requires additional behaviors
- Appears to be broken
- Difficult to control

Along with the visible pop-down layer, a transparent layer, or transparent GIF, can be used to extend the active area, allowing the user to mouse around without inadvertently closing the layer.

FIGURE 8.5

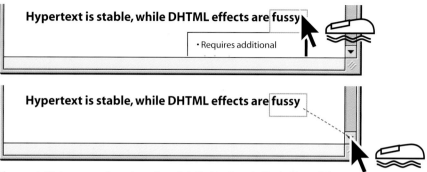

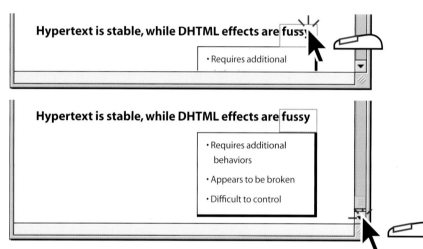

If a user initiates a pop-down layer for a link that is close to the bottom of the browser window, it can be difficult to interact with—mousing off the layer to use the scroll bar would hide it.

It's better to use a click-to-open/click-to-close interaction that leaves the layer open while the user scrolls through the browser window.

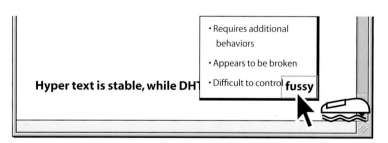

The visual relationship of the link and the layer is a persistent problem, especially when one element obscures the other. Sometimes, instead of positioning a pop-down layer relative to the link, you'll want to position it relative to the edge of the browser window using JavaScript, so that the layer will remain visible regardless of where the link appears on the screen.

FIGURE 8.6

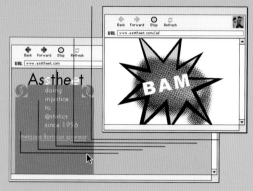

Launching a new window over the one the user was paying close attention to is like punching him in the face.

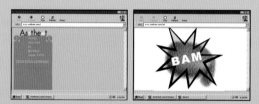

Users of PCs, especially those with smaller monitors, tend to fill the screen with the browser. When a new window is launched automatically, it covers the previous window entirely. Often the user thinks he is still looking at the original window and may try to use the Back button—to no avail.

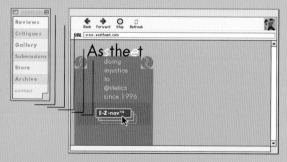

A small pop-up window without buttons, scroll bars and resize grippers, can serve as an interface element of sorts. This one is intended to provide the navigation for this site. Sweeping the navigation to the side helps the user focus on content.

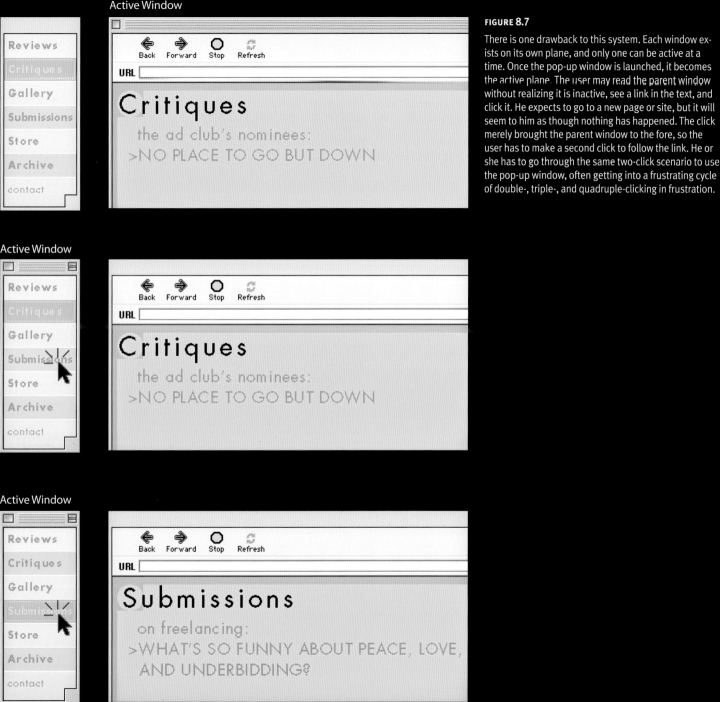

Active Window

FIGURE 8.7

There is one drawback to this system. Each window exists on its own plane, and only one can be active at a time. Once the pop-up window is launched, it becomes the active plane. The user may read the parent window without realizing it is inactive, see a link in the text, and click it. He expects to go to a new page or site, but it will seem to him as though nothing has happened. The click merely brought the parent window to the fore, so the user has to make a second click to follow the link. He or she has to go through the same two-click scenario to use the pop-up window, often getting into a frustrating cycle of double-, triple-, and quadruple-clicking in frustration.

Active Window

Active Window

Flash

New inventions in interface design are becoming commonplace thanks to Flash. Macromedia has created a powerful tool by making interactive tricks that are extremely difficult to achieve in DHTML into stock items—and presenting them in a user-friendly, WYSIWYG (what-you-see-is-what-you-get) interface. Flash also makes complex interfaces more practical because its graphics are built from outlines (splines), rather than the memory-hungry bitmaps of GIFs and JPGs.

Flash design is not actually Web design, any more than, say, Adobe Illustrator art is print design. In fact, Flash files aren't even based on HTML. Just as the Acrobat browser plug-in allows designers to display their print work as PDF files on the Web, the Flash plug-in lets people see Flash files in a browser. In essence, a Flash interface is a browser in the browser. The standard browser buttons, and the relationships that exist between domains by way of hyperlinks, are essentially unaffected by Flash. (See Fig. 8.8)

The most significant feature of Flash is that it lets you define objects with basic behaviors, instead of making you write out all the code. In most cases, it constructs mouseover events as families of frames that give the object an appearance for static, active, and used states, as well as for a state between static and active—the mouseover state. (Macromedia calls these states Up, Over, Down, Hit.) This little feature lets designers handle the majority of interaction needs with little effort. (See Fig. 8.9)

FIGURE 8.8

What with links between pages and the ability to jump from one HTML site to the next, the user experiences a boundless world of Web pages through the browser window.

A Flash applet is actually a self-contained world within the browser. Flash lets you design navigable spaces, but once users are in them, the browser's buttons and tools are ineffectual.

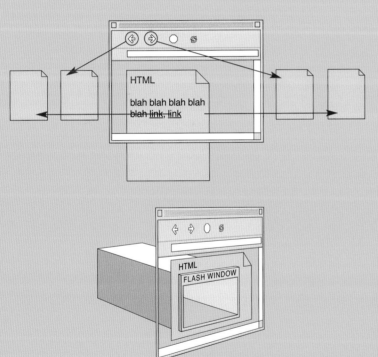

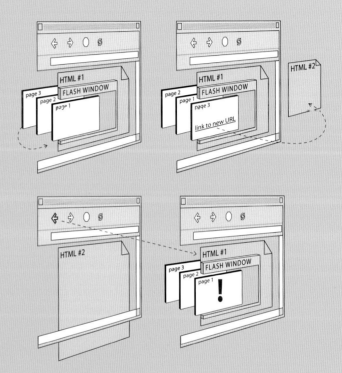

Although Flash is capable of referencing URLs, scripts, and email addresses that reside in other Web spaces, navigation between Flash and external destinations can be disorienting. If a user flips through pages within a Flash applet, decides to follow a link from the applet to a different URL, and then clicks the browser's Back button, he might expect to return to the last page he saw in the Flash site. Instead, he'll be sent back to the page that originally offered the Flash site, the applet will reload, and he'll wind up back at the very beginning.

CUSTOM INTERFACE ELEMENTS

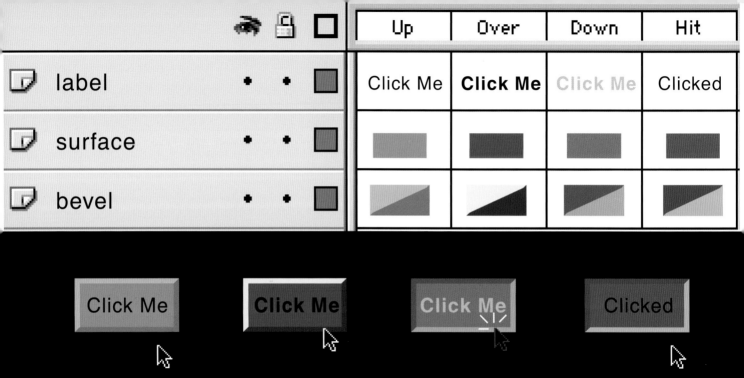

					Up	Over	Down	Hit
label	•	•	■	Click Me	**Click Me**	Click Me	Clicked
surface	•	•	■				
bevel	•	•	■				

FIGURE 8.9

Creating mouseover interactions in HTML with JavaScript requires some programming knowledge. Flash takes the difficulty out of creating object behaviors by presenting the changing states of an interactive element as a layered, or frame-based, metaphor.

The key to Flash's power among nonprogrammers is the extra dimension of glitz it enables them to create through animation—every object's interaction layer can be animated. This takes the user experience beyond simple static and highlighted appearances, and into the theatrical realm. Subsequent animations within an object can have any appearance the designer wants. An element can become one kinetic object when moused over, and yet another when clicked. (See Fig. 8.10)

The variety of possibilities that Flash's simple mouseover construction model offers is partly responsible for its success in novice interface design circles. Since the consequences of mouseovers are not as great as the consequences of clicks—mouseovers are noncommittal by nature—designers can stretch the definition of acceptable interactions. As these kinds of interactions become more common, a new paradigm of interaction will open up.

FIGURE 8.10

Flash's active feedback system can be used to create bizarre events. Here, what appears to be an ordinary button is revealed upon mouseover to be a trap. When clicked, the unsuspecting user (or at least their cursor) is devoured.

chapter 9

EXPERIMENTAL INTERFACE ELEMENTS

Most computer interfaces take advantage of a few tried-and-true interaction conventions: windows, icons, menus, and pointers (otherwise known as WIMPs). In this virtual world, where dialog between human and computer takes place within windows and menus, and icons are used as shortcuts, placeholders, and buttons, the mouse-driven pointer, or cursor, is a manifestation of the user. The speed and efficiency of interaction is tied to the power (or lack thereof) of the cursor. It comes as little surprise that most of the interactive tricks of new experimental interfaces focus on this tool.

Until recently, the pointer/cursor was treated as a sacred. Users were allowed to poke around with their mouse as their eyes darted around the interface; the interface would remain static until the user was ready to commit to an interaction; and the interface would only react to the cursor when it was clicked.

The grandfather of the new, experimental models is the mouseover effect. Perhaps as a sign of evolution among users—and certainly as a sign of evolution among interaction designers—Web and CD-ROMs have given more power to the cursor. Just as the single-click has replaced the double-click as the standard committal action, the mouseover is replacing the single click as a way to grab interface elements. (See Fig. 9.1)

Nearly every experimental interaction model online seeks to squeeze more use out of limited space. Pop-down layers and the like (discussed in Chapter 8), are just the tip of this iceberg. Other devices include hot spots that reveal additional layers of related information, as menus and tool tips do. The same architecture can be packaged in a radically different appearance, and while essentially the same as pop-down layers, it can have a profound effect on an interface.

event	traditional mouse behaviors (operating system and applications) result		new, online, traditional mouse behaviors (DHTML and FLASH) result
mouseover	nothing		reveals options, hidden layer, etc.
mouseover, hold	sometimes tool tips	REVEALING	
mouse down	gripping, used to click and drag	MANIPULATING	gripping, used to click and drag movable layers and Flash objects
mouse down, hold (stationary mouse)	sometimes reveals option. On Macintosh, this is similar to a right click in Windows. Opens menus.		
click	executes buttons and control elements (scroll arrows, close-window boxes etc.), opens menus,	EXECUTING	executes buttons and control elements (scroll arrows, close-window boxes etc.), opens menus, executes icons to open windows, launch applets etc.
double click	executes icons to open windows, launch applications, etc. In applications, options tool setting and options.		essentially unused—curiously

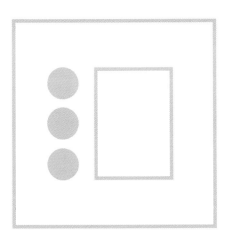

Cursor Appearance

Most people take the role of the cursor for granted. We are so accustomed to its behavior, switching from arrow to finger as it mouses over a link, that we don't consider the significance of its iconography. In a world where interaction is limited to looking and going, there is no need for a larger interactive lexicon.

Referencing stock cursors is easy with both HTML and Flash. HTML gives designers a set of predefined cursor options, or stock icons. Each browser has its own art for some of the cursor options, while others are borrowed from the operating system (like the wristwatch in Mac, and the hourglass in Windows). Flash, which runs in the browser, also has access to the browser's set of cursor icons. They may not match the interface look and feel, but since it's likely that only a couple of cursor appearances will be needed for any given element, the stock icons should suffice. (See Fig. 9.2)

As interfaces become more powerful, interface elements can serve several functions and be manipulated in several ways. The key to clarifying what the element can do is to change the appearance of the cursor.

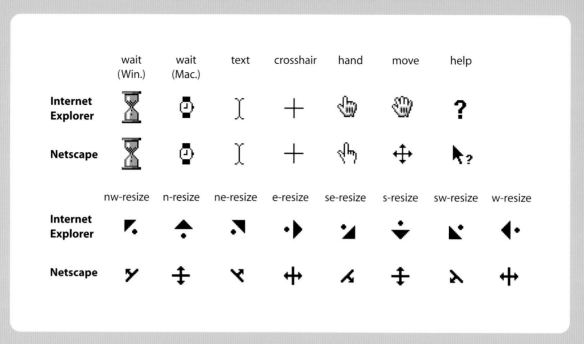

	wait (Win.)	wait (Mac.)	text	crosshair	hand	move	help
Internet Explorer							
Netscape							

	nw-resize	n-resize	ne-resize	e-resize	se-resize	s-resize	sw-resize	w-resize
Internet Explorer								
Netscape								

FIGURE 9.2: STOCK CURSORS, AS DEFINED BY BROWSERS AND OPERATING SYSTEMS

Consider the simple interaction of moving an element within an interface. Since that element is both clickable and movable, there must be a way to tell the user whether she is about to move it or execute its function. Showing the cursor as a pointer hand alone would not be sufficient—you need another means. (See Fig. 9.3)

Without custom cursors, the best way to affect a multipurpose object is to associate it with other interface elements. If you want to remove one object from a group of similar objects, for instance, you might have to select a checkbox next to it, and then click a "move" button. It is quicker and easier to directly affect the object by clicking on it, but to convey the object's movability, the cursor must change. With this model of direct interaction, the cursor becomes a primary interface element, as versatile and functional as a Swiss Army knife. (See Fig. 9.4)

When an interface does demand special cursor designs, many people are surprised at how limited the options are. One problem is that cursor art is significantly smaller than even the smallest icon. Another is that cursors must be rendered in 1-bit mode— black or white—so no color or antialiasing is possible. Cursors need to be robust little graphics that are clearly distinguishable on any background. They usually have a one-pixel wide white edge to act as a buffer

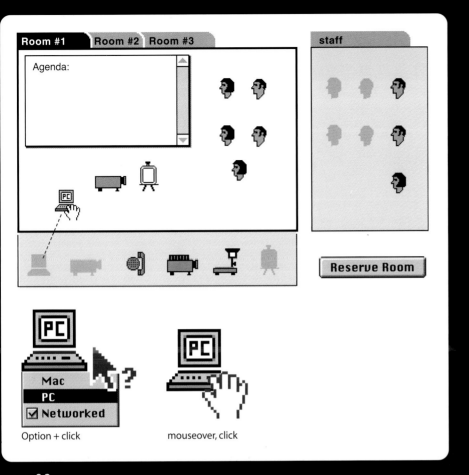

FIGURE 9.3

This interface is malleable, in that the user can drag each icon into the conference room. Each icon has two facets, accessible by clicking: the movability, which results from a simple click and drag; and the icon's options, which pop-down when clicked with the Option key pressed. The cursor appearance reinforces each behavior.

between the cursor and the background. Although it may seem small, the active part of a cursor is smaller yet. Only a single pixel actually interacts when it comes in contact with a button.

Despite—or perhaps because of—the limited pixel depth, cursor design is an art form. (See Fig. 9.5) Capturing the spirit of a specific behavior in such a tiny area is difficult, but when done successfully, it seems to extend the reach of the user and bring new vibrancy to the stunted, one-mouse, one-button interaction model common to all interfaces.

Really deviating from standard cursors requires some trickery in HTML. Custom cursors are relatively easy to create in Flash, where any graphic can be used as a cursor. You use a simple script that hides the standard cursor and renders the desired graphic in its place. As with all Flash graphics, the new cursor can have different appearances depending on the mouse event (hover, click, etc.). Since large graphics can be used to replace the standard cursor, usability can suffer if the graphic does not have a clear active point that corresponds to the mouse event.

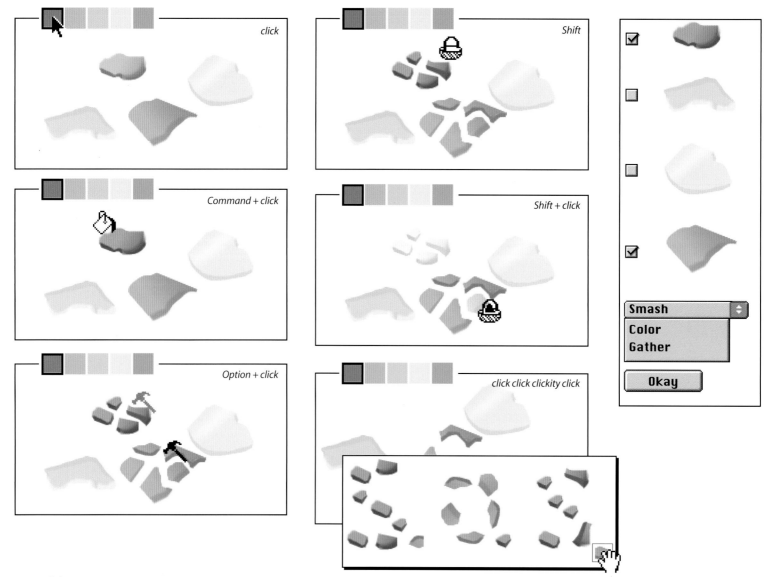

FIGURE 9.4

In this interface, several possible actions are associated with mouse clicks: choosing a color, applying a color, smashing an object, collecting objects, placing an object, and positioning an object. Each action is selected by pressing a modifier key (Command, Option, Control, Shift), and is indicated by unique cursor icons. By tying actions to keyboard combinations, and displaying special cursor designs for each one, you can cut several steps from a process that would normally involve buttons, menus, and checkboxes.

FIGURE 9.5: ANATOMY OF A CURSOR

Whether it's a pointer or a hand, stock cursors have a few standard components.

16 X 16 pixels

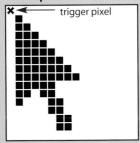 trigger pixel

 pointer

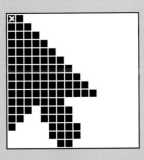  mask

A custom cursor can be made from a GIF, coded to follow the real cursor around—dude.

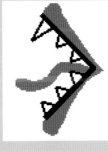

Every cursor is a 16 X 16 bit square. The black part of the cursor (in this case called the pointer) would be invisible on dark backgrounds if not for the mask.

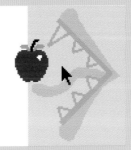

Large-sized cursor images are difficult to use. The objective here is to have the cursor bite the apple on click, but it won't happen unless the true cursor (which is only 16 px X 16 px) contacts the apple. Here, the image seems to overlap the apple. With a little effort, you can use the same tactic with DHTML and JavaScript. A GIF follows the mouse around, giving the illusion of a custom cursor.

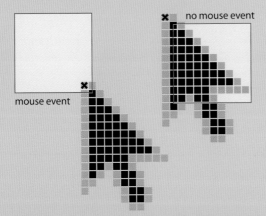

mouse event

no mouse event

There is a designated pixel that represents the trigger: mouse events only happen when the trigger overlaps the interface element.

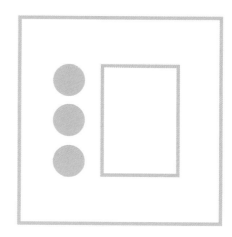

Mouse Motion

Often, the only thing that differentiates experimental interactive elements from traditional ones are animated effects that create an appearance of fluidity. In traditional interactive design, the menu responds immediately to a mouse event: mouseover the menu label, and the menu appears. Prior to that event, the element has a default static appearance; after the event, it has a new, active appearance. But when a single mouse event results in complex behaviors, the user can get disoriented. Showing the transition from one state to the next by animating the steps in between can illustrate exactly what is going on, and keep the user on track. (See Fig. 9.6)

FIGURE 9.6

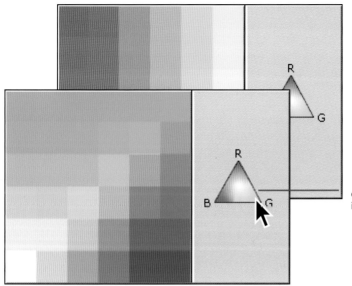

This control panel, used for choosing colors, is a fairly advanced Web interface. A palette of color swatches within a hue is swapped with swatches of other hues as the user mousesover a key.

on click, use new image for color grid

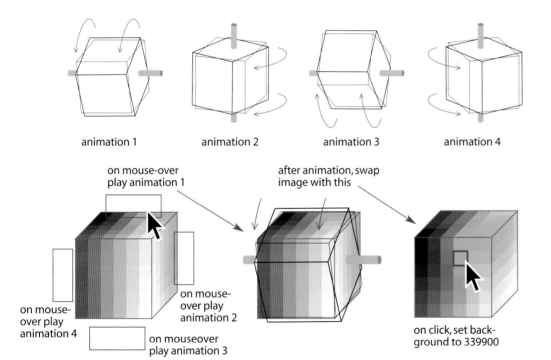

animation 1   animation 2   animation 3   animation 4

on mouse-over play animation 1

after animation, swap image with this

on mouse-over play animation 2

on mouse-over play animation 4

on mouseover play animation 3

on click, set back-ground to 339900

This 3-D color model's rotating cube allows for a more direct, and seemingly advanced, interaction.

To manipulate the cube, the user mouses over trigger points around its edges, each of which displays a different side of the cube. If the image swap happens abruptly, the cube won't appear to rotate, the illusion of solidity will be destroyed, and the user will be disoriented.

It's neither practical nor necessary to render each degree of rotation. A few animations that show the outline rotating would be enough to help the user keep track of the transition. Though providing a transitional animation makes this interface slightly more complex than the previous model, it seems more intuitive.

Panning

In its simplest form, panning is a method of navigation where the content of an interface is moved horizontally, vertically, and diagonally according to the movement of the mouse. To see an area of an image to the left of the visible boundaries with a panning interface, a user can move the mouse to the left: the image will scroll from left to right.

Panning can take many forms and offers a variety of behaviors, but there are definite properties that distinguish panning from scrolling and grabbing.

Grabbing

Briefly, grabbing an object to move it is an alternative to scrolling through an interface. To see parts of an image to the left of the viewable area, the user can grab it by clicking, and move it by dragging: both the cursor and the image move from left to right. This is a common function in application interfaces. In Quark XPress, for instance, to reveal the area to the lower left of the window, the user can grab the page and move it diagonally in a single motion, rather than having to first scroll down and then scroll left.

Tracking

With grabbing, the position of the object corresponds to the position of the cursor. With scrolling, the position of the object has an inverse relationship with the cursor: when the user moves a scroll handle down, the page moves up. Panning is related to scrolling in that the page moves in the opposite direction of the cursor. This may seem so obvious that it's hardly worth mentioning, but an interface can be designed to do the opposite.

If a user were to mouse toward the upper right of an clipped image, the image could move toward the upper right—further away from the viewable area. This is tracking, so called because the image seems to follow, or track, the mouse. Tracking is not the same as grabbing, because the image continues to move as long as the mouse remains in a trigger area, even after the mouse is at rest.

Tracking creates a very different effect than panning; you tend to apply the two models in very different circumstances. But it is convenient to discuss the architecture of both at the same time. From here on, I'll discuss panning, with the understanding that tracking can be handled the same way. (See Fig. 9.7)

Panning Interfaces

Speed, sensitivity, and direction are the basic components of panning and tracking behaviors. Interacting with a panning interface is a little like piloting a boat: Once the movement begins, it continues at the same rate and in the same direction until it is interrupted or the direction is changed. Without easy ways to modify the speed and direction of panning, the user can quickly become overwhelmed by what appears to be uncontrollable movement.

Most good panning interfaces have zones of sensitivity, beginning with a place where no panning is triggered—the static zone. As the cursor moves away from that point, the object moves in the opposite direction, with increasing speed as the distance between the cursor and the static zone increases. That speed can be a problem for the user. If the interface only has a few zones, the panning action is jumpy and hard to control, with objects zooming across the screen without warning. It's better to create many speed zones, so that the speed increases in small increments from the center. This creates a highly sensitive interface that gives much more control to the user.

The zones that trigger an object's movement can be arranged in concentric circles

Grabbing
Cursor and image move together.

Tracking
Cursor and image move in same direction,
image continues moving after cursor comes to rest.

Panning
Cursor and image move in opposite directions,
image continues moving after cursor comes to rest.

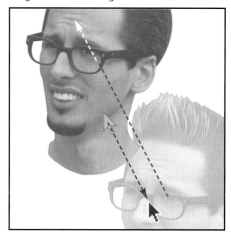

FIGURE 9.7

Grabbing and tracking are related interactions. **Grabbing** requires the most effort, but it is the most accurate way to move on-screen content. **Tracking** is like a hyper-grab: the object follows the cursor, but often continues moving after the mouse has come to rest. **Panning** is like inverted tracking, where the object moves in the opposite direction as the mouse. You can also see panning as related to the action of the scroll handles, which are moved in the opposite direction as the image.

radiating from the center of the static zone, or they can be much more rudimentary—blunt hot spots around the edge of the image that turn panning on when moused over. The latter is the least sensitive type of interface and it allows little user control, but it does have the advantage of being easier to code.

There is more to directing an object's motion than simply moving it away from the cursor. You also have to consider the vectors of movement. In an interface with just a few triggers around the edge, the image can only move along axes oriented at 90°, 45°, or 0°. Concentric zones create a more

sensitive interface, with more natural movement, as the object moves on an axis that is based on the position of the mouse relative to the center. (See Fig. 9.8)

Panning can be a powerful interaction model that gives users good navigational control in a flat space, especially when adaptive behaviors are programmed into it.

The basic architecture of concentric zones is adequate, but it only goes so far in giving the user intuitive control over an object's position. To change speed or direction, the user must be constantly aware of the cursor's position relative to the center.

Initially, the cursor moves away from the static zone, setting the object's trajectory and speed. To stop the movement, the user must move back to the center. But if the group of zones is programmed to adapt to the user's behavior by following the cursor after it has come to rest for, say, two seconds, the object will gradually come to a stop and the static zone will find its way back to the cursor. The user can then move the cursor in a new direction, sending the object on a parallel course. The user does not have to concentrate on the cursor position, but can pay attention to the object, guiding it with slight flicks of the wrist in whatever direction is desired. (See Fig. 9.9)

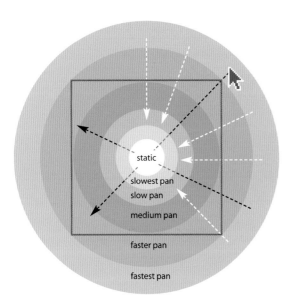

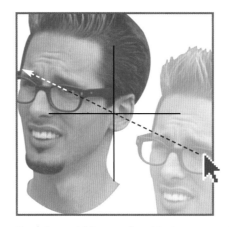

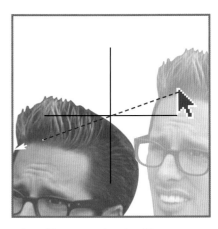

The axis on which a panning object moves can be based on either a complex algorithm or a simple grid of hot spots. The most natural panning behavior happens when the object moves on an axis that is determined by the position of the cursor relative to the center: if the mouse is 20° southeast, the image moves 20° northwest. This allows the user to quickly change the trajectory of the object by moving the mouse slightly.

The speed of a panning object can be either fixed or variable. In the case of a four-axis pan with eight triggers, there is likely to be only one speed. The most natural panning interfaces have zones of speed radiating out from a static center. The further from the center, the faster the rate of pan. Speed and sensitivity are then related, because the center of the image is the least sensitive, and has the slightest effect on its movement.

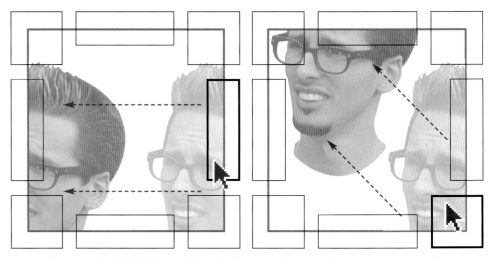

A rudimentary, but slightly less useful, method is to set hot spots that trigger movement. The East trigger sends the image West, the Southeast trigger sends it 45° northwest. This method does not allow the user to aim the image trajectory or change it midmotion, because the image can only move in four axial directions.

FIGURE 9.9: ZONES OF MOVEMENT

1. Mouse moves, image is set into motion.

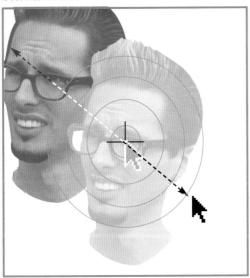

2. Mouse comes to rest, image continues to move. Static zone catches up with mouse, image stops.

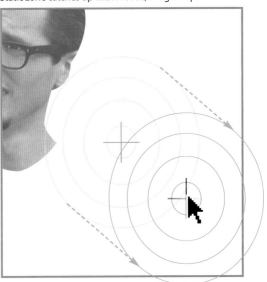

3. Mouse moves away from static zone, image moves on parralel axis …

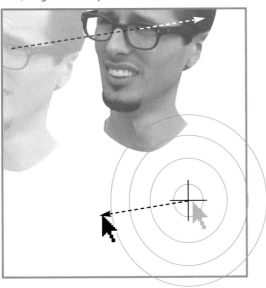

4. Until mouse comes to rest, and static zone catches up again.

In this interface, the image does not continue off in one direction indefinitely, because the zones of movement track the cursor. If the cursor comes to rest for a moment, the zones realign with it, which brings the image to rest. Since the static zone is once again under the cursor, when the user moves the mouse again, the image moves along a new path relative to the stopping point. The further the stopping point is from the original static zone, the longer it takes for everything to realign, and the further the image drifts before it stops.

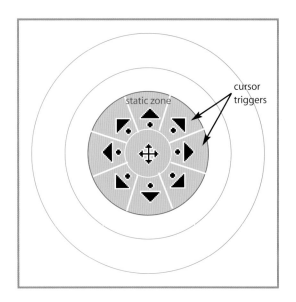

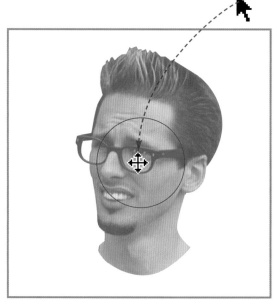

On mouseover static zone: panning is turned on. Cursor indicates active panning.

A slight mouse move in any direction changes cursor appropriately, mouse is still in the static zone.

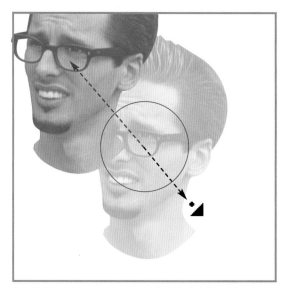

Panning occurs, cursor corresponds with the direction.

FIGURE 9.10

Since it differs so dramatically from other interaction models on the Web, panning can overwhelm or disorient a user. Anything a designer can do to help orient users will go a long way toward making them comfortable. For instance, swapping the cursor to directional icons can alert the user when panning is active and when a movement has been triggered.

Initiating the Pan

None of these examples takes into account the initial event that triggers the pan. Whether you're using concentric circles or edge triggers (hot spots), the user must mouse into the center to find the static zone. In theory, the user could inadvertently trigger a pan as the cursor moves over the outer triggers on the way to the center of the image. Therefore, you must give users a way to toggle the panning function on and off.

If panning should be off by default until the cursor is placed over the static zone, the user can get to the invisible control without triggering movement. A user could click to activate panning (though there wouldn't be any movement until she moved the mouse off the static zone), or it could be enabled automatically. Automatic enabling may be better, because using clicks can limit the way a user interacts with the object. A large map that is navigated by panning may also have hyperlinks, so that a click could take the user to a new view or a new page. In either case, a signifier that tells the user panning is available—changing the cursor to a multidirectional icon, for instance— would be a good idea. (See Fig. 9.10) You also have to give the user a way to turn the panning function off. It can be as simple as mousing beyond the outer limits of the interface, but it has to be clearly indicated.

Flinging

Without getting too wrapped up in the endless possibilities for scrolling and panning though content, I'd like to mention a little-used interaction that I found remarkably intuitive the first time I tried it. It does not appear in any usability textbooks, and there is no official term for it, but flinging (as the programmers at Hotwired dubbed it) sounds apt. The user sets a long list of content into automatic scrolling mode by grabbing the page, quickly moving the mouse in the desired direction, and releasing it. Just like throwing a ball, or shoving a toy car across the floor, flinging feels good and moves things fast. The Hotwired guys used it in a Java version of *Wired News,* where it was a handy way to set tickers into motion and determine the speed of the scrolling at the same time (the harder you flung the content, the quicker it scrolled).

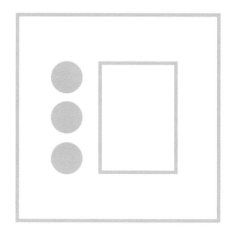

3-D Interaction

Most of the topics in this chapter have to do with the interaction between the cursor and a part of an interface. As mentioned earlier, the use of cursor icons to indicate multiple functions in a single element has brought interaction design beyond its original paradigm, and made it possible to add a new dimension to human-computer interaction: 3-dimensional space.

Navigating a virtual 3-D space with a 2-D interface (mouse and screen) is cumbersome at best. There are several ways of programming mouse behaviors to overcome this, but any solution requires the user to be patient and adventurous, and runs counter to accepted usability scenarios. However, most people will accept a degree of struggle when learning to use a game interface. For that reason, most of the behaviors described in this discussion of 3-D interaction are more common to games than to other interfaces. This may change in the future. As 3-D behaviors become commonplace, the navigation paradigm will become so ubiquitous that users will automatically understand it.

One attraction of games is the feeling of accomplishment they create when, after some effort, the user masters the interface. The very thing that makes a game interesting—challenge— makes an interface off-putting. Still, an interface does not have to rely solely on conventional interface elements and systems to be usable.

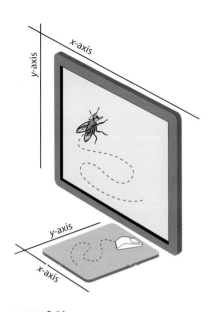

FIGURE 9.11

Panning limits the user to movement on one plane, up, down, left, and right like a fly stuck on a window.

To access a third dimension, the mouse click, which was once reserved for executing tasks, can represent movement "into" the depth of an interface, breaking the limits of the flat space.

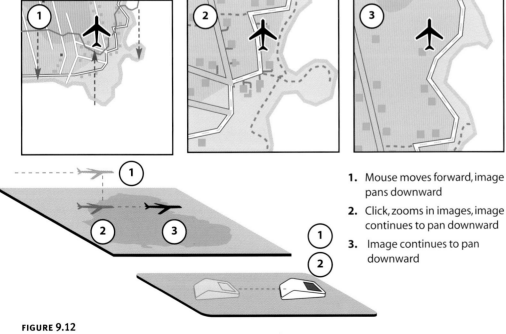

1. Mouse moves forward, image pans downward
2. Click, zooms in images, image continues to pan downward
3. Image continues to pan downward

FIGURE 9.12

Like an airplane flying over a landscape, the up/down, side-to-side panning of this map interface can easily be augmented with a mouse click, which either zooms into the image or lowers the plane's altitude.

Some intuitive interaction models can be drawn from unlikely real-life objects, such as puppets and airplanes. As long as the designer makes an effort to explain the interaction model with a key, recognizable iconography, or didactic text that doesn't interfere with the interface, a user can benefit from advanced techniques that utilize the capabilities of new online technologies.

For now, though, while computers render three-dimensional space well, input devices make 3-D movement problematic. With a rolling mouse and a flat mouse pad, the cursor is literally confined to the two-dimensional *x* and *y* axes of the flat screen. Fortunately, there are other options. If up-and-down movement along the *x* and *y* axes of a 3-D interface can be made possible through panning algorithms, then movement along the *z* axis—reaching into the screen—can be made possible through mouse clicks. (See Fig. 9.11)

The practical execution of this *z* axis can take several forms. Looking at an interface that shares some of the behaviors of the panning interface discussed above, it is easy to imagine how a *z* axis can augment usability. If we were flying over a virtual landscape, panning would help us navigate east to west, north to south, etc. Using the *z* axis, we could reduce our altitude by clicking the mouse while continuing to steer by moving it around. (See Fig. 9.12)

This model is limited, because it's one way. If clicking the mouse button means "down," you can't easily increase altitude, because there is no such thing as a reverse click.

There's no real need to give users a special tool to reverse direction. When we think of navigating a three-dimensional space, continual forward motion is the norm. You can reverse direction by pivoting. With the reverse problem solved, we have a complete set of navigational tools for three-dimensional space, based on what we know about panning, tracking and pushing. (See Fig. 9.13)

Here's another approach. When moving through a virtual space, such as a room, it helps to take the point of view of a puppet perched on your knee and controlled by a handle in its back—the mouse being the handle. The movements used to pivot a puppet's head from side to side are identical to panning: the puppeteer's hand (the mouse) moves to the left to reveal the part of the room which lies beyond the left side of the screen. To create the illusion that the user is moving, the panning algorithm moves the screen image in the opposite direction, from left to right.

To look down, the puppeteer pushes the puppet's head forward, leaning it over his knee. In tracking mode, pushing the mouse forward (which moves the cursor up) slides the image of the room up, revealing the floor. Pulling the puppet's head back (cursor

FIGURE 9.13

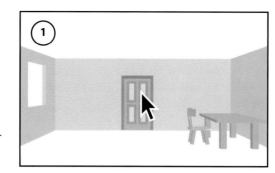

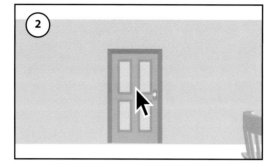

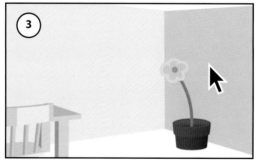

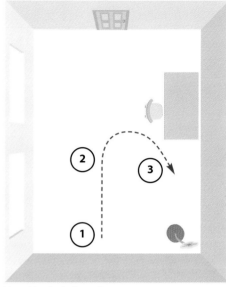

Hypothetical view of room.

prolonged click + pan right

1. Cursor is in idle position, no panning or tracking.
2. Mouse key held down, perspective is propelled forward. Mouse, cursor remains in the idle positions, so the only movement is forward until cursor is moved to the right.
3. While mouse key is still held down, perspective is both rotated and moved forward.

downward) tracks the image down, revealing the ceiling.

Holding the mouse key down could propel the puppet (and the puppeteer) forward, into the virtual space. Pivoting left, with the mouse down, could send everyone in a circle. (See Fig. 9.14) Until better input devices become standard, these are good, workable methods for creating the illusion of moving through space in a flat-screen world.

FIGURE 9.14

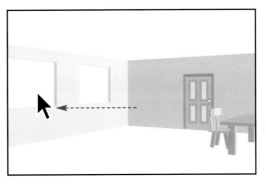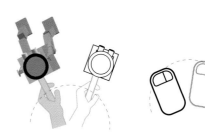

1. Move mouse left, image moves right (panning).

In a 3-D environment, navigation requires a unique combination of mouse behaviors. Side-to-side movement makes use of panning, while up and down movement uses tracking. This seemingly contradictory behavior makes physical sense because the mouse handles like a puppet.

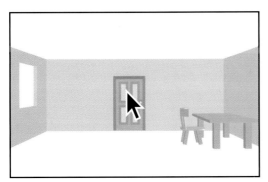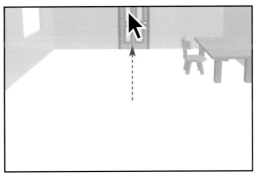

2. Push mouse forward (cursor up), image moves up to reveal floor (tracking).

Swiveling the mouse to the left to view the left side of a room is like swinging the puppet's head left, while pushing the puppet forward faces it downward. A forward push of the mouse is the right physical action for angling the view downward, even though the cursor will move up as a result.

SECTION IV:
Interface Elements in Action
REAL-WORLD EXAMPLES OF INTERFACE ELEMENTS

The Design Criteria

Users can't appreciate a Web site's look if its parts are getting in their way. Interface elements are therefore arguably the most important aspect of Web design. Paradoxically, they are most successful when the user is unaware of their presence: she is then free to consider how well the site addresses her needs and fits her personality.

You can't talk about interface elements without looking at the effects of color, language, context, and the temperament of the user. In this section, we'll consider all these factors as we look at a collection of Web sites.

Technology

Though I personally believe in building Web sites according to the original vision of HTML as a scalable platform that lets us mark up text to be read by any browser, there are times when newer technology works better. At the same time, I don't want to encourage designers and programmers to use technology that requires them to create special versions of the site for different browser platforms and forces users to get new plug-ins every six months. Circumstances and capability should determine how and when new technologies should be used.

Many of the sites in this section use Flash or DHTML sensibly, to either enhance usability or create a unique user experience. In cases where a comparable HTML or CSS solution exists, I'll point it out in the hope that designers will look for the most ubiquitous, democratic, and bandwidth-friendly solutions.

No site is perfect. All sites fall short in some circumstances because the technology of the Web is so far from perfect. Interfaces designed to work perfectly on every browser and every platform fall into one of two categories: supercustom and super-basic. Supercustom sites use extensive browser targeting and conditional code to serve each browser a special version of the site that will optimize its appearance in that environment. Superbasic sites use almost no formatting for fear that it will break in one browsing environment or another. Either solution can work—but there are other aspects of interface design that may matter more than technology.

The Designer's Intent

Very often the best interface is also hope-lessly flawed, as you will no doubt observe from the examples selected for these case studies. Designers who make an effort to compose interfaces using the tried-and-true toolkit of color, grids, language, and hierarchy, will design interfaces that have the potential to work extremely well in some circumstances, but not so well in others. In spite of the designer's best efforts, some sites fail because their owners don't permit them to succeed—as, for instance, when they insist that massive amounts of infor-mation and functionality be incorporated in a very limited onscreen environment.

It isn't hard to recognize cases when good design has been hindered by the still-adolescent technology of the Web. It's often obvious when a site has suffered from managerial problems or from a haphazard combination of third-party technologies that don't quite mesh. But a lot can be learned by looking beyond these issues, and analyzing the intent of the designer.

We can do this without reading a full case history for every site or listening to the designer explain her rationale. Instead, we will look at interface examples with a particular audience in mind, based on what we can discern from the site's name, branding, content, and context. From there we can work backwards to see what the designer was most likely thinking, and to some extent, what constraints technology and management may have imposed on the design.

The interface examples here range from corporate to personal. In most of them, basic HTML has been augmented with CSS and JavaScript. However, while few of them use old-fashioned hypertext, that is still the baseline from which we'll view usability.

Several examples are sites built by designers for designers, because that is where the most progressive use of interface elements is found. The design audience may or may not be more interface savvy than the average user, but while keeping the nature of the audience in mind, these interfaces (some quite experimental) are such that the average person should find them usable.

Blogger (www.blogger.com) Designer: Evan Williams Firm: Pyra.com LTD

Blogger is a Web log (blog) site, where individuals can publish essays or launch discussion threads and readers can comment. It has two faces—work and play—which are emphasized visually through bold, complementary colors. Every content panel or interactive tool is contained in a rectangle bordered by black, which creates a bold grid reminiscent of comic book panels. Such a graphic style might cause the diminutive interactive elements to get lost in the mix of strong colors and thick lines, but this site's clear delineation helps the user to tune out the rest of the page when focused on any given rectangle. Visual noise within each panel is kept at bay by removing the link underlines and altering the color of the system buttons to create a visual harmony with the overall look of the site.

Blogger emphasizes its work and play faces with two bold, complementary colors—blue and orange. The color scheme creates a visual system that helps users distinguish among Blogger's content, navigation, and tools. Hypertext links are always orange—the color of architecture and navigation—and buttons are always blue—the color of utility. News and text are always on white.

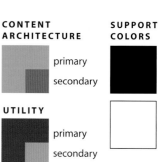

CONTENT ARCHITECTURE
primary
secondary

SUPPORT COLORS

UTILITY
primary
secondary

NAVIGATION PANEL

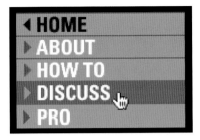

The site navigation relies on text, with minimal affordances, rather than mouseover effects. Blogger reserves buttons (that is, dimensional, clickable rectangles) for signing-in, submitting queries, and the like. Black arrowheads in the menus serve a dual function. When pointing left, they direct the eye to associated content; when pointing right, they work like the rotating triangles in operating systems that tell the user "more inside: click to display." The navigational hierarchy, which unfolds as section heads are clicked, is reinforced by type style—section heads are uppercase, while subsections are lowercase.

SIGN-IN PANEL, INITIAL STATE

SIGN-IN PANEL, UPDATED

Users need to log in to access some of the site's functions. The sign-in panel is updated to reflect the logged-in state but remains visually and functionally simple.

Blogger — *continued*

Blogger does a decent job of providing access to two kinds of blogs in the "recent-blog" list. Without leaving the page, a user can toggle between indexes of the last ten updated blogs and the last ten created blogs. Mousing over the inactive tab reveals a more explicit description of the hidden index.

Tabs are a good interface convention for this utility, but the color scheme creates a slight hierarchical problem. The active tab comes to the fore and assumes the blue color of the content screen. The inactive tab is bright orange, and seems so important that it is easily mistaken for the active element. In this example, at a glance, a user could easily think Updated was the active list.

A more monochromatic color system would make it easier to distinguish between the active and inactive tabs.

Dot Dot Dot (www.dot-dot-dot.org) Designer: Peter Bilak

This site deserves mention for its lyrical use of raw, unmanipulated screen type. The links in this online 'zine are reversed text that look like highlighted type in a word processor. This device gives a immediacy to the links, as if someone has gone through the page with a highlighter.

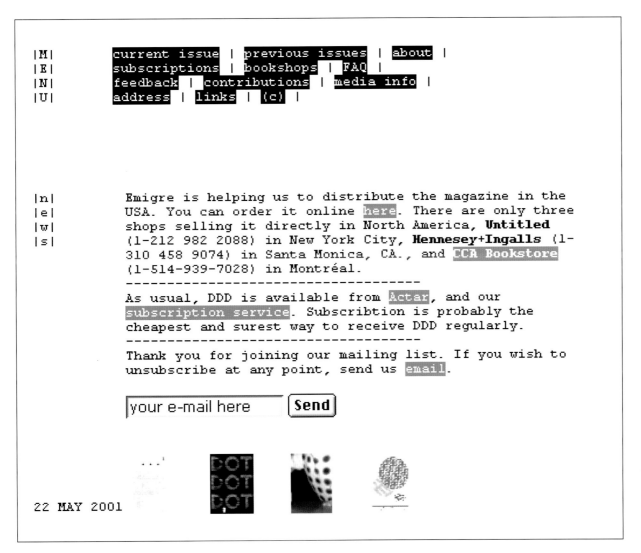

```
|M|      current issue | previous issues | about |
|E|      subscriptions | bookshops | FAQ |
|N|      feedback | contributions | media info |
|U|      address | links | (c) |



|n|      Emigre is helping us to distribute the magazine in the
|e|      USA. You can order it online here. There are only three
|w|      shops selling it directly in North America, Untitled
|s|      (1-212 982 2088) in New York City, Hennesey+Ingalls (1-
         310 458 9074) in Santa Monica, CA., and CCA Bookstore
         (1-514-939-7028) in Montréal.
         ------------------------------------
         As usual, DDD is available from Actar, and our
         subscription service. Subscribtion is probably the
         cheapest and surest way to receive DDD regularly.
         ------------------------------------
         Thank you for joining our mailing list. If you wish to
         unsubscribe at any point, send us email.
```

`your e-mail here`   `Send`

22 MAY 2001
```

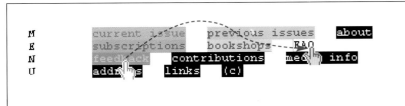

As you mouse over each link the text reverts to positive type, which makes links easy to interact with and gives the page a liveliness that belies its old-fashioned appearance.
```

Factory 512 (www.factory512.com) Designer: Dmitri Utkin

This is the tip of the European Web design iceberg. It seems that the farther a designer is from Silicon Valley (computing's Fertile Crescent) the more liberties are taken with usability. Factory 512, a side project of Russian designer Dmitri Utkin, is a portal for designers and geeks that borrows much of its aesthetic from such old media forms as television test patterns.

Die Fabrik512 Nackt-Haus Video Production.

inspirations	covers	links		
email	got news?			
	surfstation	media inspiration	kiiroi	the best designs
	infront	digitalthread	dform	adobe
	moluv	retinal sin	praktica	netdiver
	a list apart	coolhomepages	design-agency	newdream
elena	shando			
	at web design mag	f512 in impress mag		
	reboot at impress	reboot '01 splash		

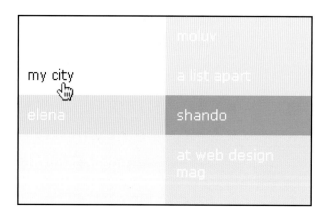

Much as the Swiss Punk movement blurred the relationship between language and abstract visual devices, this site allows the type to disappear in low-contrast relationships with the background patterns. However, since the page is very structured, the user is not apt to miss much. The consistent placement of links within the color blocks helps the user find even the least visible link: mouseovers reveal them just where the user expects them to be.

Die Fabrik512 Nackt-Haus Video Production.

	covers	links	
email	got news?		
surfstation	media inspiration	kiiroi	the best designs
ntront	digitalthread	dform	adobe
moluv	retinal sin	praktica	netdiver
a list apart	coolhomepages	design-agency	newdream
elena	shando		

erotik im beruf, enoian, factory512: outro gurl, tama68, missfiction, part5, uncovered & mailbox, addikt, heterofactory, astraphoby, share me with your hate letters, how much is total, plain cd orgy, morgan, congo, viagra happytime, sexuntagged, hyperdog, pressculture, flexometry, frisky, pick up the skin, i, pick up the skin, ii, donate, ___indesicao, 360uno_partida, fucking american patriots, novene.com, 153f, tokyo_mojo, 15XX8593B9-67, level 18, global galaxy inspirit service, panic!, 512 metal ladies, absolut models (you know this), factory roots 1, factory roots 2, factory roots 3, factory roots 4, factory roots 5, 1024x768 dot year 2000 promo wallpaper, florida, you'll see (to L.), pocket paris, reactor critical (web splash screen), what a lucky man he was, touch me (i'm in sorrow), design for sale, virtually everything made of plastic, salut, comment tu vas?, sunnyday, this game has, the end of advertising, nato sucks, it's the end of the world as we know it / and i feel fine, not a dream, coming soon, letterevolution, gentle gap, ayashi, modern architects, 1956: fest of popular music, 1970: factory's the best

erotik im beruf, enoian, factory512: outro gu
uncovered & mailbox, addikt, heterofactory,
your hate letters, how much is total, plain cd
viagra happytime, sexuntagged, hyperdog, p
world against brand new, frisky, pick up the
donate, ___indesicao, 360uno_partida, fuck
novene.com, 153f, tokyo_mojo, 15XX8593B9
inspirit service, panic!, 512 metal ladies, abs
factory roots 1, factory roots 2, factory roots
roots 5, 1024x768 .dot year 2000 promo wallpaper, florida, you'll see (to
L.), pocket paris, reactor critical (web splash screen), what a lucky man he
was, touch me (i'm in sorrow), design for sale, virtually everything made
of plastic, salut, comment tu vas?, sunnyday, this game has, the end of
advertising, nato sucks, it's the end of the world as we know it / and i
feel fine, not a dream, coming soon, letterevolution, gentle gap, ayashi,
modern architects, 1956: fest of popular music, 1970: factory's the best

Clicking one of the categories at the top of the page causes an enormous list of links to pop up in a content panel. A subtle shift in hierarchy takes place on the page when this happens: except for the scroll bar, which helps distinguish the content panel from the rest of the page, the long list might blend in too much.

The designer makes little effort to categorize the links or add structure to the list with labels or metainformation. The user must use the cursor to focus each link. While this may be a pain, there is a nice side effect: a kind of interactive poetry emerges from the interaction. Not exactly good usability, but it does go a long way toward creating a unique experience that may appeal to Factory 512's creative audience.

Suffocate
(www.suffocate.org/s3/nonshock/?pg=art&nr=20)

Designer: Christopher J. Falvey Firm: Media Basement

A simple site that assembles the musings of several artists in one place, Suffocate is essentially a jumping-off point for interested readers. To that end, the site is a quick-loading piece of HTML that relies on hypertext links for most of its navigation. HTML also allows quick-and-easy edits, and since the artists' stories are frequently updated, it's a very good choice—GIF links would be far harder to change.

Sometimes the simplest sites benefit most from interactive effects that give the page a livelier, more alluring appearance. Here, the links are bold in their static state. To show what's active and to add a little energy, the designer chose to make them larger on mouseover. Rather than take care not to disturb the rest of the layout with this technique, the larger type pushes the list apart considerably, to comical effect. This would be annoying on a page with more content.

There is, however, one unfortunate consequence: depending on the size of the browser window, a scroll bar may appear when part of the list is pushed below the fold. This is easy enough to fix—add a little space to the navigation area.

ioResearch (www.ioresearch.com/flash/index.html)

Designer: Kris Griffith Firm: ioResearch

ioResearch is a design studio that specializes in interactive interfaces. Its portfolio site is one of the company's simpler pieces. It also has a few successful interaction models that draw upon familiar interface systems.

Sites that serve a single purpose—to lead the user through a selection of images—have an advantage in that most of the interface elements can function with minimal affordances. Since they don't have to compete with other widgets for attention, links can be indicated as text. Users understand right away that any short piece of text is a link and the role it plays is indicated in plain English. The up and down arrows at the bottom right are not links, but controls. This lack of affordances is not an obstacle to usability: since there is so little on the page, users will be willing to experiment to find out what each element does.

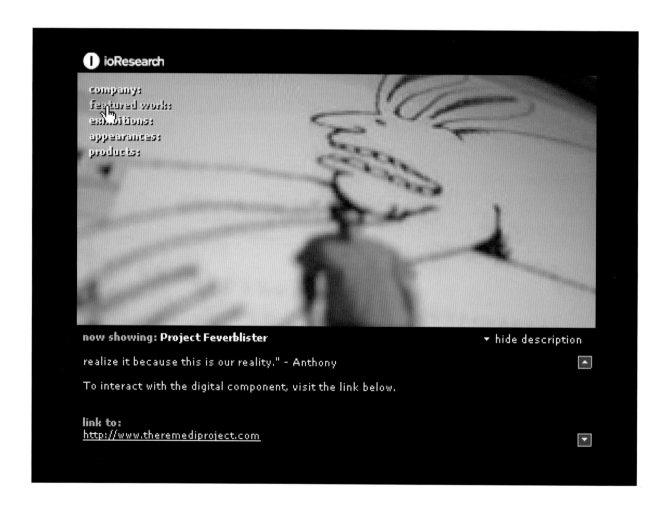

now showing: **Project Feverblister**   ▾ hide description

realize it because this is our reality." - Anthony

To interact with the digital component, visit the link below.

link to:
http://www.theremediproject.com

Each category link—company, featured work, exhibitions, appearances, products—has a subset of links that load new pictures to the image window beneath it. Though there is no iconography or labeling to convey the depth of each category, this interface is so simple that one click is sufficient to show the user what's available.

company:
featured work:
exhibitions:
appearances:
products:

company:
featured work:

Kind Radio
ioRacing
Jim Russell Racing
NCAA Final Four Brackets
Larry Rouch Company
Stick Networks
The Remedi Project
The Bill Bowerman Story
Dreams

exhibitions:
appearances:
products:

When the user clicks on a category link, a list of sublinks drops down and any remaining category heads move to the end of the list. Users could easily become disoriented when a short list of links is replaced by a longer list of links that looks much the same, but this site uses motion to guide them through: When a category is clicked, the sublinks visibly push the remaining categories down. Since animation lets the user see the change in layout while it's happening, he is less likely to be disoriented by the new list. If the sublinks were to suddenly pop onto the screen, it would be easy to lose track of the navigation's original structure.

now showing: The Remedi Project

Named from 'REdesigning the MEdium through DIscovery', The Remedi Project was created in 1997 as an online collection of digital media that challenged the capabilities and preconceptions of interactivity on the web. Since its first exhibition, invited artists from around the world have been adding their experiments to the collection▾ hide description

Every quarter, artists are asked to present their personal explorations into new ways of communicating in this medium with the hope to inform and direct the future of interactivity on the web. ioResearch supports this evolving installation, developing and designing its framework around the belief that the content is king.

link to: http://www.theremediproject.com

Named from 'REdesigning the MEdium through DIscovery', The Remedi Project was created in 1997 as an online collection of digital media that challenged the capabilities and preconceptions of interactivity on the web. Since its first exhibition, invited artists from around the world have been adding their experiments to the collection▾ hide description

now showing: The Remedi Project present their personal explorations into new ways of communicating in this medium with the hope to inform and direct the future of interactivity on the web. ioResearch supports this evolving installation, developing and designing its framework around the belief that the content is king.

link to: http://www.theremediproject.com

In order to keep the layout simple, all content adheres to a grid based partly on the proportions of the central image. Rather than insisting that text be written to fit the grid, the overflow is clipped and up and down arrows let readers scroll through. Each entry can thus be written to any length. A single click moves the text one line at a time (more or less), while a prolonged click scrolls the text smoothly.

now showing: **The Remedi Project**   ▾ hide description

Every quarter, artists are asked to present their personal explorations into new ways of communicating in this medium with the hope to inform and direct the future of interactivity on the web. ioResearch supports this evolving installation, developing and designing its framework around the belief that the content is king.

link to: http://www.theremediproject.com

now showing: **Nike: The Bill Bowerman Story**   ▴ show description

A simple link with a rotating triangle makes a convenient toggle for the text portion of the interface.

Designer Shock
(www.designerdock.de/designershock/ds003/inhalt.html)

Designer: Stefan Gandl Firm: Designer Shock

Conceptual art meets interface design in this site for an imaginary operating system called DSOS. Designer Shock is a collaboration between three designers and engineers who approach Web development as musicians approach recording projects—they jam, with solos. Different facets of the site reflect one or another individual designer's sensibilities, but the sum holds together as a cohesive work.

Every aspect of Designer Shock is written and designed as an inside joke. Even the start page requires deciphering: The navigational elements are not labeled to indicate purpose or destination. The result is a case study in the ways people perceive and interact with interface elements.

Compositionally, this page is divided neatly in half, with interactive elements on the right and content on the left. In the steadfast tradition of Dutch design, there is a relationship between the visual form of the text on the left and the interface elements on the right, which share a flush-left/ragged-right format. That visual relationship leads the user to expect that interacting with the elements will affect the content side—yet it does not. The sole purpose of the visual repetition is to create harmony.

The interface elements themselves look like page or document icons, which gives a clue to the nature of the site—it's an online magazine. The unequal number of elements on each line helps the user gauge the amount of content. After a few clicks, the user understands that each line represents a week's worth of publications (and an erratic publishing schedule).

Within the site, the interface elements in DSOS are very simple. They generally take the page-icon appearance and require the user to interact with them to elucidate their purposes. This over-simplification may make the user work a bit, but it also helps the interface succeed—elements with extensive labeling and affordances would begin to compete with the content.

Though the DSOS site is evercryptic, deciphering it is always easy: In the screens above, mousing over the interface elements resolves the display text to reveal information about the content's author. One might reasonably ask what is gained by obscuring the information in the first place if revealing it does not dramatically enhance its meaning, but the lesson here has more to do with how obscured content can indeed function, to some extent, as content.

Designer Shock — *continued*

:BACKISSUE	:CONTENT
DS 001	THE BRAND NEW ISSUE™
FEATURING	LOPETZ (BÜRO DESTRUCT/CH) IAN ANDERSON (THE DESIGNER'S REPUBLIC/UK) PIA BETTON (META/GER) OLE SCHUMANN (S&F/GER)
FONT(-GAMES) +	DS PEEP™ DS AUSTRIAN SPACE INVADERS™ PERMUTATIONS™
DS 002	THE MOST WANTED MISS YOU ISSUE™
FEATURING	STEFAN SAGMEISTER (SAGMEISTER INC./USA) TANJA GOMPF (RGSQUARED/USA) RUND&AMOEBA (RUND.ORG/GER) RINZEN (RINZEN/AUS)
FONT(-GAMES) +	DS MEEK 10™ DS EPM SERIES™ DS MR GREEN™
DS 003	THE 100% 420PROOF ISSUE™
FEATURING	DSOS) (DS OPERATING SYSTEM 1) THE USER'S MANUAL ISBN 3-931126-64-1
INCLUDING +	4 DS TOOLS 80 DS FONTS 25 DS SCREENSAVER 55 WALLPAPERS

:CONSUMER	:INFO
TC1	DS MADE IN BERLIN
TC2/A	ARE YOU A DSR YET? SCHON EIN DSR?
TC2/B	IF YOU WOULD LIKE TO BE INFORMED ABOUT IRREGULAR UPDATES OF EACH DESIGNERSHOCK EDITION, PLEASE SUBSCRIBE
TC2/C	WENN SIE ÜBER DIE UNREGELMÄSSIG ERSCHEINENDEN AUSGABEN DER DESIGNERSHOCK SERIE INFORMIERT WERDEN WOLLEN, TRAGEN SIE SICH BITTE EIN
TC3	EMAIL klug@deluxe-ate-design.com
TC4	NAME Eric K. Eaton
TC5	COMPANY Deluxe-ate Design
TC6	COUNTRY USA COMMENT

SEND

In keeping with Designer Shock's predilection for nontraditional interface design, this page is rendered vertically for no apparent reason other than to distinguish it from the rest of the site. In spite of the odd configuration, the page has two clear purposes, well delineated: one is to provide an index to three Issues of DSOS, and the other is to provide a form users can use to subscribe to update alerts. Though the two are similarly designed, the icons in the index distinguish it from the form.

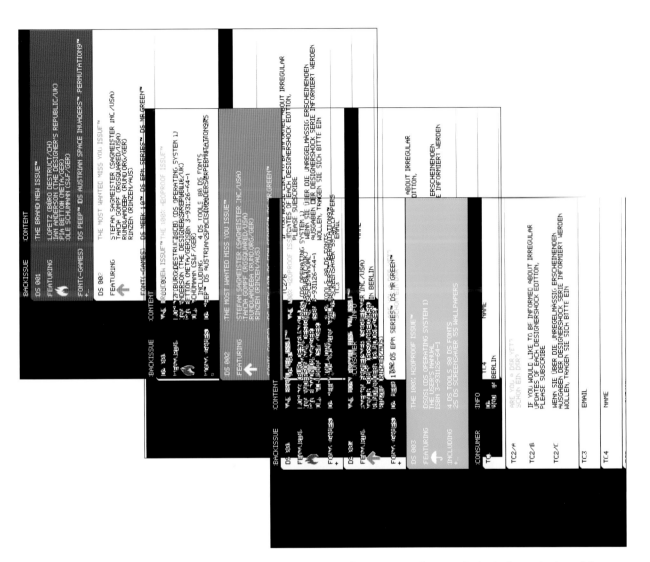

What appears to be a conservative use of color in the static view of the index/form interface actually supports a deeper functionality. In their static mode, the three sections of the index are on an equal footing. As the mouse moves over the index, each section it touches is highlighted in the same color as the icon, and shown to be unique. The mouseover effect also helps convey clickability—a necessary cue in an interface that does not employ many affordances.

```
:BACKISSUE    :CONTENT
:DS 001       :THE BRAND NEW ISSUE™
:FEATURING    :LOPETZ (BURO DESTRUCT/CH)
              :IAN ANDERSON (THE DESIGNER'S REPUBLIC/UK)
              :PIA BETTON (META/GER)
              :OLE SCHUMANN (S&F/GER)
:FONT(-GAMES) :DS PEEP™ :DS AUSTRIAN SPACE INVADERS™ :PERMUTATIONS™
+...

:DS 002       :THE MOST WANTED MISS YOU ISSUE™
:FEATURING    :STEFAN SAGMEISTER (SAGMEISTER INC./USA)
              :TANJA GOMPF (RGSQUARED/USA)
              :RUND&AMOEBA (RUND.ORG/GER)
              :RINZEN (RINZEN/AUS)
:FONT(-GAMES) :DS MEEK 10™ :DS EPM SERIES™ :DS MR.GREEN™
+...

:DS 003       :THE 100% H20PROOF ISSUE™
:FEATURING    :DSOS1 (DS OPERATING SYSTEM 1)
              :THE USER'S MANUAL
              :ISBN 3-931126-64-1
:INCLUDING    :4 DS TOOLS :80 DS FONTS
              :25 DS SCREENSAVER :55 WALLPAPERS
+...

:CONSUMER     :INFO
:TC1          :DS
              :MADE IN BERLIN
:TC2/A        :ARE YOU A DSR YET?
              :SCHON EIN DSR?
:TC2/B        :IF YOU WOULD LIKE TO BE INFORMED ABOUT IRREGULAR
              UPDATES OF EACH DESIGNERSHOCK EDITION,
              PLEASE SUBSCRIBE.
:TC2/C        :WENN SIE ÜBER DIE UNREGELMÄSSIG ERSCHEINENDEN
              AUSGABEN DER DESIGNERSHOCK SERIE INFORMIERT WERDEN
              WOLLEN, TRAGEN SIE SICH BITTE EIN.
:TC3          :EMAIL
              :kluge@deliberate-design.com
:TC4          :NAME
              :Eric K. Eaton
:TC5          :COMPANY
              :Deliberate Design
:TC6          :COUNTRY
              :USA
              :COMMENT
              :[-----]

SEND
```

The sign-up interface lacks the telltale type-in boxes of most Web forms, but the user should have no trouble discerning its function from the text. Furthermore, the obvious segmentation and labeling actually make it look more like a real-world form than a Web form—the language of forms nonetheless. If the user is initially uncomfortable with the atypical design, he will adapt soon enough to fill it out, partly because the form is shorter and less angst inducing than most forms on the Web.

One very real drawback to typing vertically has to do with using the keyboard's arrow keys to move through the text—the vertical and horizontal keys don't work intuitively. If you make a mistake, and try to move the I-beam backwards to make a correction, the natural tendency would be to use the down key, which actually moves the I-beam horizontally.

The page's visual harmony is partly the result of a minimal use of interface elements, but usability does suffer. The submit button is a pointing finger that looks more like "go to next page" than "submit," and thus requires investigation.

Say what you will about the irreverence of Designer Shock's take on interface layout, it does follow most of the important interaction models. Once the user has submitted the subscribe form, she is assured by a confirmation screen that the organization behind the interface has received it.

Incidentally, DSOS addresses internationalization bluntly, by rendering the text in German and English simultaneously.

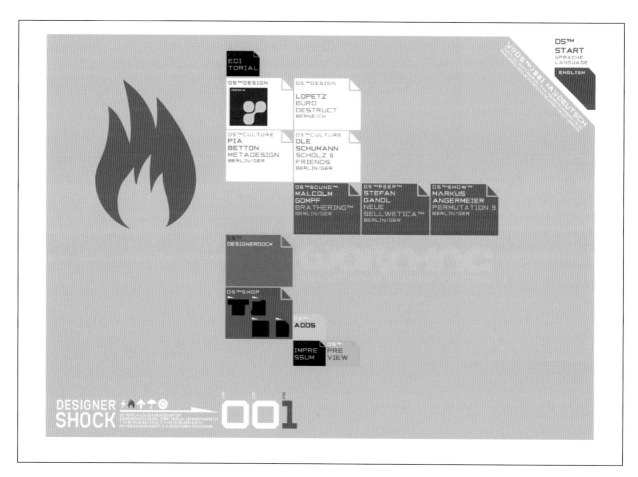

The initial simplicity of Designer Shock is somewhat misleading. Once the user has clicked through several pages, it becomes apparent that the site has many layers of content and interface, each of which is distinguished by a unique appearance, and all of which are part of a larger, conceptually cohesive design system.

This is the index page of one of the issues users can link to from the vertical, site-index page. Its layout and color scheme bears no relation to the site index. Only iconography sustains the connection: the large fire icon here is an enlarged version of the one that labels this section in the index. The dramatic change of color and layout gives this issue a life unto itself—the user will sense that it is a new space, with new content and navigation, then find that it reassuringly maintains many of the interface conventions of the rest of the site.

Another way in which Designer Shock challenges the conventional use of form elements is with its custom take on the toggle. Rather than using checkboxes or radio buttons to toggle between two states, this interface uses a large polygonal button. To change the language from German to English, one need only click the button.

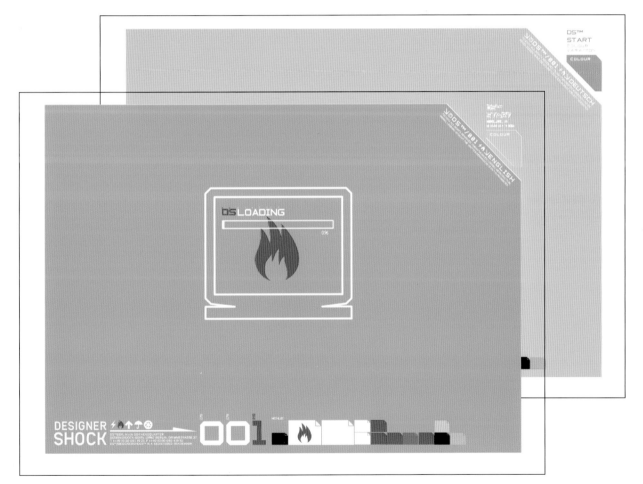

Toggling works well for the German/English toggle because there are only two languages to choose from. It might continue to work with three or four languages, but any more might arouse frustration as users would have to keep on clicking and waiting for the page to refresh until they found the language they wanted.

One layer down, the same element lets users toggle between two different color schemes for the section. This brings us into murky usability territory. The language toggle is only available on the index page, which is okay because users are only likely to change the language once. Why offer similar-but-different functionality deeper in the section? Why not let users choose a color at the beginning, too, instead of springing new choices on them and making them wonder what others choices await?

Designer Shock — *continued*

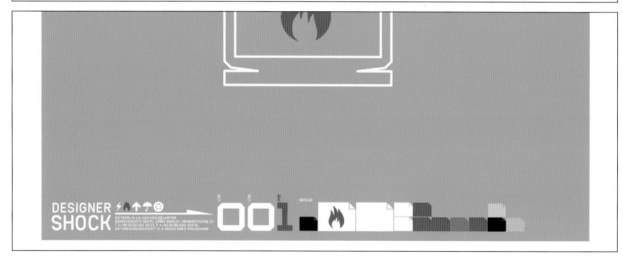

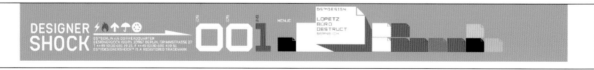

Designer Shock consistently displays its navigation and way-finding devices at the bottom of the page. Within the individual issues, which have considerably more content, the interface elements have dual functions: navigational and informational. They link to content, of course, and also give the user intuitive information about the content through size and color, as well as explicit information through text panels that pop up on mouseover.

Boeri (www.boeriusa.com)

Designer/Firm: Red98

Boeri, makers of high-end helmets for a variety of sports, uses this site to sell its merchandise and increase its reach. The language, the evocative imagery, and the edgy design go a long way to position Boeri as a hip company, while the direct nature of the site, which immediately gets down to the business of selling helmets, conveys a no-nonsense philosophy that is in keeping with its audience's active lifestyle.

For all intents and purposes, Boeri.com is an effective e-commerce site, although it does succumb to many of the pitfalls of highly visual, highly functional sites.

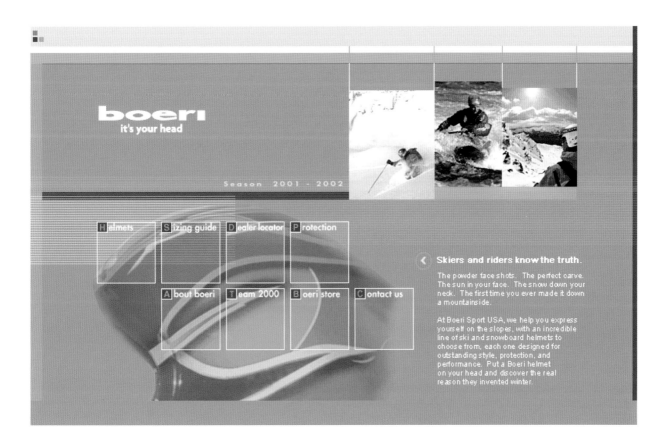

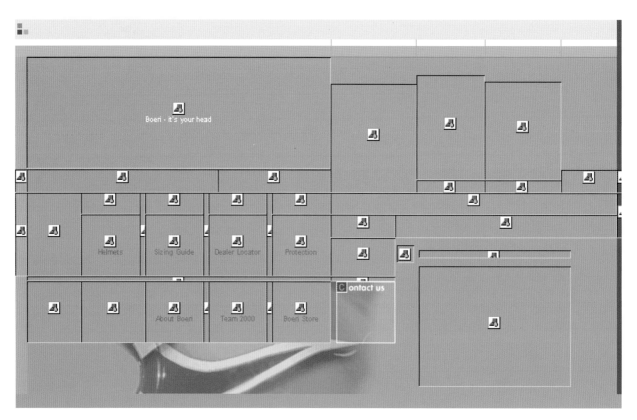

When the sole purpose of your site is to sell a product, it is often necessary to rely heavily on imagery. (What better way to entice the user into wanting your goods?) The unfortunate consequence of this is lengthy downloads as GIFs and JPGs stream into the page. That problem is exacerbated by the mouseover effects that the Boeri interface relies on so heavily. This site's usability would be greatly enhanced if the interactive area was presented as a separate image. It would load faster and, at the same time, make a clearer distinction between interactive tools and content.

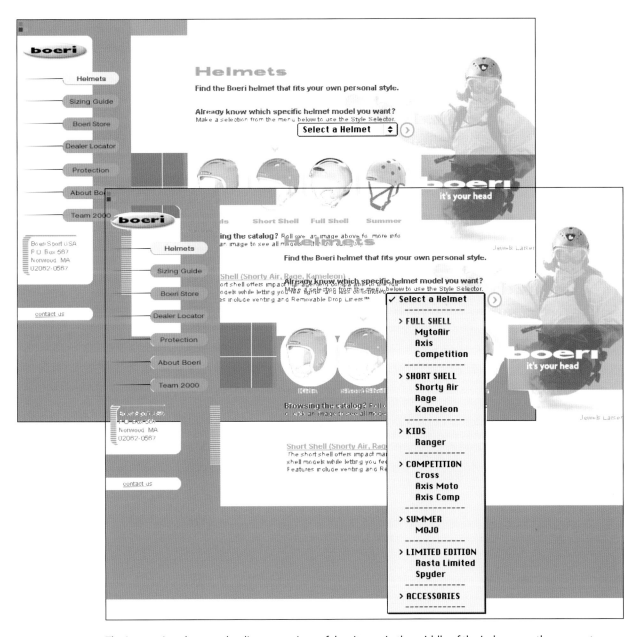

The interactive elements leading to sections of the site are in the middle of the index page, then move to a vertical, left-hand list on later pages—a typical interface convention Boeri does nothing to categorize or subdivide the list, which is okay because there aren't that many sections and the most important links are at the top. The page offers two other ways to drill into the core offering: by clicking on the helmet images or by selecting from a menu that lists all the helmet categories. This serves the site well. It offers a way into the products for two types of users: those who are drawn to images and may be unsure of what they are looking for; and those who know exactly what they want, and would like to go directly to it.

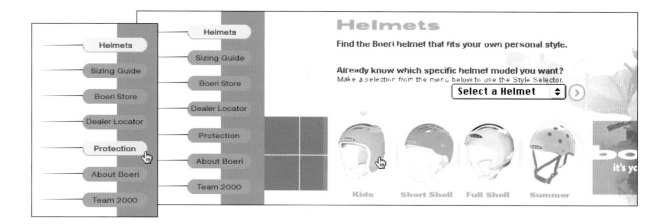

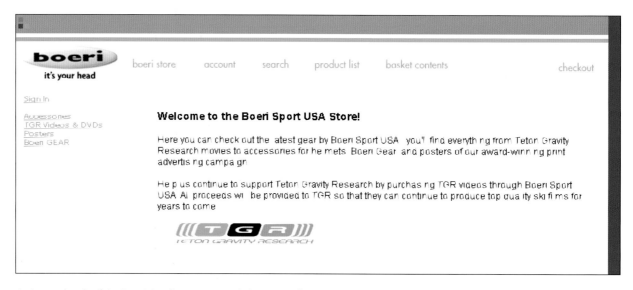

At the top levels of the Boeri site, the navigational elements offer all the usual interaction affordances—dimensionality, passive, and active appearances, mouseover effects—to reinforce usability, but they are too soon abandoned when the user goes deeper. Clicking on the store link takes the user to a page that, oddly enough, lacks imagery, though stores are where you would most expect to find visual displays. The site navigation, which on higher-level pages is a vertical column of gray buttons on the left, is now a horizontal row of word links across the top. The subnavigation for the store is in a left-side column, and is appropriately rendered as hypertext, but has no visual relationship to the navigational scheme of previous pages. To some extent, the user can reconcile these inconsistencies with the knowledge that they are going into the nuts-and-bolts section of the site, but a consequence is that the site feels less and less considered and, perhaps, less and less valuable.

Form 1 (top):

Bold = Required
Italic = Optional

Ship To: **Bill To (If Different):**

First Name   [_____]   First Name   [_____]
Last Name   [_____]   Last Name   [_____]
Email Address   [_____]   Email Address   [_____]
Phone Number   [_____]   Phone Number   [_____]
Fax Number   [_____]   *Fax Number*   [_____]
Company   [_____]   *Company*   [_____]
Address   [_____]   Address   [_____]
City   [_____]   City   [_____]
State/Province   [Alaska   ▾]   State/Province   [Alaska   ▾]
Other State/Province [_____]   *Other State/Province* [_____]
Zip/Postal Code   [_____]   Zip/Postal Code   [_____]
Country   United States   Country   United States

                                                                [Continue]

Form 2 (bottom):

Bold Required
Italic Optional

Ship To: **Bill To (If Different):**

First Name: [_____]   **First Name:**   [_____]
Last Name: [_____]   **Last Name:**   [_____]
Email Address: [_____]   **Email Address:**   [_____]
Phone Number: [_____]   **Phone Number:**   [_____]
Fax Number   [_____]   *Fax Number*   [_____]
Company   [_____]   *Company*   [_____]
Address: [_____]   **Address:**   [_____]
City: [_____]   **City:**   [_____]
State/Province: [Alaska   ▾]   **State/Province:**   [Alaska   ▾]
Other State/Province [_____]   *Other State/Province* [_____]
Zip/Postal Code: [_____]   **Zip/Postal Code:**   [_____]
Country: **United States**   **Country:**   **United States**

Attributes in **bold** are required.

Color: [Blue   ▾]
[Continue]

                                                                [Continue]

The purchasing form is typical of e-commerce sites, but has a couple of minor problems. While it's common for a form to use a combination of required and optional fields, this one uses flawed cues for distinguishing between the two. Required fields are labeled in bold type, which many screen fonts are incapable of displaying at small sizes. A user might think the interface above doesn't have any required fields (unless she happened to go back into her browser's setup screen and set a larger default font size that could render the boldface well).

Some form elements only require the user to specify one thing. In the one above, it's color. The text label, "Attributes in bold are required," implies that there are multiple fields to fill in, which there obviously are not. Just as obviously, the display text comes from a stock template. If you have to use generic display labels, they should be written to work with every scenario. Another problem with this label is that "bold" is relative. Without other fields nearby in a Roman font that the user can compare with this type, it is not clear that the label is in boldface.

Boeri — *continued*

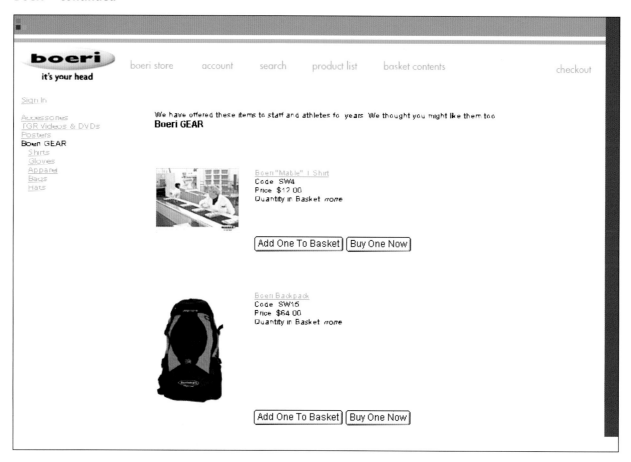

Boeri is on the right track with this short shopping interface, which allows the user to purchase an item by clicking a single button. But the grid in which each item is displayed is not cohesive enough. Each item has three components: an image, text-based information, and some purchasing buttons. Rather than hold together, the three components seem to float in space. Worse, in some cases, the buttons for one item look as if they belong to the image of the next.

Boeri Cap
Code: SW14
Price: $14.00
Quantity in Basket: *none*

[Add One To Basket] [Buy One Now]

One solution would be to give each item a box of its own and use tinted backgrounds to add visual weight. Regardless of the design solution chosen, the goal should be to let the user jump from one item to another visually and quickly identify the components that relate to each item.

Boeri Cap
Code SW14
Price $14.00
Quantity in Basket *none*

[Add One To Basket] [Buy One Now]

Boeri "Mable" T-Shirt
Code: SW4
Price: $12.00
Quantity in Basket: *none*

[Add One To Basket] [Buy One Now]

What probably looked like a cohesive grid in the production phase of development turns out to be less than optimal.

Without the aid of grid lines, this item falls apart— so put them back in.

Boeri Backpack
Code: SW15
Price: $64.00
Quantity in Basket: *none*

[Add One To Basket] [Buy One Now]

Boeri Cap
Code: SW14
Price: $14.00
Quantity in Basket: *none*

[Add One To Basket] [Buy One Now]

Omnia (www.omniband.com) Designer: Mathew Mejia Firm: Droppod

An exercise in simplicity, this site provides news about the band Omnia. The designer chose to stick to a rigid grid, so text is confined to a scrolling window, with up and down arrows to let the user scroll to overflow text. This is a simple, self-explanatory device that contributes to the overall slickness of the site, but it has two drawbacks. First, since there is no scroll bar, the user doesn't know how much text is available and can't see how much of it they've read. Second, the text continues to scroll as long as the cursor remains over the down arrow. Using a mouseover to initiate scrolling is perhaps the wrong choice, because it requires the user to move the mouse on and off the button constantly to navigate the text. It might be preferable to let the user leave the cursor over the button, and click to see more text—but since mouseover interaction is supported by more browsers than mouse and click, the existing interface will probably work on more platforms.

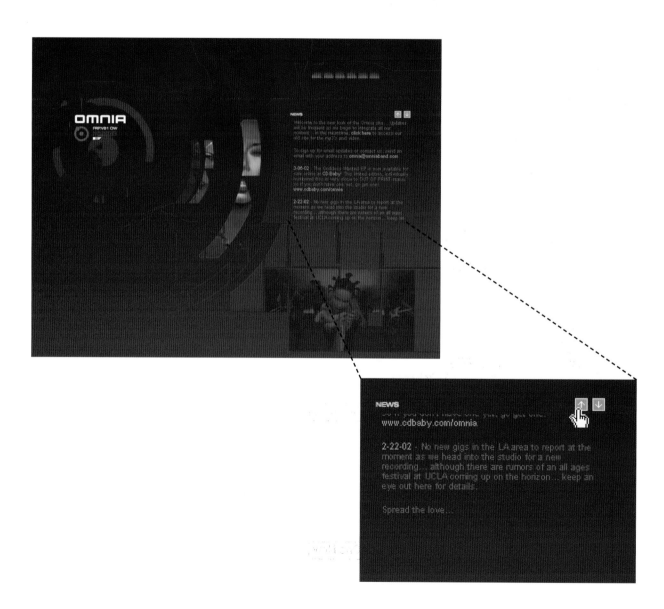

Media Basement
(www.mediabasement.com/mediabasement/default_main.asp)

Designer: Christopher J. Falvey Firm: Media Basement

Media Basement is a simple portal to six artistic sites, each dedicated to "a different aesthetic discipline." Such a portal could easily overshadow or obscure the underlying sites. Media basement avoids this by limiting the portal to a single page, and using DHTML and JavaScript to provide deeper information, news, and gateways to each site while maintaining its own sense of individuality.

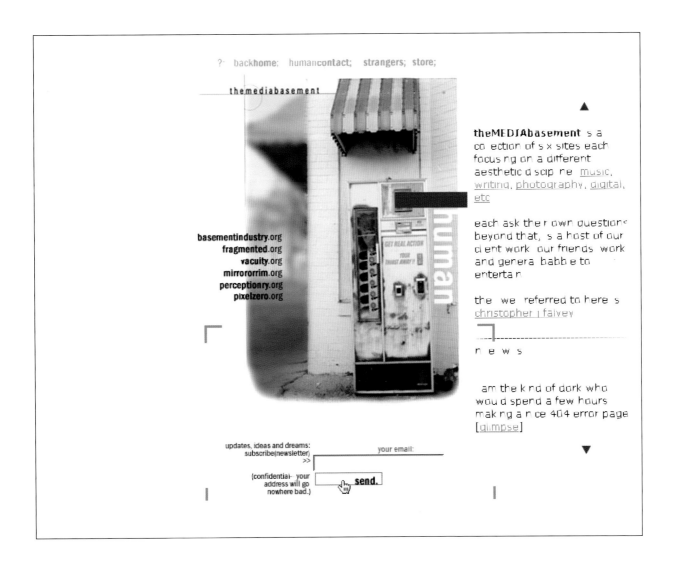

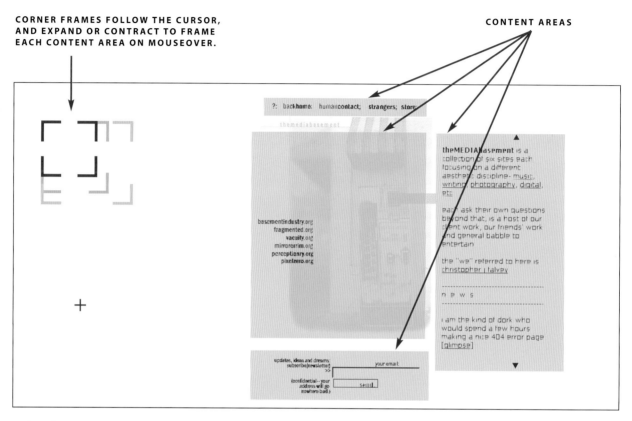

CORNER FRAMES FOLLOW THE CURSOR, AND EXPAND OR CONTRACT TO FRAME EACH CONTENT AREA ON MOUSEOVER.

CONTENT AREAS

At first glance, this site looks chaotic, but the user is quickly oriented to its page architecture thanks to some clever, cursor-oriented JavaScript. Like a divining rod, the mouse reveals content areas with four corner icons that follow the cursor until it finds a content area, at which point the corners lock to the boundaries of that area.

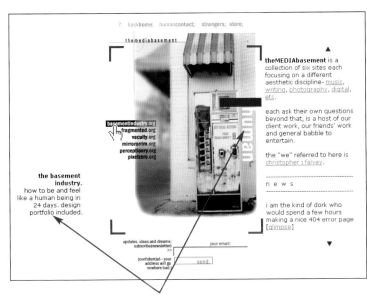

MOUSEOVER EFFECTS BOTH THESE AREAS

The framing corners (which I've rendered here in red) define an area that represents a type of content. When the cursor is over the large image or its associated links, the corners snap to the boundaries of the entire area (actually they move around a little—you have to see it to understand). Even though mousing or clicking on the links makes information pop up in two unconnected areas, the framing corners provide enough focus to prevent the interface from seeming too unstructured.

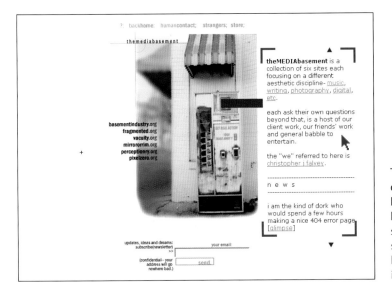

The long, scrolling, text window uses up and down arrows to lead to more content, much like the Omnia site. It also suffers from the same handicap: there is no way to tell how far you've scrolled or how much more content is yet to be seen. Somehow it doesn't seem like a problem here because the overall effect of this dynamic interface is one of imprecise elegance.

Three.oh (www.threeoh.com/v09)

Designer: John Widegren, Stanley Wolukau Firm: three

This is one of those rare sites that strives to present every possible kind of usability, in a unique visual language, while adhering to the spirit of established interaction models. It draws upon many conventions of application design, but does not mimic the WIMP (windows, icons, menus, and pointers) appearance of most interfaces. Unlike most sites, where the home page is just a veneer of links that lead to the more important content pages, Three.oh.com presents layers of text-based information, discourse, and musings in an interface confined largely to the one page.

Unlike Flash interfaces, or certain frames-based interfaces that seek to confine interaction to a tidy and inflexible aspect ratio, this site takes advantage of the browser's natural ability to present more information on a single plane than will fit within a single page. Like most Web sites, the interface has several areas. Only some of them fit above the fold, but once the user has scrolled to an area, the space required for it is minimal, because the designers found ways to expand the information by adding visual and conceptual layers. First, the interface provides conceptual gateways to content by way of expressive imagery and simple blurbs. ("Fizzarum: So good that we heard one track and did a Special Feature…") Users can then click on control elements to display additional, and navigable, text on top of that area. Text that overflows its space has a custom scrolling widget (one that is superior to traditional scroll bars in some respects).

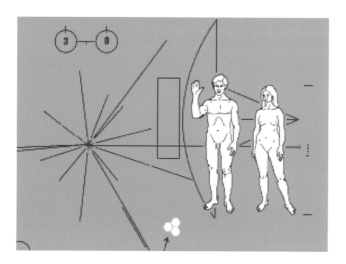

Unlike most sites, which put all the branding across the top and a big logo on the left, Three.oh's 2001 portal splashes its look and feel across the page.

Three.oh uses a crisp visual language that was flat, monochromatic, and based on aliased-pixel imagery perfectly suited to the medium. The interface design offers only the slightest visual affordances. The interactive elements don't need big bevels or drop shadows, because the site adheres to the notion that everything on the page should be interactive.

Ambiguous imagery was used to set the tone of each content area. The hieroglyphic key to humanity (launched into outer space in the 1980s to give extraterrestrials contact info for earth and its naked, white people), at upper right, is an apt image for "credits and contact." While the iconography bordered on techno-trivia, the text labels directly above it are clear, and clicking each one fills the rectangle with corresponding text. Areas that represent the outside world used more modeled, tightly cropped, graphics that act like little windows onto other worlds.

[EXTERNAL] [INTERNAL] [RELATED] [JOBS]

EVENTSCAPE

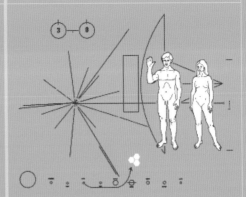

EXTERNAL NEWS

■ 18/04/01 05:41
PLEIX is a virtual community of digital artists.
My Pet Skeleton – Art.

For your information: I'll be in NY between
today 18-23 April thus no updates. See you
soon and come with us to OFFF in May.

■ 18/04/01 01:29
One of our past Special Features SIKKO (TMB)
just redesigned his site, and he's looking for a
job in Vancouver.

■ 16/04/01 18:52
Dennis Interactive redesigns.

MAY 1st REBOOT
CURATED BY THREE.OH

stealing eyeballs
designing media

VIEW NEWS ARCHIVE ⬈

TIP US! NEWS@THREEOH.COM ⬈

SPECIAL FEATURES

Fizzarum
So good that we heard one track and did a
Special Feature...

[LAUNCH ⬈]

Austin Young
Austin Young threw in his degree in Art in
Paris for a career as an artist in New
York...

[LAUNCH ⬈]

SITE OF THE WEEK
Planet of the Drums

[Archive ⬍]

SITE OF THE MONTH

Designgraphik
continuing a re-evaluation
of graphic and real space
through visual form.

[MORE ⬈] [ARCHIVE ⬈]

SEARCH	NEWS / TECH	ENTERTAINMENT	SHOPPING	MAIL
ALTAVISTA	WIRED NEWS	TIMEOUT	AMAZON	HOTMAIL
YAHOO	DESIGN IN MOTION	THE SKINNY	CDNOW	NETADDRESS
GOOGLE	CNET	SPUTNIK 7	GEMM	YAHOO MAIL
ASK JEEVES	RED HERRING	MR SHOWBIZ	LAURENCE KING	RSUB

POINT OF VIEW
OPINIONS ON DIFFERENT TOPICS

[ARCHIVE ⬍]

How interactive can typography be if it does not react
uniquely to every instance of a letterform?

Jeremy Tankard 1:3 / Jimmy Chen 0:1
We have seen the ability for and of intelligent type
(Letterror's types). On another level there is/were
Multiple Masters – allowing the user to adjust the type
image accordingly. Not only width, weight (Myriad) but
also optically (Minion). Thus allowing for a visually
correct type size (in the eyes of some that is,
remember it may not be what the job requires). MM
fonts have been discontinued, due (I feel) to problems in
printing and lack of understanding the potential.

Over the years font formats have been dreamed about
that would allow intelligent mutation of type. Apples
fated GX fonts (now called AAT - Apple Advance
Typography) are similar to Adobe's Multiple Master
technology. But AAT also allows for 'glyph substitution'
– we see this in some applications when typing f and i =
fi ligature automatically.

[NEXT ⬍]

TOP THREE
CULTURAL ARMOURY

↓ Herald Tribune   NORMETICA-A   Graphics In

WEB SITES	TYPEFACES	MAGAZINES
Int. Herald Tribune	Normetica	Graphics International
Art and Culture	Helvetica	Eye Magazine
Kaliber 10000	Univers	Stockholm New

↓   21   critical   Graphics

BOOKS	RECORDS	FILMS
Typography 21	Tipper - The Critical Path	Koyaanisqatsi
G1	Flanger - Templates	The Matrix
Hybrid Space	Mirwais - Production	The Crouching Tiger

GIFT GUIDE
CONTEMPORARY AND NICE STUFF

Our own Inspector Gadget Anders from DFORM1 – helps us find cool
technology gadgets, furniture and more – all reviewed.

[LAUNCH ⬈] [ARCHIVE ⬈]

RECOMMENDED
We recommend a 4+ browser like IE. Site is best viewed
with Geneva font, PC users download here. Make
THREE.OH your startpage.

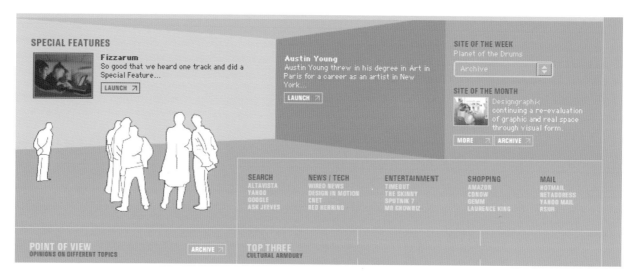

The Special Features interface uses the same interactive devices. Though the illustration suggests a public space where art is consumed, Three.oh didn't take the reference too literally or too far. Clicking the Launch button fills this area with text, while rest of the interface is grayed by ingeniously positioning a semitransparent GIF over the page. This helps the user focus on the text, which necessarily took up much of the middle of the page.

Graying the inactive areas of the page is a visual technique borrowed from application and operating system design. It implies that the rest of the interface is not usable while allowing it to remain visible and keeps the user oriented while forcing him to address the active content. This turns out to be an elegant (if latent) way of handling the conceptual rift between vertically oriented Web interfaces (which scroll through disparate sections) and Flash sites or interactive CD-ROMS, which tend to have self-contained, fixed-ratio interfaces.

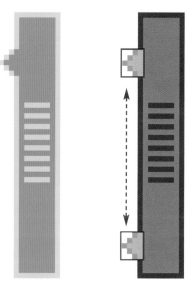

Three.oh's most impressive invention is the custom Scroll handle in the External News section. Unlike the scroll arrows in Omnia and Media Basement, this element both gives access to hidden content and shows where you are within it. The adjacent tick marks correspond to individual news items. When the cursor is placed over a tick mark, the header of the entry is displayed: click on it, and you jump to the top of the item. This custom scroll device is more attractive than an operating system scroll bar, as well as more versatile.

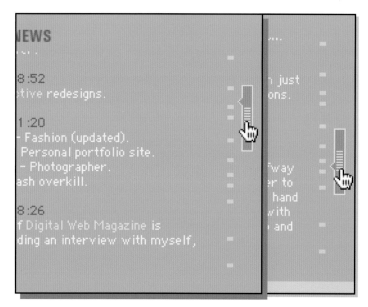

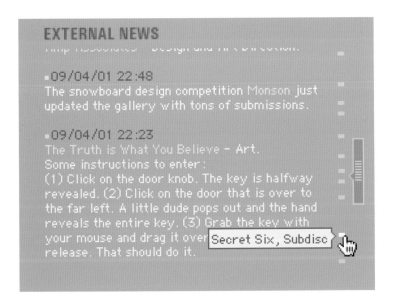

EXTERNAL NEWS

■09/04/01 22:48
The snowboard design competition Monson just
updated the gallery with tons of submissions.

■09/04/01 22:23
The Truth is What You Believe - Art.
Some instructions to enter:
(1) Click on the door knob. The key is halfway
revealed. (2) Click on the door that is over to
the far left. A little dude pops out and the hand
reveals the entire key. (3) Grab the key with
your mouse and drag it over [Secret Six, Subdisc]
release. That should do it.

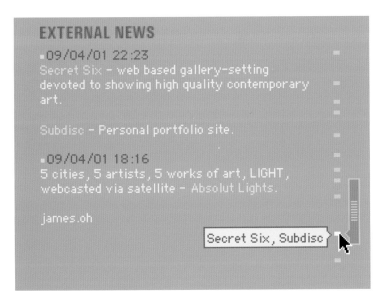

EXTERNAL NEWS

■09/04/01 22:23
Secret Six - web based gallery-setting
devoted to showing high quality contemporary
art.

Subdisc - Personal portfolio site.

■09/04/01 18:16
5 cities, 5 artists, 5 works of art, LIGHT,
webcasted via satellite - Absolut Lights.

james.oh

[Secret Six, Subdisc]

Mousing over the tick mark displays the title of an overflow entry.

Clicking on the tick mark lets you jump to the top of the item.

HUGE (http://hugeinc.com/2001/huge_1000.html)

Designer/Firm: HUGE

Huge is a design firm that uses Flash on its own Web site to help potential clients navigate the online portfolio, case studies, and news blurbs. While Flash allows Huge to create some interesting interaction models, the site could also have been built with DHTML.

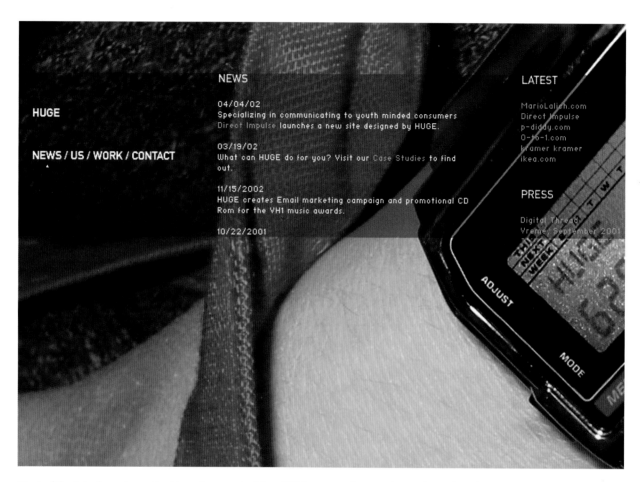

Most of the interface elements at hugeinc.com build on HTML conventions, such as using colored text links as the main gateways to deeper content. As with conventional HTML design, link text is set in a different type style than the rest of the page. The cluster of section names—NEWS, US, WORK, CONTACT—gives two cues to clickability. First, the text is set in bigger, bolder, uppercase letters; second, the small arrow below NEWS is a standard device for identifying active elements.

The clickable elements of this interface share many visual qualities with the surrounding text, which could cause them to get lost. But overall, the simplicity works to the interface's advantage. The clever use of branding, which is woven into the background image, is another advantage. The image of the wristwatch, cropped close and carrying the name HUGE, is on a separate plane from the interface, apparently and stylistically, which allows the user to easily turn her attention to the text, without getting bogged down by trying to find the line between branding and interface.

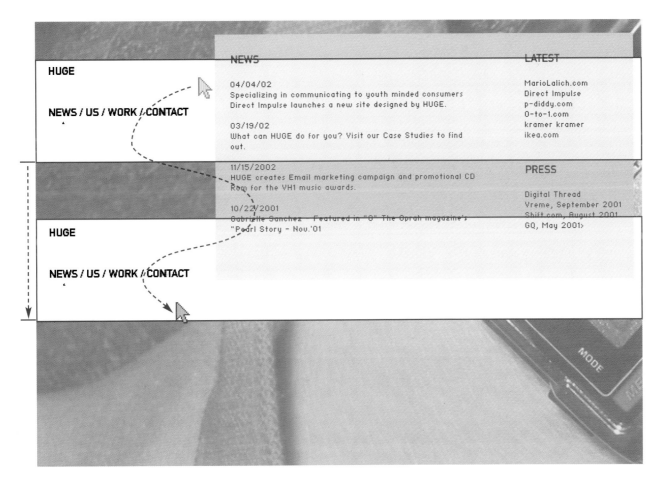

HUGE

NEWS / US / WORK / CONTACT

NEWS

04/04/02
Specializing in communicating to youth minded consumers
Direct Impulse launches a new site designed by HUGE.

03/19/02
What can HUGE do for you? Visit our Case Studies to find
out.

11/15/2002
HUGE creates Email marketing campaign and promotional CD
Rom for the VH1 music awards.

10/22/2001
Gabrielle Sanchez - Featured in "O" The Oprah magazine's
"Pearl Story - Nov.'01

LATEST

MarioLalich.com
Direct Impulse
p-diddy.com
O-to-1.com
kramer kramer
ikea.com

PRESS

Digital Thread
Vreme, September 2001
Shift.com, August 2001
GQ, May 2001>

HUGE

NEWS / US / WORK / CONTACT

Rather than animating portions of art or type (as is often done in Flash sites—think "blinking type"), Huge uses static imagery as a backdrop for a moving interface. The site navigation and text are presented on a panel that floats over the photograph and follows the mouse vertically. This panel has a fixed height, so the user can see most of the background image at any given time. The text is in a fixed position on a hidden layer, and the panel acts as a window to reveal whatever section of text lies below it. The effect is similar to scrolling, but instead of moving the text within the panel, the user moves the panel up or down to reveal the text.

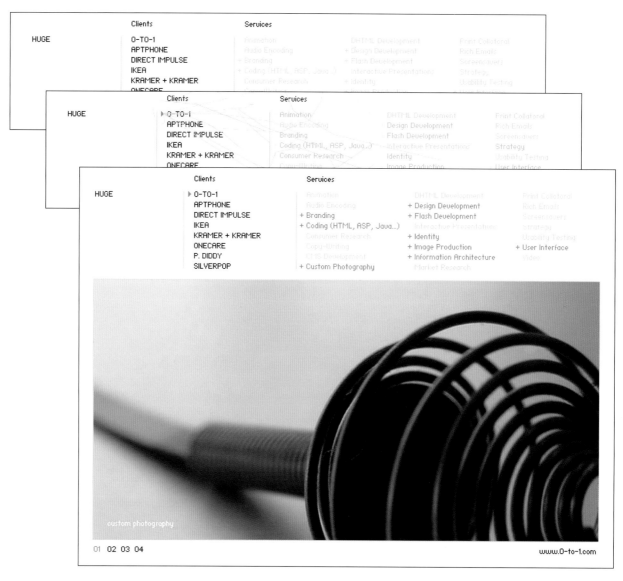

In the portfolio section, the screen is divided into two sections: content and architecture. Huge devotes a lot of space to listing its broad range of capabilities, then takes advantage of interactivity to make the navigation do dual duty as a cognitive guide. When a client name is clicked, organic trails slowly branch out and connect it with every relevant service. After clicking a few links, the user can build a mental model of the extent of each project, conveying far more information than the portfolio images could on their own. Perhaps the tentaclelike branches are unnecessary—highlights would suffice—but their gradual crawl helps distract and amuse the user while the large portfolio section loads.

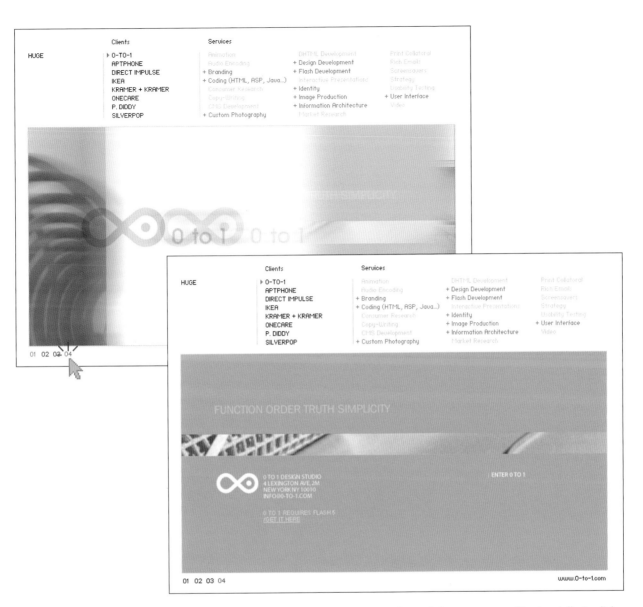

Each portion of the portfolio presents a group of sample images arranged horizontally. By clicking the image number in the lower left, the associated sample is brought into view, as the rest of the images slide by. On the surface, this seems like gratuitous animation, but it actually serves a purpose. While jumping to a sample, the user can still benefit from seeing the others, however briefly. If you were to return to this site after a few days, and were looking for a specific sample, you might mistakenly click 04 when the image you want is 03—but you'll see the desired image as it flies by.

Shift (www.shift.jp.org/banner)

Designer/Firm: Paradise Graphics and Shift Productions

Shift is an online magazine that publishes items of interest to the international design community. This example is just a small corner of the publication that promotes some of the studios that contribute art to the viral art project "Mind the Banner."

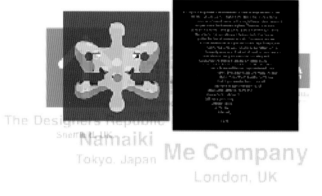

This kinetic interface uses both tracking and panning to provide access to a large group of thumbnails that would otherwise take a less interesting form. A dozen thumbnails representing individual content offerings appear to rotate on a vertical axis. A user may reveal information about a thumbnail my mousing over it—which is tricky since the cursor position also controls the speed and direction of rotation. The result is something of a moving target. Some patience is required. If the user misses an image on the first pass, he has to wait for the images in the back to come around again before interacting with them.

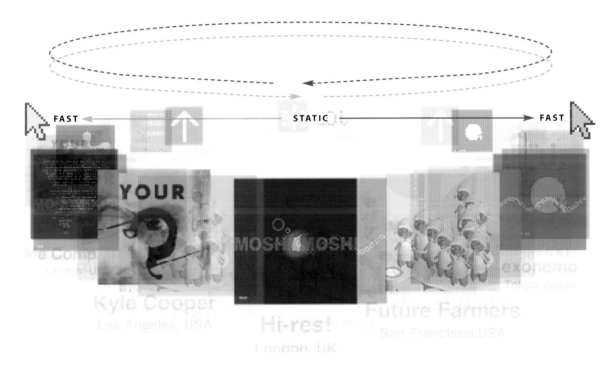

FAST ← STATIC → FAST

The group rotates from right to left when the cursor is positioned on the right, and switches direction when the mouse moves to the left. The farther left or right the cursor is, the faster the images rotate. If the cursor is placed in the center, the group comes to rest, which makes it a little easier to cope with.

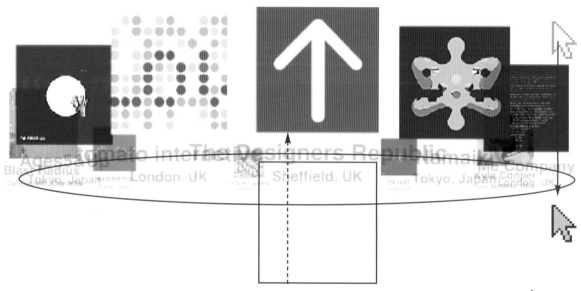

The axis on which the images rotate may be pitched, depending on where the mouse is on the screen's vertical axis. This is more than a trick, however, since the more you tilt the axis, the easier it is to read the images that have rotated to the back.

Wireframe Studio (www.wireframe.co.za) Designer/Firm: Wireframe Studio

This site serves to demonstrate Wireframe Studio's capabilities in Flash interface design. Though it's hard to imagine how this interface could be built in DHTML (much of its usability is based on the fluid motion of elements) both DHTML and HTML designers can learn a great deal about advanced interactive models from this site. The clarity of the rendering contributes to the site's success. The designers at Wireframe use crisp, aliased pixels to define the edges of interfaces elements and to render type. The resulting sharpness gives this site the visual authority of an operating system.

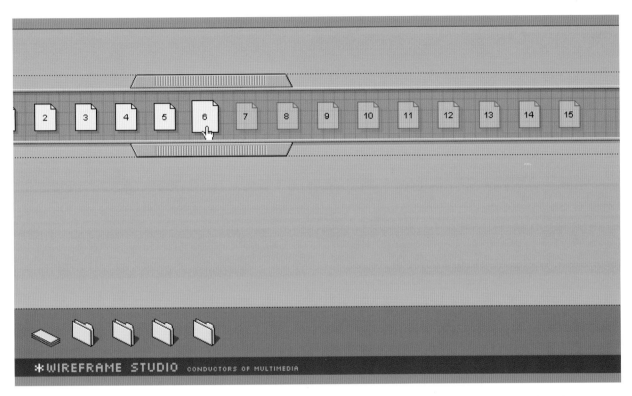

Wireframe builds layers of interactivity into its interface by using color and horizontal lines to distinguish interface elements from architecture. Control elements, such as the horizontal scroll handles, are generally gray, while elements that lead to content have a slight color tint that relates subtly to the orange background.

These horizontal scroll handles use a visual texture of vertical lines to imply grippability, as do title bars and scroll handles in operating systems. In this case, the affordance is meant to explain the element's interactive purpose, for it is not intended to be gripped or clicked at all. As soon as the cursor approaches, the scroll handles separate to reveal the panel's content and display its true interactivity: content automatically scrolls horizontally based on the cursor's position. The scroll handles track the cursor while the content pans in the opposite direction. The effect is of a supercharged control element.

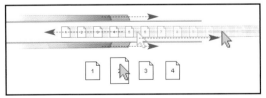

As each page moves under the cursor, it expands to connote clickability.

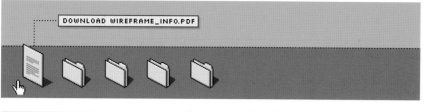

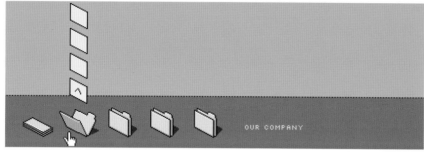

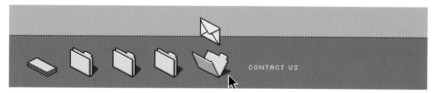

In addition to interesting interactive models, the Wireframe interface makes good use of iconography to build a clear and useful navigation system. As with all good systems, the navigational elements follow a consistent set of conventions, each having a similar color and spacing. The folder icons tell the user that multiple items are apt to be contained within, while the small stack of pages to the left is obviously not a container. Mousing over it reveals the item to be a downloadable document.

When mousing over a folder, items spring out vertically, revealing the content within. The number of items varies from folder to folder, showing the relative depth of content in each. There is real value in this because it helps the user build a mental map of the depth of the site, much as we judge books by their thickness. Consistent with this model, mousing over the individual items reveals whether there are one or several pages in that section.

Oddly, the Contact Us folder only contains one item (perhaps more items will be added later), but at least its purpose is obvious from its design: the envelope icon defines a mail-to link.

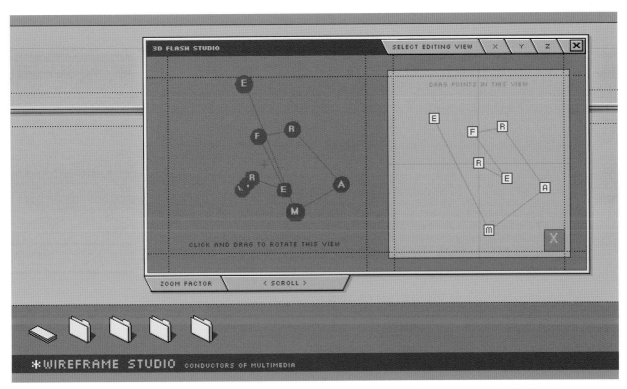

Clicking on an item within the horizontal scrolling panel loads an interactive piece in the content area. Each piece has an amusingly inane purpose, such as this tool for arranging the letters of WIREFRAME on three axes. In keeping with the rest of Wireframe, the control elements are slightly beveled, gray devices, while content-oriented elements have some color. This particular interface begins to solve the 3-D conundrum by providing a simple map of each axial view on the right, and a perspective view to the left. Rather than wrestle with pushing and pulling elements into the z-axis, the user can see the model from any angle, and move the elements up or down to affect any axis.

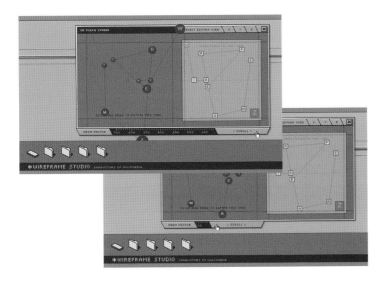

An interesting device: the Zoom tab allows the user to easily zoom in and out of the model.

CONCLUSION

Don't close this book and go straight off to design an interface in direct imitation of the examples in this section. It won't work. One important component of site design, which we have not been able to share here, is the context in which these interfaces have been built. Some use new interaction models to address the particular needs of a specific audience, while others are deliberate efforts to go against the grain of convention and usability. Such irreverence towards the common WIMP paradigm is fuel for much-needed change in computing—a conceptual kick in the pants for the complacent. But when your audience is engaged in time-sensitive or complex tasks, they may prefer more tried-and-true solutions.

On the other hand, the face of computing is rapidly changing, thanks both to the speed with which developers can launch new interface ideas and the Web audience's occasional willingness to try out adventurous interaction models under the right circumstances. Some seemingly experimental interactions address handicaps in the browsing environment, such as screen real estate constraints. When an invention solves such a problem efficiently, without straining bandwidth and sending the user on a treasure hunt for plug-ins, it can quickly be assimilated into the Web at large (JavaScript and CSS can be copied from the source code very easily). Make a habit of using new, experimental interfaces when you think they'll work. Then test your hunches by watching which inventions are adopted by established sites. If you find an interface that shows promise, don't be afraid to email the site's owners to ask if they have had positive feedback on it. Very often, a failed experiment will endure not because it worked well, but because the owner didn't have the time or capacity to replace it. That's something you'll want to know before following suit.

Many of the examples, both in this section and throughout the book, have been isolated, exaggerated, or simplified to illustrate a point. Once you begin to execute the ideas you've found here, you will quickly notice that each interface brings with it a specific set of constraints that make some solutions less viable than others. Use this book, the Web, and your own experience as data points for judging the probable success of your intended design. Then ask impartial people to check your thinking—user tests, formal and informal, should become a part of your everyday design process. Finally, never forget that while interface elements are the building materials of Web sites, people are more important than widgets. Don't focus on the technology, focus on the person who will have to use it.

When copying source code from JavaScript, be cognizant of the author's rights—and hard work. Some scripts are open source (public domain), while others are not. Copy scripts only if the code includes comments giving permission for public use, or if you are certain the script is open source. And give the author credit in your own code for others to see. If you think nobody will notice when you "borrow" code that isn't in the public domain, think again. HTML and JavaScript are much more visible than the hotel towels in your closet.

BIBLIOGRAPHY

Books and Articles:

Apple Computer. *The Macintosh Human Interface Guidelines.* (1992).

Aunti Opiate & MCN, 1994

Aunti Opiate's Pick-me-up-mag, Volume 1 #11

Beyer, Hugh, and Holzblatt, Karen. *Contextual Design.* (Morgan Kaufmann Publishers, Inc., 2002)

Bowman, Shayne, and Willis, Chris. *DesignWhys: Designing Web Sites That Sell.* (Peachpit, 2002)

Brand, Stewart. *How Buildings Learn.* (Penguin USA, 1995)

Bringhurst, Robert. *Elements of Typographic Style.* (Hartley & Marks Publishers, 2001)

Cooper, Alan. *About Face: The Essentials of User Interface Design.* (Hungry Minds, Inc., 1995)

Fontana, David. *The Secret Language of Symbols.* (Duncan Baird Publishers, 1993, London)

Gill, Eric. *An Essay on Typography.* (Hague and Gill, 1931)

Helmoholz, Herman. *On the Sensation of Tone.* (Dover, 1954)

Kotch, Rudolph. *The Book of Signs.* (Dover Publications, Inc., 1955)

Kurg, Steve. *Don't Make Me Think: A Common Sense Approach to Web Usability.* (2000)

Mayhew, Deborah J. *The Usability Engineering Lifecycle.* (Morgan Kaufmann Publishers, Inc., 1995)

McCloud, Scott. *Understanding Comics.* (Kitchen Sink Press, 1994)

McLean, Ruari. *Typographers on Type.* (W. W. Norton & Co. LTD, 1995)

Miller, J. Abbott and KIOSK. *Dimensional Typography.* (1996)

Mullet, Kevin, and Sano, Darrell. *Designing Visual Interfaces: Communication Oriented Techniques* (Sun Microsystems Inc., 1995)

Norman, Donald. *The Design of Everyday Things.* (Currency/Doubleday, 1990)

Oldsen Jr., Dan R. *Developing User Interfaces* (Morgan Kaufmann Publishers, Inc., 1998)

Per Mollerup. *Marks of Excellence: The History and Taxonomy of Trademarks.* (Phaidon Press LTD, 1997)

Reiss, Eric L. *The Complete Talking Machine: Second Edition,* (Sonoran Publishing, LLC, Chandler, 1996)

Salvendy, Gavriel (ed.). *Handbook of Human Factors and Ergonomics* (Wiley-Interscience, 1997)

Segalat, Roger Jean. *How Things Work.* (Bibliographisches Institut and Simon and Schuster)

Strandh, Sisvard. *A History of the Machine.* (A & W Publishers, Inc., 1979)

Tschichold, Jan. *The New Typography.* English Edition. University of California Press, London, 1995

Tufte, Edward. *Envisioning Information.* (Graphics Press, 1990)

Tufte, Edward. *The Visual Display of Quantitative Information.* (Graphics Press, 2001)

Tufte, Edward. *Visual Explanations.* (Graphics Press, 1997)

Veen, Jeffrey. *Hotwired Style: Principles for Building Smart Web Sites.* (Wired Books Inc., 1997)

Veen, Jeffrey. *The Art & Science of Web Design.* (New Riders, 2000)

Vredenburg, Karel; Isensee, Scott; and Righi, Carol. *User-Centered Design: An Integrated Approach.* (2001)

Willett, John. *Heartfield versus Hitler.* (Editions Hazan, 1997)

Web Sites and Listservs:

Taylor. "Captain Cursor and His Cursor Styles." (Webmonkey.com, 1997). www.webmonkey.com/html/97/38/index1a.html?tw=authoring

Face@veen.com (1999–2002)

Savio, Nadav. "Giant Ant: on DHTML and contextual information." (2002). www.giantant.com/antenna/archive/00000007.php3

Hays, Grace. "Successful User Interfaces for Mobile Devices." (Developer.com, 2002). www.developer.com/wireless/article/0,,10836_1143541,00.html

Thau, Dave. "Thau's JavaScript Tutorial." (Webmonkey.com, 1998). www.webmonkey.com/98/03/indexoa.html

INDEX

interactive buttons, 103–104
source code, use of, 250
JPEG buttons, 78, 79
JPGs graphic links, 44, 49–51

K

Knobs as output controls, 145–147
Krug, Steve, 39

L

Labels, button, 90–99
Layers (HTML objects), 165–167
Layout, 16–19, 29–33
    information visualization, 29–30
    organization of content and categorization, 31–33
    outline for, 33
Legacy interfaces, 6
Linear interface elements, 40–41.
        See also Buttons; Checkboxes; Form elements;
        Hypertext links; Link elements; Menus
Link arrangement, 51–52
Link density, 52–53
Link descriptions, 56–63
Link elements (links), 9, 42–67. See also Text links
    active, 61
    autonomy of links, 51, 52
    buttons vs., 72–75
    color of, 58–60, 62–63, 202, 217
    cross-browser and platform link presentation, 64–67
    legibility, 61–62
    link descriptions, 56–63
    linked text, 46, 56–57
    nontext link types, 48–55
    presentation of, 58, 62–63
    typography, 61–62
    visited, 58–61
Link grouping, 53–54
Link placement, 55
Linked text, 46, 56–57
Lists, 37, 116–117, 122–123

M

Macintosh
    desktop, 152
    form input text fields, 114
    link presentation on, 66
    stock cursor, 183–184
Macromedia Dreamweaver, 103, 133
Macromedia Flash, 7, 38, 78, 133, 200
    control elements, 135
    cursor, design of, 183, 185
    custom interface elements, 165, 176–179
    entertainment vs. functionality, 23
    examples, 240–243, 247–249
    interactive buttons, 103, 106
    output controls, 145
Margins, placement of links in, 53–54
Market niches, 11, 14
Mayhew, Deborah, 8, 39
Media Basement (www.mediabasement.com),
        208, 231–233
Mejia, Mathew, 230
Mental models, 148–163
    applying metaphors to Web interfaces, 153–159
    directional signage, 154–157
    metaphor hierarchy, 150–152
    tabs, 160–163
Menus, 9, 40, 116–122, 181
    items as buttons, 72
    style of, 37
Metaphors, 22–23, 80–81, 149
    applying to Web interfaces, 153–159
    desktop, 151–152
    environmental, 158–159
    hierarchy, 150–152
    page, 153
    reasons for, 23
    tabs, 160–163
Microsoft Internet Explorer (IE), 66, 183–184
Mouse events, 181. See also Mouseover effects
    cursor design and, 185–186
    motion of mouse, fluidity of, 188–195
    table of, 182
    3-D interaction, 196–199

Mouseover effects, 181–182
    Dynamic HTML (DHTML) custom interface elements,
        168–170
    examples, 204, 205, 206, 209, 215, 217, 230
    experimental interface elements, 188–195, 244–246
    for icons, with tool tip text, 57–58
    interactive buttons, 103–107
    links, reinforcement of, 62–63
    pop-down layers, 169–174

N

Name of interface, 150
Name of user, 14
Navigation images, grouping of, 37
Neilson, Jacob, 39
Netscape (NS), 66
    buttons, 78
    form elements, rendering of, 114
    stock cursor, 183–184

O

Omnia (www.omniband.com), 230
Organization. See Layout
Output controls, 145–147

P

Page metaphors, 153
Panning, using mouse for, 188–195, 244–246
Paradise Graphics, 244
Passwords, 14
Paths, user/site, 34–35
PC, link presentation on, 66
PDAs, link elements on, 67
Platforms, various. See also Browsers
    buttons, cross-platform rendering of, 78
    link presentation on, 64–67
    PDAs, link elements on, 67
Pointer. See Cursor
Pop-down layers, 169–174
Pop-up windows, 171, 174–175
Production phase, 12
Project scope, 12–14
Pyra.Com LTD, 202

Eric Eaton, former design director at HotWired and Lycos, spent five years creating some of the Web's most influential brands, including *Wired News,* Webmonkey, and HotBot, receiving several honors including American Center for Design: Award for Excellence in Interaction Design; *PC World*'s Best Web Search Interface; and *Communication Arts*' Award for Excellence in Information Design. He was involved in creating Wired Digital's usability lab, and was a content contributor to *Wired News* and Webmonkey.

Currently living on an island off the coast of Maine, Eaton is principal and founder of Deliberate Design. In his spare time he is developing a curriculum for experimental typography.

Series editor Cynthia Baron is technical director in the department of visual arts at Northeastern University, and she teaches in the department and the multimedia studies program. She was a contributing editor for *Critique* magazine, has been published in several periodicals, and has authored or coauthored four books, including *Creating a Digital Portfolio* and *The Little Digital Camera Book.*

Acknowledgments

I'd still be biting the tips off crayons if not for the support and tutelage of: Jeffrey Veen, Matthew Nutter, Judd Vetrone, Mike Kuniavsky, June Cohen (who never calls), J. P. Louie, Erik Adigard, Barbara Kurh (especially), Eric Courtemanche, Scotty Ton, Shirly Ton, Bab and Ruffus, and Chris Porter, who is dead.

Thanks to Satoru Nihei for research assistance; to Cynthia for lending lucidity to my words; to Maximilian for his unwitting distractive power; and, of course, to Dame Holly, for her unending support and well-timed snack breaks.